The Lucky Ones

The Lucky Ones

✦

Airmen of the Mighty Eighth

Erik Dyreborg

Writers Club Press
San Jose New York Lincoln Shanghai

The Lucky Ones
Airmen of the Mighty Eighth

Writers Club Press
an imprint of iUniverse, Inc.

For information address:
iUniverse, Inc.
5220 S. 16th St., Suite 200
Lincoln, NE 68512
www.iuniverse.com

ISBN: 0-595-24990-6

Printed in the United States of America

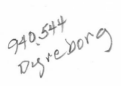

Contents

Foreword

By Tom Clay

In December of 1903, two young men, challenged by the laws of nature, yet driven with an unprecedented curiosity about aeronautics, made the first powered flight. For only a few seconds, over a windswept beach called Kitty Hawk in North Carolina, these sons of a clergyman did what no human had ever done before.

Little did Orville and Wilbur Wright realize that such a significant event would change the world forever. Fast forward a short 39 years later. The world is in the midst of a world wide conflict. A war that pitted evil and captivity against goodness and liberty. The hobby that once tickled the interest of a couple of bicycle builders from Dayton, Ohio, became the critical factor that would lead America and its Allies to victory.

On January 28, 1942 the Eight Air Force was born. Initially its first units were assembled to provide the air element of a projected invasion of North-West Africa. Only four weeks after its inception, the build up for the North-West African invasion was cancelled and the Eight Air Force found itself without a home. By early April however, the Eighth was headed to England, to become the nucleus of the entire Army Air Force in Great Britain. From the rolling green fields of the English countryside, the Eighth Air Force became one of the greatest forces during the war in the European Theater.

During World War II, under the leadership of such generals as Ira Eaker and Jimmy Doolittle, the 8th Air Force became the greatest air armada in history. By mid-1944, it had reached a total strength of more than 200,000 people, and by some estimates, there were more

than 350,000 Americans who served in the Eighth Air Force throughout the duration of the war.

At peak strength, the Eighth Air Force could dispatch up to 3,000
planes on a single mission. The Eighth Air Force thus became known
as the "Mighty Eighth."

The Mighty Eighth compiled an impressive record in the war. This
achievement, however, carried a high price. The Mighty Eighth lost
6,537 heavy bombers and 3,337 fighters. Half of the U.S. Army Air
Force's casualties in World War II were suffered by the Eighth Air
Force.

The mortality rate for 8th AAF crew men was 12.38 percent, i.e. over
26,000 dead and in total there were more than 47,000 casualties.

More than 21,000 became POWs. These men sat behind barbed wire
to await their liberation, while their commrades continued to fly above
them, hastening the end of the war.

The Lucky Ones is a collection of memoirs from a few of the many
brave young men of the Mighty Eighth. These are the experiences of
those Airmen who beat the odds and lived to tell their stories, which in
reality have both happy and tragic endings.

The world will forever be indebted to the courageous Airmen of the
Mighty Eighth !

About The Author—
A Dane's Story

Narrated by Erik Dyreborg

I was born June 30, 1945 at Rønne Hospital on the Danish Island of Bornholm in the Baltic Sea. The Island was occupied by the Germans from April 9, 1940 until May 8, 1945, at which time the Russians took over, after they had bombed the two major cities Rønne and Neksø.

The bombing caused very heavy damages. Of the 4,400 houses, 1,700 were either destroyed or damaged by the bombing. My family in Neksø lost everything they ever owned in just a couple of hours time including the family photo album. Losing the family photo album was in my opinion a real loss—as if my family didn't exist before 1945.

Apart from the devastation, caused by the bombing, the bombing itself was a stupid act, committed by the Russians as the war was already over even before they bombed the two cities.

One could say that the Island had a very quiet, almost peaceful occupation by the Germans and an extremely violent Russian "liberation". The Russians stayed on the Island for almost a year, leaving in 1946. The Island was occupied for more than 6 years.

The people on Bornholm were lucky that the Russians didn't stay on the Island. We could easily have ended up just like the Baltic States and thus have been some 40—50 years behind western European standard.

In 1950, my permanent Bornholm era was over, we moved to the Copenhagen area, where we have lived ever since.

As long as I can remember I've always taken a great interest in history. I consider myself a 'history buff'. This is probably mainly due to the fact that my paternal grandfather was a history 'freak' as well.

When I, as a boy, spent time with him, we were practically "living" in all kinds of museums. My grandfather served on the German side during World War I, as that part of Denmark (south west–the Island of Als) had been German "occupied" territory since 1864. However, it again became Danish in 1920.

Looking back, I owe my Granddad a lot, even if most of the visits at the museums in my young years usually were very tiresome for me.

The family on my mother's side were all living on Bornholm for many generations and it was here, in my grandparent's home, that I became especially interested in the history of the Island. They had a lot of books on the subject, as well of many photographs.

There was one particular book titled *100 Years of The Rocky Island* which had one special story, with an accompanied photo (below) that had made such an indelible impression on my young inquisitive mind, that it has been there ever since.

B-17G "Big Stoop" 447th Bomb Group crash landed April 11, 1944 4 miles from my parents home on Bornholm.

My father seeing the plane coming in over the town of Neksø at very low altitude, jumped on his bike and raced to the crash site. He arrived approximately 20 minutes after the landing but at that time, the American Airmen had already disappeared. Four of the crew members were captured by the Germans but the other six evaded capture and escaped to Sweden.

As a school boy I spent every summer holiday on the Island and as my family was related to several fishermen, I spent most of my time either at sea or at the harbor of Neksø on east Bornholm.

I remember one summer day back in the late 1950's when two fishing boats came in with quite a catch. It wasn't fish though but almost a complete German plane with wings, tail, engine, cockpit etc., quite an exciting experience for a young schoolboy. This happened often all over the Island but again there were hundreds of planes that had ended up in the Baltic Sea during World War II.

My school time ended in 1963 and I spent the next three years as an apprentice with Maersk Line (shipping) in Copenhagen. After the apprenticeship and after having done my time in the Army in 1968, I entered International forwarding and transportation and have been working in this business ever since, doing mainly sales and marketing.

My job has taken me to many places. I've been travelling all over Europe, except Austria and Finland. I've even been in Greenland, most of the eastern European countries, Russia, Saudi Arabia, Yemen, Nigeria in Africa, Malta in the Mediterranean Sea (there you can talk about history) and last but not least the States. I have been to the States several times and have visited Florida, Georgia, South and North Carolina, Virginia and New York. The visits to the States have mainly been during summer holidays.

Back in 1978 I managed, through a friend, to get flying lessons, free of charge, and just enough hours to get my license. But only a couple of years after I had to give it up and turn in my license as the charge per hour for flying was at that time more than 100 Dollars with a minimum of 12 flying hours per year.

I would love to fly again but I guess this will not be possible, at least not for the time being, as a license in Denmark, today, would cost almost 10,000 Dollars. Well, gotta have some dreams!
Army time in Denmark for me included 3 months as a Rookie, 6 months at the Sergeant School in Sonderborg on the Island of Als and 14 months as Sergeant. I had a good time in the Army and only good memories, apart from one particular drill we were doing in 1968 with the English SAS (Special Air Service), when a sudden and unexpected heavy explosion very close to me, resulted in an ever-lasting bad hearing in my right ear.

In 1999, and by coincidence, I found myself again reading the very same book that I was so fascinated by as a boy *(100 Years of The Rocky Island)* and when I saw the photo and read the story again, I got the idea that it might be interesting to do some research about what happened to the crew, and the local people on the Island who helped them evade and escape.

I got in touch with some good people on Bornholm and the research started rolling. First I read all I could on the subject. I read all the books, newspaper clippings etc., about the crash landings on the Island and in the Baltic Sea, near the Island. After that, I got my hands on of all the photos related to the events that I could possibly get.

After having researched the stories of five planes and crews I decided to concentrate on one plane from the 401st Bomb Group, 615th Squadron, the B-17G (#42-31619) named "BTO in the ETO". This plane was shot up pretty bad by flak over the target on a mission to BIG "B" (Berlin) May 24, 1944 and crash landed on the Island later in the afternoon.

By pure luck I got hold of the e-mail address of the Pilot of the plane, John S. Whiteman, who lives in New York and the two of us started e-mailing regularly back in March 2000.

Soon after, the crew members were about to have their third reunion May 24, 2000 in Savannah, Georgia.

I wrote a letter to introduce myself to the remaining six crew members. I explained to them that I would like to have their life-stories, especially regarding their war time experiences and that my intention was to gather their stories in a book, along with the stories of the locals who helped them on Bornholm.

After a short while their stories started coming in by e-mails and letters with photos etc. By October 2000 the draft was done in English. After that, I got this crazy idea about having the book published in Danish. (One of my greatest wishes has always been to write a book and have it published). Now was the chance!

Furthermore I decided that if the book should be published, it had to be done by the local and only publisher on Bornholm—Bornholm's Tidende's Publishing Co. I therefore mailed the editor a copy of the English draft. The editor had someone else read it and inform him what he thought about it, as well as his ideas regarding the selling of the book if published.

Eventually I got the message from the editor that he thought the book was worth publishing and that he would print it.

The book was published May 14, 2001 in 1,000 copies. In this connection, a friend of mine on Bornholm arranged an interview for me with the local TV station (the only one) in order to promote the selling of the book. The interview was conducted at various locations on the Island. The TV station broadcasted the interview the day after the filming—imagine 7 whole minutes on the evening news.

The selling of the book went well, and in May 2002, only one year later, more than 900 copies were sold!

In the summer of 2001, my wife and I went to the States, where we visited the Navigator, Seymour Ringle in Palm Beach, Florida and the Ball Turret Gunner, Nelson Liddle in Blacksburg, Virginia.

It was a very special experience for me to meet with two of the "actors" from my own book, for the first time.

In September last year I started designing and editing my own web page: usairmen.com and in October, I decided to write another book on the subject but this time it should "only" contain narratives from various Airmen from various Bomb Groups. However, later I decided to also include my first book, "The Escape from Bornholm 1944" in this book.

The beginning was difficult—whom should I contact and how? Then the idea struck me, that Nelson "Nels" Liddle and myself could do this together. Nels agreed and we both started looking for Airmen from World War II who served with the 8th Air Force Bomb Groups in England. I met a few on the Heavy Bombers Forum on the Internet and Nels simply just found the rest.

The question to the Airmen was very simple: "Would you consider giving me the story of your war time experiences? It's for a book".

I guess we have been in touch with 25—30 Airmen during the past 6-7 months, resulting in stories for the book from 22 narrators. This was beyond any imagination!

I want to thank all the Airmen and their families, for sharing their stories of their personal experiences during World War II with the readers of this book.

Personally, I want to thank Nelson Liddle, Karen B. Cline and Tom Clay for doing such a great job and for helping me out with this book-project.

Erik & Nels, Summer 2001 in Blacksburg, Virginia. Discussing war stories—as usual.

It was a very exciting and interesting time for me, but also a lot of hard work. I knew it would be a *maximum effort*, every day, but I enjoyed every minute of it, and furthermore, I gained many new friends.

This book is about The Lucky Ones—Airmen of The Mighty Eighth, their courage, their heroism, their pain, their loss, and their joy. Future generations will forever be in debt to them for the price they paid for the freedom that we all enjoy today.

The Mystery Crew Photo

Narrated by Erik Dyreborg

The following coarse of events and correspondence took place in the lives of a few "history buffs". Men passionate about understanding, and telling, the stories of the brave young men of the United States Air Force during World War II. Unfortuanately, the stories they discover and tell about aren't always happy.

The following are excerpts from e-mails, during the research of The Mystery Crew Photo:

Nelson Liddle to Erik Dyreborg: My friend , Charles Vaughn, a pharmacist here in Blacksburg, was a radio operator on B29 bombers but not during World War II. He was too young for that war. We talk about our experiences of our days in the Air Force. He has read the book about the experiences of my crew: *The Escape From Bornholm 1944.* He is very interested in my World War II experiences.

His wife is from Grundy, Virginia. Her aunt, Mrs. David Crocket, died about three years ago. She was 83 years old and had no close relatives. Her husband and all her children died before she did.

Charles and his wife and maybe some other relatives were cleaning out her house. They were going thru a collection of old photos and came across the mystery photo. No one knew anything about it and no one wanted it. Charles said he would take it. He was thinking of me and knew that I would be interested in seeing it.

He brought it home and gave it to me. I guess I have had it a couple of years. When John Chopelas, a friend of mine, expressed interest in World War II Air Force items, I sent it to him…

Charles also said that he thinks she lived in Kentucky. May be during the war years.

Erik Dyreborg: March 16, 2002. After this, I contacted John Chopelas and asked for a copy of the mystery photo. John got the copies made of both front and back and mailed it to me. Meanwhile John did some research in order to find out about the crew of the mystery photo and sent an e-mail to Nelson "Nels" Liddle .

John Chopelas to Nelson Liddle: March 19, 2002. Nelson: That really IS a mystery photo. I've checked the 8th AF "Roll of Honor" but none of this crew is listed. I also went to the "American Battle Monuments Commission" which lists most of the military KIA during WWII but not a mention of any of these crewmen. I'm sending an enlarged photo (front & back) to Erik and hope he can solve it. I note in my copy of Freeman's "Mighty Eighth War Diary" that there was NO activity by heavy bombers on 9-5-43 (he shows only medium-bomber missions) so I wonder if the "mystery crew" crashed that day during a practice mission or if they were with the 15th AF?

Erik Dyreborg: March 25, 2002. When I received the photo by mail, I scanned front and back sent both by e-mail to Bruce Carson in Bump-ass, Virginia. (I "met" Bruce on the Heavy Bombers Internet web site). I knew that Bruce possessed great knowledge. (Bruce once helped a German guy with information about a plane that crashed in Southern Germany during WW II—boy did this German get a surprise when he received 23 pages of reports, information etc.) So I was hoping that Bruce would be able to dig up some information about this mystery crew photo. A few days after I got a message from Bruce.

Bruce Carson to Erik Dyreborg: March 29, 2002. Eric: Making some progress—the date is 9/5/43 = 5 Sept 43, B-17F, standard training crew photo—tracking down the particulars by crewmen names...Dates and losses just don't seem to fit—definitely not 8th AF, ...Might not be combat related at all. Where did the picture come from?—it seems a mite worn and tattered...
Should have more shortly...
Cheers
BC

Erik Dyreborg: I few days later I got another message from Bruce.

Bruce Carson to Erik Dyreborg: April 3, 2002. Eric: The very short (53 day) history of the aircraft shows it doesn't make it into the ETO. The picture is indeed a B-17F and a standard crew photo taken during training.

The date annotated on the picture is 9/5/43 = 5 Sep 43, aircraft is #42-30690—It is a B-17F-115-Boeing built, delivered to Cheyenne Wyoming Modification Center on 12 July 43; then on to support the second phase of B-17 training, B-17 transitional training at Dyersburg, Tennessee 27 July 43; during transitional crew training at Dyersburg Army Air Field, this aircraft crashed in Kentucky on 5 Sept 43 with the crew fatalities listed on the back—the aircraft was Written Off (WO) 30 Sept 43.

Dyersburg Army Air Field, 3rd Air Force, was active from 1942-45. A WWII B-17 training facility. The 3rd Air Force: Constituted as Southeast Air District on Oct. 19, 1940, activated on Dec. 18, 1940, and redesignated Third AF in early 1941. The Bomber Command, III Bomber's mission was to train units, crews, and individuals for bombardment, fighter, and reconnaissance operations.

I'll have more shortly through the accident report but during that period of time, this was not all that un-common—most 'pilots' had

~20+ hours at the controls before trying to fly across the big pond—not too much mystery now.

Cheers
BC

Erik Dyreborg: April 6, 2002. Received accident report from Bruce which has been attached to this "story". After this we were now trying to locate the survivors—or hopefully just one of them. Bruce would give it a try and I also got a message from Nels.

Nelson Liddle to Erik Dyreborg: April 7, 2002: Hi Erik, We are going to try to find info on the survivors of the mystery crew, my daughter in law works for the Veterans Adm. She is sending me some forms to fill out and send to the National Archives in Washington DC. She thinks that is the best place to start.

Erik Dyreborg: Only problem with the forms for the National Archives in Washington DC was that the reply would probably take up to 4 months, so we decided to forget about it.

Meanwhile Bruce was still checking, and on April 20 I got this e-mail:

Bruce Carson to Erik Dyreborg:

Erik: I am drawing a blank—can't find anything on any of the survivors of the mystery pix…

The "Mystery" Crew Photo.

Back row L to R: S/SGT Milton Gersfeld Engineer, SGT Clyde Mullins Radio Operator, SGT Clement J. Funai 2nd Armorer, SGT Donald A. Goodner Assist. Engineer, SGT Forland F. Nincehelser Gunner and (not shown) SGT O. R. French 1st Armorer.
Front row L to R 2nd LT Leonard J. Morence Co-Pilot, 2nd LT Harry N. Anderson Pilot, 2nd LT John A. Jr. Stinson Navigator and 2nd LT Andrew G. Kohlhof Bombardier.

<u>*Erik Dyreborg:*</u> Not all research work has a "happy" ending and some times you simply just have to give it up and quit. Anyway I find that research, in general, is about knowing people who know how and where to dig up information and after all, the whole thing started with just an old photo and we ended up with a lot of information of what happened to the plane and the crew.

The following are excerpts from the reports of the three survivors and the Aircraft Accident Committee.

The report of the Co-Pilot 2nd LT L. J. Morence dated September 5, 1943:

At 8,000 feet, in the overcast our flight indicator went out. We had a little trouble getting the plane under control and getting used to flying without it. At about 11,000 feet we broke into the clear and decided to go up to 20,000 feet and over the top of the soup. We heard flight control call us to go to Port Eads and rendezvous at 20,000 feet at 16:30. We were climbing all this time.

At about 16,000 feet we ran into the soup again. We were climbing straight ahead and everything was okay. The pilot turned on the A.F.C.E. to warm it up as we intended to fly that way once out of the overcast. I noticed excessive cylinder head temperatures on engines 1, 3 and 4, and opened the cowl flaps.

Then there was an explosion that jolted the plane and we went off into a spiral to the right. We leveled the plane off but immediately it went off to the left in a spin. Then after a few seconds of being tossed around the fuselage broke right at the top turret and I managed to get out that way.

The engineer was sitting behind us and may have been thrown clear but I don't know whether he had on his chute. I noticed the pilot, LT Anderson, getting out.

My chute was buckled at the thighs only and not across my chest and when it opened, I was coming down head first. I managed to turn and land flat on my back.

A Mr. Frields located me as I stayed right where I was at, hoping and think that would be the wisest. They told me when they came to me that they saw only three chutes open.

SGT Mullins called in and as yet I don't know about the rest of the crew.

The report of the Bombardier 2nd LT Andrew G. Kohlhof dated September 5, 1943:

We were flying at 21,000 feet and trying to gain altitude to get over the overcast. We were briefed that there was overcast up to 12,000 feet and that it would be clear after that, but we went up as far as 21,000 feet and were still in the overcast.

About five minutes before the crash we were gaining and losing altitude, excessively, because of rough weather. At this time the Pilot, Harry N. Anderson, ordered us to put on our chutes. I also heard the Pilot call over the interphone that the Flight Indicator was inoperative. At one time we lost 3,000 feet in a matter of seconds, and then were pushed upwards with equal violance. Then we went into a dive, during which time I saw the airspeed indicator hit 300 MPH. After that I tried to make my way to the escape hatch in the nose, when a terriffic explosion occurred. I was thrown from the plane as a result of the explosion. After I pulled the rip cord, I looked around and saw two chutes below me, and peaces of the plane was falling nearby.

As far as I know there was no ice on the plane, because the nose was still clear. I am of the opinion that the cause of the crash was purely a mechanical failure.

The report of the Radio Operator SGT Clyde Mullins dated September 5, 1943:

Weather very cloudy and rough. Plane seemed to rise and fall 2,000 feet. Noticed no ice on aircraft prior to accident. I was sending position report at time, when I heard a loud crash and plane went into dive. I lost consciousness and was thrown out of ship. Navigator told me that ship was flying at approx. 17,000 feet. All personnel on ship (was) notified by Navigator before to put on parachutes. After I bailed out I saw ship falling in several pieces, no smoke or fire noticed.

The report of the Aircraft Accident Committee September 1943:

At 8,000 feet the flight indicator went out and the pilot had considerable difficulty in flying the airplane under instrument conditions. It appeared as though after getting into the clear, the pilot continued to climb and went into the overcast again trying to reach 20,000 feet though the flight indicator was not functioning. While on instruments, the co-pilot and bombardier state the airplane exceeded the maximum safe operating conditions which placed a great strain on the airplane. It is believed because of the statements of the co-pilot and the bombardier concerning the attitude of flight and the loss of control that the airplane went out of control and into a spin, thereby disintegrating and crashing.

Responsebility: It is the opinion of the board that the responsibility rests with the pilot of that eleven (11) airplanes were cleared for an over water mission at Gulfport, Mississippi, seven (7) of which reached their destination without trouble, two (2) developed mechanical failure and landed, one (1) returned due to weather. The pilot of the airplane in question failed to follow his flight plan and encountered weather which was not anticipated thereby getting in the trouble as outlined in narratives.

Recommendations: More emphasis be placed on actual weather flying under closer supervision.

The Americans in England

Narrated by Christine Armes, Norwich, England

The Americans left the USA which is a continent of 3 million square miles and arrived in Great Britain, a small country of only 59,000 square miles.

England was smaller in area than North Carolina or Iowa. The whole of Great Britain—that is England, Scotland and Wales together—is hardly bigger than Minnesota. To the Americans it seemed cold and drab and dirty as well.

In June 1942, when the ETO was established, there were fewer than 60,000 US troops in the British Isles. By May 1944 an Invasion Force of 1,526,965 combat and service troops (including air and ground forces) was stationed in an already overcrowded Island, with a population of just over 48 million in an area smaller than the state of Oregon.

The US troops occupied 100,000 buildings, either newly built or requisitioned, ranging from small nissen huts, cottages and bell tents to sprawling hangars and assembly plants in more than 1,100 cities, towns and villages.

The accommodation at some airfields that had previously been R.A.F. bases, was quite good, with brick built barrack blocks. These contained some central heating (assuming that the fuel supplies were available), and washing and latrine facilities were all inside these buildings. Living conditions on most of the American Air Bases, which were built in 1942 and 1943 were much less comfortable.

The men were located in nissen huts which were scattered around amongst the trees, and the living conditions in them were pretty rugged.

The only heating they had were little coke heaters (tortoise stoves) about three feet high. As they were strictly rationed with coal and coke, (usually enough for only two days a week), many tricks were used to obtain extra fuel.

It was also difficult to dry out wet clothing in the damp and often rainy weather experienced, especially in the winter.

Air crews, both officers and enlisted men shared such miserable accommodation.

Enlisted men slept in bunks, sometimes double-tiered, while the officers had small beds or "cots".

Narrow and made of two frames of iron, these were "Sheer torture...the frames were about three feet long and the iron cross bars where they joined would cut you right about the hips".

The mattresses consisted of three separate, unforgiving little biscuits stuffed with excelsior (packing material) and they tended to separate in the night, and at 2 a.m., "You would be woken with a cold draft coming from below. In the end most of the crews sewed their mattresses together and that was much better".

The troops slept without sheets, covered only by thin blankets which were scratchy to the skin and often drifted in the night; flying crews who could wear their warm sheepskin—lined jackets day and night in the long, damp, chill British winter were much envied.

The ablution areas were often widely dispersed "You bathe, wash, shave etc. in separate and distinct places, usually from a block to half a mile apart".

Washing could be almost impossible…. "Small tin tubs stand on a brick and concrete pedestal. They are filled from a leaky spout which drizzles cold water or drenches you by turns. To empty you simply dump the contents onto the pedestal which has a trough down the center. If two dump at once, the pedestal overflows and both get their feet wet. The room is unheated".

When the men had really had enough of barracks hygiene, they would take a bus into the nearest town and go to the Red Cross Club for a hot shower and then take the bus back to the camp.

For many Americans the "Taste of (Britain) was of brussels sprouts, old mutton, spam, powdered eggs, dehydrated potatoes and strong tea".

An infantryman from Michigan, who had to wait all day for a meal when he arrived at Tidworth Barracks, found when it finally came that it was "The regular British ration…. Predominantly mutton, cabbage, Brussels sprouts, boiled potatoes and heavy dark bread and tea".

A radio operator stationed in R.A.F. quarters in Wales found the food—"Bad—thick globs of grease which someone found to be mutton(which the cook claimed it to be), whole cold potatoes and lukewarm tea. I quickly located The Salvation Army Hall where I lived on hot tea and biscuits".

Eventually more American food was shipped in from the USA. About 68% of their food was purchased locally—but the other 32% made the difference.

A technical sergeant stationed at Wendling near Norwich was dramatic: "I think the first shipment of peanut butter saved our lives!"

Many G.I.'s who were invited into British homes would arrive with cans of peaches, sugar, tins of luncheon meat or other delicacies unobtainable in wartime.

Some of the Americans eating customs seemed rather unusual to the British.

When A.T.S. girl and her friend were invited to an American Base in Wales, she noticed that "Every man had a queer mixture of food on one plate…. Tinned peaches and jam were indiscriminately mixed up with slices of veal and ham and sautéed potatoes and vegetables. A kindly orderly handed us two plates…saying 'I know you Limeys don't like to mix food on a plate like we do'…We were grateful because I doubt if we could have eaten the delicious meal the way everyone else was doing".

The one item in the British culinary desert that did seem to find favour with the G.I.'s was fish and chips.

"There is a national dish over here called fish'n chips", explained a US colonel in a letter home: "It is fried fish and fried potatoes which are cut into long, thin cubes before frying. I don't think they are very good, but they are popular".

Soon G.I.'s became accustomed to saying, "Fish'n chips with a dash of vinegar and plenty of salt", rather than "Hot dog, please".

In every city and town throughout Britain there seemed to be a fish and chip shop (fish was never rationed in the war, though some varieties became scarce and the Ministry of Food encouraged people to try the 'more unusual varities'—whalemeat for example), and fish and chip shops were often the only place to get any food in the evening.

It was often the fish and chip shop that a G.I. had his first experience of another British phenomenon—The queue.

"Over here", the observant Colonel reported, "The people are very orderly. They stand in line for everything—it is called queuing. It is pronounced 'cue' and you do this for a bus, for a shave and for practically any merchandise and food".

It didn't take the G.I.'s long to fall hand-in-glove with the fish and chips queue...You stood in line for buses, at the movies...and of course, the chow line", explained an infantry man from Georgia.

Pubs were another local institution which most G.I.'s embraced whole heartedly. For many troops stationed in rural areas, the pub was the only place to go in the evening if they wanted to get off the base.

It wasn't all that different in towns and cities, particularly in the early days before the American Red Cross set up clubs for the US troops.

Pubs accustomed to a couple of farmers and a sheepdog in the corner had fresh life injected into them with the arrival of American Forces in the area.

And the troops had already been briefed on pub behaviour by their handbook: It was described as a "Poor man's club where the men have come to see their friends not strangers...If you want to join a darts game, let them ask you first (they probably will)".

In fact it wasn't just a poor man's club; G.I.'s were surprised to see that men and women often went to the pub together, something that was rarely seen in The States at that time, where in any case some states were still enforcing prohibition.

The pubs provided companionship, often darts, cribbage or shove ha'penny—and weak, warm and watery beer.

It was explained to the G.I.'s that British beer is "Not an imitation of German beer like our beer is, but ale (though they usually call it beer). The British are beer drinkers—and can hold it. The beer is now below peacetime strength".

As one American found out when he tried the mild and then asked for something stronger: "We tried the bitter. It was weak and sweet and warm. We tried the brown ale. We tried the stout. We tasted the Guinness. We ended up by drinking the light ale, which was the only variety that seemed strong enough to put foam on a glass!"

Later he came to like, or at least, become accustomed to, 'arf and arf'". (Mild and bitter mixed.) "I think your beer's an aquired taste, and somehow I can't get round to aquiring it," regretted a G.I. from St. Louis, while another thought the beer tasted as if it had been boiled and then boiled again".

The Yanks shocked many locals by adding shots of whisky to their beer to give it strength, or salt to give it taste.

Troops stationed in the west country had another choice—cider. (Called rough cider—or scrumpy).

The average, hard drinking American would walk in calling "Cider, bud". This was gleefully provided and, once the first drink had gone, another soon took its place, often paid for by one of the locals in the interest of Anglo—American relations.

When the American rose to his feet at the end of the evening—that was the moment that he discovered he'd mislaid his feet, that the previously still room had started to rotate. Willing hands helped him outside. If lucky, he was taken back to the base in a Jeep, by M.P.'s.

"The Americans were incredibly generous at all times", remember a Dorset man, "but in a pub they were really crazy the way they threw their cash around. I don't know whether it was just to be big, or if they thought the money wasn't going to be of any use to them much longer".

"We did alright out of the Americans" a Dorset pub owner recalled, "that's how the Missus got this place. Them yanks were crazy for whisky. The Missus used to nearly fill a bottle with cold tea and then add a tot of whisky.
Then she'd shake it all up and sell it to the Yanks for a couple of quid".

Another pub keeper was more generous: "Whisky was always scarce and more than once I was offered as much as £ 10 for a bottle, but I always said that to sell it would only please one person. By selling it behind the bar, I brought pleasure to a lot of people".

It was hardly surprising that some local tensions developed. With free evenings and a lack of other entertainment, the G.I.s would head for the pubs as soon as they opened and would soon consume the limited stock available, with the result that "the agricultural workers, who, because they are working long hours and cannot get to the public houses as early as the American troops, find on their arrival that there is no beer left for them. This is causing very considerable resentment". It was by no means unusual for the G.I.s to drink a pub dry halfway through the evening, or even all the pubs in the town, as the 820th engineers did: "On Tuesday night, "The Dog" went dry—and the landlord hung out a sad little sign on his door—"No BEER"—and closed his inn for the evening—the first time in 450 years of The Dog's history".

The Americans would never get used to the complexities of pub opening hours—a cartoon in Stars and Stripes showed a parachutist bailing out of an aeroplane with the caption "Say, I just hope I come down near a pub that's open". Equally bewildering were the social graduations involved in the design of some pubs—places they called 'taverns' back home.

An infantry man remembers a pub round the corner from Grosvenor Square in London, where there were "Separate doors for family bar, saloon bar, public bar. Ladies' bar etc.... A person had to be really sober when he went in...."

But the G.I.s were almost universally taken with the phrase of British publicans, "Time, gentlemen, please". This and "You Cawn't miss it"—the standard response whenever they asked for directions—became the most mimicked sentences of their times in Britain.

"It's a pity", mused a sixty-nine-year-old woman, "They speak our language. If their language was a foreign one, we could make excuses for them and expect them to be different". For the G.I.s did—and didn't—speak English.

Conversely a G.I., when he arrived in Britain was told by a British woman "You're very homely". She clearly meant it as a compliment and "she couldn't have known that it meant "You are downright ugly".

The advice given to the British was blunt: Some Americans consider that our English accent is affected when it is 'standard' and repulsive when it is 'dialect'. There are also Britons who resent all American accents and phraseology on the grounds that they are a sign vulgarity, pretentiousness etc. Some people in these islands even believe the Americans "put on" their accents in order to emulate the movies.... It would be helpful, however, if Britons to day would acquaint themselves with some of the more common differences between American and British phraseology, especially such differences as may lead to practical misunderstandings—e.g. when an American speaks of the hood of a car, he means what we call the bonnet; when he says vest he means waistcoat, and when he says undershirt he means vest; when he says crackers, he means biscuits and when he says biscuits he means scones.

One G.I. went into a chemist in Birmingham: "Wanting a torch, I asked for a flashlight, and was sold a flyswat". But the language difference which seems to have caused almost the greatest ire was when Americans used British phones.

"On our first weekend in England officers and men were given permission to go to London.... We skipped the noon meal and thought we'd get an early start. Fourteen thousand of the fifteen thousand men in the division had the same idea". Remembers and infantry officer staioned at Tidworth Barracks.

London was a magnet to the G.I.s, the place where they headed to spend their furloughs. "Wartime London was special", recalled a nineteen-year-old from Oklahoma: "It is difficult to describe it now, but...it became a Mecca for just about all members of the nations in the war".

According to one G.I. at the time, "The conviviality of London in wartime is unimaginable—unless you have actually experienced it. I have seen people who literally hadn't seen each other five minutes earlier become comrades.... You could reckon on striking up a conversation in about five minutes of getting off the train. Everyone was real friendly".

"Battered and dirty, worn and scarred, the city swarmed with scores of different uniforms and it spoke in a hundred different tongues", one veteran relates: "No matter how long you stayed, you never saw it all, wherever you were going in the U.K. you had to go through London. London was the Babel, the Metropolis, the Mecca. London was IT".

London was the nerve centre of US Army activity in Britain: "It had a higher concentration of important personnel, a greater variety of installations than any other area in Britain...and in addition it was the principal leave centre in the U.K., ministering to the wants of a transient population half as large as its assigned strength".

By D-day there were 33 officers' Billets (including 24 hotels) and 300 buildings in use for troops and their accommodation. Whilst more than 2,5 million square feet had been taken over in offices, depots, garages. Shops, and various others places to house such American facilities as PX's, messes, a detention barracks, the Military Police Headquarters in Piccadilly, and a Gymnasium, as well as clinics and dispensaries.

The grandest of the US installations was undoubtedly the Officers' mess at Grosvenor House in Park Lane which had taken over the Hotel's spacious and elegant ballroom. Opened in 1943, it was nick-named "Willow Run" after the car assembly line in Detroit; eventually it was able to serve between 6,000 and 7,000 meals a day.

On his second visit to wartime London in 1943, Ernie Pyle, an Ameri-can journalist, was struck by the extent to which the city was crawling with Americans, both Army and civilian. All headquarter cities were alike in their overcrowding, their exaggerated discipline and what appeared to be overstaffing.

There were those who said that London was as bad as Washington. Others said it was worse. Certainly the section where American offices were most highly concentrated was a funny sight at lunchtime or in the late afternoon. Floods of American uniforms poured out of buildings. On some streets, an Englishman stood out as incongruously as he would in North Platte, Nebraska...There were all kinds of cracks about the way Americans had flooded the island and nearly crowded the English off....One American said to another, "The English are beginning to act as if this country belong to them".

But there was more space for pedestrians in London streets as petrol rationing meant many private cars were laid up for the duration of the war. At weekends traffic was light. In Hyde Park, U.S. troops joined British servicemen in listening to the harangues of the speakers, and in Green Park, British visitors—and the sheep who grazed there as part of the 'produce more food' wartime campaign and occasionally escaped into Piccadilly itself—watched the Yanks play hectic and noisy games of baseball and softball in the shadow of the anti-aircraft rocket batter-ies.

The trips by special trains to London for the two days off each month had the supercharged aspect to be expected. Some used their energy on the British Museum, and some burned it on a non—stop binge, but for the most it was just a continuation of the lonely sense of being strangers in a strange land.

"The gigantic bigness of London never ceased to overwhelm G.I.s. Nobody can ever again tell them that New York is the biggest city in the world", mused the Stars and Stripes correspondent, Ralph Martin.

The most popular leave towns for G.I.s., once they had torn themselves away from the delights of London, were Stratford-upon-Avon and Canterbury. Also Edinburgh was popular. Charles Taylor, who came from Ohio, found the Scottish people much more cheerful and friendly than the English.

Troops who visited Canterbury were amazed at the antiquity of the city as they strolled along and saw signs hanging out reading 'Sun Hotel, founded 1505'; there were streets that "We'd almost call back alleys, and many antique shops lined the way where people coming on pilgrimages could purchase relics and souvenirs".
Robert Arbib found "barrage balloons over the close at Canterbury and the city badly damaged by a Baedeker raid in 1942.... But the Cathedral itself was still a thing of beauty".

Eileen Smithers was living in Norwich 'surrounded by US Army Air Force Bases', and her mother's house was on a list for providing emergency beds for officers when the Red Cross Club was full: "I was also on the list! Most of the Bases ran Saturday night dances for which transport was sent to Norwich to collect the local girls. However, there were two distinct types of Saturday night dances. Those in Bases that just sent trucks to several pick-up points in the city and collected any waiting girls and those that were 'vetted' by the City Hall. The latter dances were only attended by girls with an official invitation issued from the CO of the Base.

To get such an invitation, a girl was interviewed at City Hall and, if approved, her name would go on the official invitation list. I went to quite a few of these dances, some were G.I. dances and some were officers dances. They were very different to the Mess parties I'd attended at RAF-fields prior to the Americans' arrival. No hilarious games for one thing".

But the best way for the Americans and the British to get to know each other wasn't at organized social events; it was made by British families inviting G.I.s. into their homes for tea or Sunday lunch, or even to stay for their furloughs.

The American Red Cross alone arranged over a quarter of a million such visits between November 1943 and the end of the war, and Anglo-American Hospitality Committees also put hosts and guests in touch with one another. People were often eager to act as hosts to the newly arrived troops. But sometimes things misfired, as when an American officer arrived with his company in Wales, where they were stationed: "When we first arrived, these town people used to gather at the camp gate—sometimes thirty at once—all of them with invitations for soldiers to come to their house for dinner. They kept coming and there didn't seem any way to handle them. I'd go down to the gate and fill my pocket with their invitations and then—we were pretty busy getting settled—I'd forget about them. One day I heard that a local family was very offended. They'd prepared dinner for two of the soldiers and the soldiers never appeared. I found the invitation still in my pocket!"

This particular unit solved the problem by forming a 'Friendship House', run by a committee of local people, who arranged sports, dances and entertainment for the troops—and a weekly hospitality schedule. "On average 125 invitations to the soldiers from the Welsh people were received. One village, twelve miles out in the country, sent buses and forty soldiers went, dined at separate houses and had a dance in the Village Hall".

Food rationing could be a problem—British difficulties with hospitality had been well drummed into most G.I.s. Their short Guide warned them: "One thing to be careful about—if you are invited into a British home and the host exhorts you to "Eat up, there's plenty on the table", go easy. It may be the family's ration for a whole week, spread out to show their hospitality".

Embarrassment about the paucity of the spread was undoubtedly one reason why many British families were initially less than eager to open their homes to G.I.s: "After four years of war, they are ashamed of their meagre rations—a 3 ounce ration of cheese cut into tiny cubes, 2 ounces of tea, 2 ounces of butter spread thinly across a "National Loaf"—and drab, threadbare homes—particularly when they think of America as a land of luxury".

A G.I. from Virginia was invited home by a girl he met at a dance: "We had a meal which even by American standards was great—complete with ham and much more. Only afterwards did I discover that I had eaten the family's special rations for a month. So I soon corrected that. I went to see our Mess Sergeant and then the next time I turned up at the girl's home, it was as if I were Santa Claus. I brought a large can of pears and a pork loin or something like that—and a lot of more stuff.

Commanding officers began to encourage their men to take official 'Hospitality Rations' when they went visiting—and the troops supplemented these with food begged from the cookhouse or treats bought from the PX.

This was done both in the spirit of friendship, and with the aim of minimizing the natural envy of American plentitude in the midst of British scarcity. Fathers received cigarettes, or even cigars, and a whiskey called Bourbon, while mothers were presented with tinned fruit, ham, chocolate and candies.

It was often "MOM" that the young soldiers far from home missed most. In many places the authorities—recognizing this, and seeing it as an ideal opportunity for creating the right sort of stable links with the British community—encouraged schemes whereby a local woman would 'adopt' a lonely G.I. for the duration, inviting him home for tea.

The fourth Sunday in Lent was traditionally linked with Mothering Sunday, but 'Mother's Day' on the scale it was celebrated in America in May—trailing only Christmas and Thanksgiving as a family festival since its introduction in 1914—was unknown in Britain.

In the middle of the war, President Roosevelt called on "The people of the United States to express the love and reverence which we feel for the mothers of our country": A number of G.I.s turned to British surrogates and 'adopted' a British mother for that special day, taking her to tea and a concert laid on by various Red Cross Clubs throughout the country, while wearing a carnation in tribute to his own mother—red if she was still alive, white if not. In the same spirit, a regular visitor to a Liverpool family paid for a party for the couple's twenty-fifth wedding anniversary and "Even bought my mother a corsage of orchids. She'd never had anything so lovely. After her death in 1971, thirty years later, we found the flowers pressed in her Bible".

If it was hard to be away from home and at war in a foreign land on Mother's Day, it was even harder at Christmas.

As many troops as possible were given the day off, Jewish soldiers would volunteer for duty, and for those men who could not be spared, the Army cooks prepared a traditional Christmas dinner.

But if possible the troops were to be entertained in British homes—"Filling the chairs left empty by British fighting men". The soldiers who accepted invitations to family meals were provided with special rations for each day's stay: "A typical package will contain fruit or tomato juice, evaporated milk, peas, bacon, sugar, coffee, lard or shortening, butter, rice or available substitutes". In view of this cornucopia, perhaps it is not surprising that so many invitations were extended to the US troops that first Christmas in 1942 that "The ratio is estimated at fifty invitations for every one soldier available" and a plea went out for more G.I.s. to come forward "and accept some more of those invitations".

One G.I. was invited to spend Christmas at a Land Army Girl's home which was "a two storey stone cottage. No plumbing, but gorgeous fireplaces". He turned up on a bicycle laden down with—legal rations of spam and powdered coffee, chocolate and soap, and other items from the camp stores...."we all sat down that day to a Christmas dinner"—and scene—that might have made Charles Dickens the only true recorder...."I don't recall what we had for dinner, but a long last the plum pudding—and all the renewed laughter at the clumsy struggle I had...till with a victorious 'whoop', I gained the threepenny bit".

It wasn't only extra rations that the G.I.s. brought into British homes at Christmas: "They taught us about Advent Calenders and Advent Candles and hanging gingerbread biscuits on the Christmas tree—but we showed them Christmas crackers, which they'd never seen before and were greatly taken with!"

If the US troops brought new delights to many young British women, it was the same with the children. Many G.I.s. were not long out of childhood themselves and the uninhibited curiosity and open admiration which British children usually displayed for the Yanks made it easier to get to know them than their elders. And for family men, time spent with the children was perhaps some compensation for missing their own children who were growing up while they were away at war.

The currency of their relationship was chewing-gum. A Hertfordshireman, seven years of age when the Americans came to his home town, recollects: "My friends and I constantly chased them with cries of "Got any gum, chum?". It must have been very irritating to say the least and

I don't recall actually getting any gum, whatever that was, but my uncle told me that this was the correct way to greet Americans".

The "gum-chummers", as a Seething airman labelled them, seemed to materialize like magic whenever a G.I. appeared. Chewing gum was a prized possession, to be asked for, cajoled for—and bartered for. Connie Stanton used to swap hard-boiled eggs from her mother's hens for sticks of gum with the Base Guards at Milton Ernest; chewing gum was also used as a bribe to get local kids to go for fish and chips, or exchanged for jam jars, coat hangers—which the satorially minded G.I.s. always seemed short of.

At a time when sweets and chocolate were almost nonexistent, and sugar was strictly rationed, chocolate Hershey Bars, "Baby Ruths", and hard candy (boiled sweets) like "Life Savers" were much coveted. A thirteen-year-old living in Bude in Cornwall "on meagre British wartime rations…couldn't believe the food available to the 29th Ranger Batialion stationed there". He and his friends would stand around the mess hall and were usually invited in to clear up some of the surplus meat balls, tinned fruit, etc.

It was customary for the Americans to give lavish parties for the local children at Air and Army Bases. "Christmas, New Year, Birthdays—any old Birthday—Hallowe'en, Fourth of July, Thanksgiving, whatever celebration the G.I.s. cooked up, there was always—bombs or no bombs—a party for the kids", relates Jean Lancaster Rennie.

A Hertfordshire man who was evacuated to Middlesborough as a child recalls how "At Christmas the Americans threw a superb party for the school children in the Town Hall. It was one of those grim public buildings of the time, with sandbags all around the lower ground floor. The G.I.s. had decorated the interior with lots of flags—Stars and Stripes and Union Jacks—together with tinsel and paper chains…They served an immense amount of food, not only the cakes, jellies and blancmange but many sweet dishes that we hadn't seen for ages due to rationing. We were all given a present from 'Santa', who had an American accent…I had a box of cardboard infantrymen. They had 'Stars and Stripes' stickers and my hosts had to reassure me that they were on 'our side'".

For those who were invited to 'Operation Reindeer' at Shipdham Air Base in Norfolk, "Coming into the hangar was like coming into Aladdin's cave…With coloured lights, streamers, silver bells and a Christmas tree reaching up to the skies". Such trees would often be festooned with 'chaff'—the thin strips of metallic foil thrown out of the aircraft to confuse German radar during raids.

"There were sweets, sacks of sweets, stacks of sweets everywhere and every now and then a great shower of sweets would be thrown into the air and the children scrambling and screaming in sheer delight tumbled into an exuberant mass for a fistful of this treasure".

The G.I.s. would have saved up their sweet rations for weeks to provide this feast, and spent many evenings making toys, collecting money so they could buy whatever they could find in the shops, and writing home for small toys to be sent for the high point of the party—the arrival of Santa Claus. Usually he came by Jeep, but at Shipdham "A droning was heard in the sky…. Nearer and nearer it came. It was silver and 'snow' covered….A Piper Cub plane straight from Santa Claus land. The propeller slowed and stopped—and sure enough there he was. Father Christmas, with a red robe and white beard and a big bulging sack, stepped out of the plane".

On one occasion, the venerable old man 'arrived' in a Flying Fortress and the children were allowed to scramble in and out of this huge 'sledge'.

The parties were thrown to foster good relations with the local community, and to bring some pleasure to wartime children for whom fun was pretty thin on the ground and who were growing up deprived of toys and treats—and often of at least one parent as well.

Many of the children who came to G.I. parties were evacuees: At Colchester in 1943 the Military Police stationed there threw a Christmas Party for ninety children whose fathers were prisoners-of-war, and many G.I.s. held parties for local orphanages and entertained children in hospital or in homes for the handicapped.

The American Red Cross and Stars and Stripes joined forces to start an orphans fund; each unit which collected £ 100 could 'adopt' an orphan, or a child who had lost one parent, for a year. They could specify their requirements—'a blue-eyed, blonde girl'. 'a red-haired boy, no older than five'. These children, and there were nearly 600 of them, would be sent sweets, toys and new clothes by their benefactors, as well as being taken on trips and entertained; they would often visit the units, where miniature uniforms might have been made for these 'mascots'.

The 306th Bomb Group at Thurleigh had wanted to adopt and had even settled on a name, 'Butch'; when the day came, there weren't any boys available, so instead they took a three-year-old girl, Maureen, nicknamed her 'Sweet Pea', and got her to christen a bomber after herself by dipping her hand in red paint and holding her up to plant her palm print on its fuselage.

Local newspapers would report the G.I.s. generosity: 'U.S. host Northants children', 'Yanks play Santa Claus at Wellingborough', 'U.S. Santa Claus at Kettering'. But a Staff Sergeant with the 820th Engineers thought a headline that appeared in the Rushden Echo and Argus was particularly apt: 'Americans Revel in Children's Visit', it read.

"The sky was always full", remembers a Norfolk man who was fourteen in 1942. A woman working in the American Red Cross Club in Norwich was struck by the fact that "In a district that had for centuries heard few other sounds than the monotobous mooing of contented cattle, and other farm animals…A new sound now dominated the air…. Dawn brought the drone of bombers".

Throughout the thousand days that the 8th Air Force was operating from Britain, its bombers flew a total of 330,523 sorties—including bombing raids (or missions), training flights, and transport flights to drop supplies over occupied Europe. By 1944 a mission—flown on one of the 459 days between 17th August 1942 and 8th May 1945 on which heavy bombers set off from the U.S. Bases in Eastern England to attack enemy targets—would take off with an average of 1,400 heavy bombers supported by up to 800 fighter planes to drop an estimated 3,300 tons of bombs.

The most significant building in the life of the bombardment group stationed on one of these 8th Air Force Bases might seem to have been the operations briefing room, but preparations for a mission started long before that tense moment when the crews were let in on the secret of the target for that day.

The decision to fly would have been taken at the 8th's H.Q. at High Wycombe (code-named 'Pinewood'), where General Ira Eaker and his staff, working from a list of priority targets supplied by the supreme allied H.Q., had sifted through intelligence and operational information to determine both how many bombers should be sent to the target and how many planes the various bomb groups would be able to muster (depending on how heavy their recent losses had been, and whether replacements had arrived), which fighter groups should be used, what was known about enemy anti-aircraft batteries, and which was the best route to avoid their flak. But the one imponderable which kept everyone on alert was the weather.

The bombers had to be able to assemble in formation, and they couldn't do that in fog, or low, heavy cloud; they had to be able to fly across occupied Europe at higher than 18.000 feet or, on daylight missions, German flak would pick off the planes at a suicidal rate; and a formation was very hard to hold flying blind through cloud. And over the target there had to be enough breaks in the cloud for the bombardiers to aim their bomb loads—until the introduction of P.F.F. or pathfinder planes, in which the ball turret had been removed and radar equipment installed, made targeting a different matter.

The crews who were 'on alert' were those who would be flying the next combat mission—and in 1942-43, the shortage of replacement staff meant that pilots and crew were on alert for most missions. Crews on alert were restricted to base.

On the base at Grafton Underwood there was an amber light in the bar: if it was switched to green during the evening, the forecast was unpropitious and the mission was off. A red light meant that the mission was on. The bar would then close around eight o'clock and everyone who was scheduled to fly would try to get some sleep.

While the air crew slept, the operations crew planned and checked the details of the raid, and the ground crew set to work to get the planes ready to fly, delivering and loading fuel and bombs—high explosive for buildings, fragmentation bombs for moving targets, trains and troops. Loading would take from around 11 o'clock at night until 3 or 4 next morning. It could be dangerous work.

At Alconbury in May 1943 the ground crew was loading bombs into a B-17 when one of the bombs detonated and set off several others. Nineteen men were killed and twenty-one injured, and four B-17 standing on the runway were destroyed.

At Ridgewell in the early hours of 13. June 1943, bombs being loaded into a B-17 exploded, destroying the Fortress and another plane, damaging another eleven and killed twenty-three men.

The work was usually freezing cold—as it was for the armament section, loading the 50 calibre links for the waist gunners, checking gun turrets and bomb sights, and for the crew chiefs taking off the canvas covers and testing the four engines and running an instrument check, turning the engines off as soon as possible to conserve the expensive high-octane fuel.

There were reckoned to be about ten ground-staff for every man in the air; and they worked through the night before each mission, servicing, checking and loading—as responsible in their way as the flight crew would be in theirs for the success of the mission.

It was still pitch black when the mechanics—or 'grease monkeys', as they were known—tapped the final rivet back and firmly secured the last bomb door.

The flying crews were woken at about 4 a.m. for a 6.30 take-off. The orderlies would flash a torch in the faces of the sleeping crews to wake them. The men who were scheduled to fly would have tied a towel round the end of their bunk, but it was firmly believed that anyone seen to be sleeping with a smile on his face would be woken up for the hell of it.

Lateness for a briefing wasn't tolerated, so as a pilot stationed at Grafton Underwood recalled, " You had to get your clothes on real quick…you had to take time to shave though, because you wore an oxygen mask real tight against your face, and the mixture of breath condensation and gun smoke would irritate your face badly even if you had shaved".

Then it was off by Jeep or bike or on foot, carrying a torch (which the Yanks called a flashlight) covered in not less than two thickness of tissue paper, to the mess hall for breakfast. Most days that meant that the men were served up what the G.I.s dubbed square eggs' (powdered eggs cut into cubes), but on mission mornings the air crews tucked into 'combat eggs' (precious fresh eggs), toast and mugs of coffee. As the war correspondent Ernie Pyle observed: "A young airman died clean-shaven and well fed".

After chow, it was off in the Jeep for a briefing session. The men filed into the base briefing room—often a Nissen hut—and sat on benches or wooden chairs. Many would be smoking—"we put up a haze that rivalled a Pittsburgh smog"—and talking and joking nervously. There was none of the usual reluctance to sit in the front row; everyone wanted to get a good look at the target map, though this was covered with a curtain or sheet until the base commanding officer strode into the room an gestured to the S-2 (the intelligence officer), who then dramatically pulled it aside.

There were catcalls and jeers from the men, and someone usually called out the wartime slogan, "Is your journey really necessary ?". It was at this moment that the men learned that whether their mission was likely to be a 'milk run'—over targets in occupied countries, from which the crews were reasonably likely to get home without being hit by flak or enemy planes. Not that there was ever any guarantee that a mission would be a 'milk run' for attacks could appear from nowhere—or the stomach-churning prospect of a long and dangerous flight into Germany, which by 1944 could even include a daylight mission to the 'Big B' (Berlin).

Elmer Bendiner, who flew with the 379th Bomb Group stationed at Kimbolton, remembers when the curtain was swept across the map of Western Europe on 17 August 1943. The red yarn indicating their flight route began at the assembly point over The Wash, stretched over the Channel across Holland to the German border and across the Mosel and the Rhine before ending in a pin "Puncturing Germany at a place called Schweinfurt".

It was, in fact, the 8th Air force's first raid into Germany and it was to prove perilous—yet it was the prime purpose for which the 8th had been sent to Britain in May 1942. They had come to prepare for—and then support- a combined Allied land, sea and air operation across the Channel to continental Europe, and this meant first smashing the heart of the German war machine from the air.

The crews were given details of the mission by the various experts involved. Allan Healey recounts, in his history of the 467th Bomb Group stationed at Rackheath, that "By map, picture and diagram the whole operation was explained. S-2 (Intelligence) put on the route, target and expected reaction from flak and fighters, S-3 (Operation and Planning) gave the operational data; Weather told of the conditions to and from the target…All (was) cut and dried; an operation of death told like a commuter's timetable".

Next came the synchronization of watches or 'time tick': "The C.O. would say something like Gentlemen, it is now three forty-five minus twenty seconds…ten seconds…nine seconds…two…one hack'". Finally, navigators were given a special additional briefing, as bombardiers and radio operator queued up to receive 'flimsy' sheets of information about their own particular duties.

The crews piled into the equipment room to pull on their flight gear: electrically heated flying suits—essential for high flying altitudes, given that the temperature could drop to minus 50 degrees, the planes were unheated and the air rushed in through the waist gunner's windows (which weren't windows at all but openings cut out of the fuselage behind the wings).

Some airmen refused to wear the suits, because "when I sweated, I'd short the damned thing out" On top of the suits came flak jackets, aprons lined with metal panels, and flying jackets, and over this lot, bulky 'Mae Wests', inflatable life jackets named after the film star 'for obvious reasons'.

Sheepskin-lined boots, helmets with ear pieces and an oxygen mask. A throat microphone on an elastic band round the neck, and a parachute completed the outfit. At least one airman always checked his pack as he strapped it on, after hearing rumours of G.I.—issue blankets being stuffed into the pack after the parachute itself had been given away to a girlfriend—for silk was much in demand to make dresses during war-time rationing.

An air crew would routinely check their oxygen supply, including the portable bottles they used if they needed to move around the plane; at the altitude the crews would be flying, oxygen was essential to the men as petrol was to this planes. An escape pack, containing a phrase card in English, German and French and four photographs in civilian clothes, would be slipped into a special zip pocket at the knee of their trousers so that there would be no danger of losing it if they had to bale out, and sometimes a small knife between their shoes and flying boots.

The queue at the fish and chip shop was considered a good place to meet Yanks—or maybe at a dance or at the Red Cross Club. It was often the daughter of the house who would first invite a soldier or an airman she'd met home for tea. And it was not all that unusual for the visitor, like all invaders, to end up by carrying off the woman. Some 70.000 British women were destined G.I. brides—though the course of wartime true love did not always run smooth.

Elieen Smithers, whose mother's house in Norwich was an emergency billet for U.S. officers, "only ever dated one of then, a Texan called 'Red' because of the colour of his hair". He was a "very serious formal young man" who would insist on walking her to wherever she was going and make sure that if she had a date she had her 'mad money'—enough for a taxi home if necessary.

They went for long walks and cycle rides, sailing in the Norfolk Broads—and "of course to the cinema!", but it wasn't an entirely compatible friendship. "He was the only Yank I ever knew who didn't dance and I was mad about dancing, especially jive and jitterbug", so it was something of a surprise when, after about a year, "my mother informed me that he had asked permission to get engaged and to marry me, having previously written and obtained his father permission to marry a Limey ? I was considerably shocked and not a little annoyed by this.

When I asked him why he hadn't discussed the matter with me first, he replied that was how it was done where he came from. As we hadn't even held hands, let alone kissed each other, I just wouldn't take him seriously. I think I hurt his feelings".

One woman remembers that the G.I.s she dated as an eighteen-year old civil servant in 1942 would often 'want to get engaged' after a few evenings out, but she concluded that 'this was only the war talking', while her family and friends "were surprised to see me dating a G.I".—A not uncommon reaction. Sometimes this was simple snobbery.

A Liverpool woman recalls neighbours saying to her mother:" I saw your Pamela out with a Yank last night"—with the use of your as opposed to our denoting North Country disapproval. Father's were often suspicious of the man's intentions: The girlfriend of a ferry pilot was instructed by her father to "question me on (I) did I have a wife ? (2) Did I have a girl back home ? I remember it was at The Swan Hotel and (Jean's) face was as red as the portwine we were drinking".

A woman from Aberdare, who had frequently sworn she would never "be seen dead with a Yank", decided that she wanted to marry the one she'd met on the eve of D-day. Her father sent her out of the room when her suitor arrived for tea in order to grill him about his marital status. "My Louis got the 'third degree'…and when we finally left the house he said "boy, that was tough—but I respect your father for what he did".

Parents often opposed such wartime romances. Because they were likely to mean that their daughters would emigrate to The United States at the end of the war. In the days before frequent air travel, a single flight across the Atlantic cost around £ 175, a sea passage between £ 40 and £ 65, while the average weekly wage in Britain in 1940 was £ 4=10. Many feared they would never see their daughters again—and to the daughters going to America seemed like going to the moon !.

"Mum kept asking me what was wrong with British boys", one woman recalled, and many dads wern't to keen on their daughters dating 'those bloody Yanks'- let alone marrying them. The father of a Cornish land girl expressed 'heartfelt feelings of relief' when the 291st infantry moved out of Newlyn in June 1944 'without capturing any of us'.

A woman who became a G.I. bride recalls that for several months her father refused to sign the necessary papers for her to marry:" I guess he was anxious for the future of his daughter, but of course I was very young and headstrong. The months crept by and I never gave up. I would put them on the table every evening where he would sit. He always picked them up and put them on one side without a word…it was so frustrating. Many nights I sobbed into my pillow. Finally one night my father sat at the table and looked down at the papers.

He looked at me and I could see that there were tears in his eyes". "You both mean business, I can see there is nothing to be gained by going on like this"- and he signed the papers".

Indeed some parents were full of encouragement. A woman who met her future husband while working as a hostess at Rainbow Corner found that her parents gave her "a lot of support…they felt there was no future for young people in England—and I would have a much better life in the States".

On the whole, the U.S. authorities discouraged their servicemen from marrying—and particularly from marrying abroad. A single man undistracted by family responsibilities was considered more likely to be single-minded in this war effort, and more likely to make a strong ties with his 'buddies' which could generate the selfless courage that war might demand. It was common currency, too, that wartime marriages were doomed to failure.(In fact, the evidence rather contradicted this: It was estimated that some 80 per cent the 8.000 marriages contracted overseas during the first world war were successful—or at least lasted).

And then there was public opinion back home, which was hardly enthusiastic about having the flower of American manhood return from foreign wars accompanied by foreign wives, at the expense of American women seeking husbands.

In June 1942 , the U.S. war department issued a regulation requiring troops stationed overseas to seek the approval of their commanding officers two months in advance of a proposed wedding. Furthermore, a potential bridegroom was warned that 'he will not be allowed any special privileges or special living arrangements different from those provided for single men and women', and the wife of a U.S. serviceman married in the E.T.O ' will not necessarily be allowed to accompany her husband to a change of station or on his return to the U.S'. Failure to comply with the regulations could lead to a court martial and sometimes immediate despatch to a combat zone. But if the woman was pregnant the waiting period was sometime waived.

The G.I.s commanding officer also interviewed the potential bride—though this could be delayed by bureaucratic red tape for more than a year after the initial application had been filed. A G.I. who applied to marry a Worcestershire woman in the autumn of 1942 was granted permission only in December 1943:" They tried to discourage us at first because so many servicemen were marrying British girls. They thought they would later regret it". Her G.I. fiancé was transferred to Northern Ireland for three months. On his return, he asked if his application had been sent out. It had not, but the C.O. conceded:" So you still want to marry this girl? Well, I guess we'll just have to go ahead and send it in!"

And a woman then living in Leicester relates that "one of my husband's officers remarked that he should wait until he was back in The U.S. and marry an American girl. My husband replied that is was a matter of opinion. He was demoted in rank". Enquiries were made about the girl's background.

The American Red Cross was supposed to be enlisted for this task, until they refused to do so. The men had to get letters from home confirming that they had jobs to return to, savings in the bank and parents prepared to support the young couple if need be. The girls dreaded the form-filling and the interviews with their fiancés C.O. or chaplain, during the course of which they were interrogated as to their fitness to be the wives of Americans—and as to whether they were pregnant. Before marrying a G.I. sergeant "I had to sign fifteen documents in all", remembers a civilian employee of the 68th General Hospital. The Commanding Officer had to sign them, my father had to sign them, my mother had to sign them, and Arnold had to sign them…and then they talk of Americans and lightning romance…non sense!".

It was not only the C.O.s who proved obstructive an occasions: Letters appeared in newspapers all over the U.S. protesting against the outbreak of overseas weddings. One G.I.—a former correspondent for Stars and Stripes, who had himself married an English woman—roused a storm of protest on both sides of the Atlantic by an article he wrote in The New York Times at the end of the war, explaining why, in his view, such marriages so often happened.

Women overseas—seemed to be there for the sole purpose of being pleasant to the men…while American women insist on a big share in the running of things. Few European women want to be engineers, architects or bank presidents. They are mainly interested in the fundamental business of getting married, having children and making the best homes that their means or conditions will allow. They feel they can attain their goals by being easy on the nerves of their men folk. But despite the obstacles, and the clampdown forbidding all weddings prior to D-Day, thousands of British girls overcame their families' reservations, their neighbours disapproval and the rigidity of the U.S. authorities to marry their G.I. in wartime Britain, wearing a corsage on their uniform, or a borrowed wedding dress, or a pre-war suit set off with a new hat (hats were never rationed), or perhaps even an entirely new outfit obtained with saved and borrowed coupons.

Their bridesmaids might wear dresses made from damaged parachute silk provided by my fiancé, or maybe butter muslin. A woman working as a volunteer at the Red Cross Club in Newbury decided that neither she nor her husband-to-be was greatly in favour of wartime marriages, but the padre warned that unless they were married it might be years before she would get transport over to America.

With the wedding arranged, transport difficulties meant that her fiancé only arrived the lunch time before the big day. There was no time to assemble the choir, but the organist played and the family rallied round to provide 'jellies and blancmange and other goodies for the reception' and Norma Lambert became Mrs. Schneider in a dress borrowed from a friend who had just got married, her mothers veil and orange blossom with the bride maids in dresses which she had brought through an advert in the local paper ("so, no coupons!").

The wedding ring was often sent from the States in a set with an engagement ring—"as if your jewellery wasn't good enough". Bristled a woman, reviving memories of her war years in Norwich. The wedding cake might be a wartime rations sponge with an iced cardboard confection borrowed from the baker plopped on top; there was no icing sugar in wartime (Roses are red, violets are blue, sugar is sweet, remember?' was inscribed in one bride's card). A corner-shopkeeper's wife, invited to a wedding, was so envious of the marzipan on the young couple's cake that she did a deal with them for a piece in exchange for several glasses of wine.

The food at a wedding reception was likely to be a masterpiece of improvisation. Guests ate whatever was available—in one case, reported by Norman Longmate, peas on toast fingers in place of the traditional canapès. If the groom was on good terms with his cook-house, there could be joints og ham, tubs of icecream and tins of fruit. When a Bristol girl married a G.I., her brother remembers that she was—"bashful in her borrowed wedding dress and her bridesmaids' dresses, none or which fitted properly, but no one seemed to notice…They had a nice reception thanks to the generosity of the yanks who brought enormous tins of spam and peaches, and Doreen's customers (on her milk round) clubbed together with their meagre rations and made her a lovely wedding cake".

An American ferry pilot who proposed to his wife in Barbara's Bun shop in Bedford—and was accepted—managed to secure a precious bottle of vodka and watched in bemusement as his best man thought-fully poured it into a large jug of orange juice reserved for the elderly ladies at the reception." When I last saw them they were crying and laughing…and one of them told (my mother-in-law) what a lovely wedding it was, and what was that exquisite drink?". There was also an excellent trifle at the reception and a wedding cake which his co-pilot enjoyed so much that " he took big chunks…with him when he left for a mission. I never saw him again. He was lost over the Channel on a foggy day".

Honeymoons, if possible at all, were often brief. One G.I. had fifty minutes in which to get married and return to his unit. He sought the help of the Red Cross:

He burst into the office at 1.10 p.m. and said he had to be married and back with his unit by 2.00 p.m. as the unit was pulling out that afternoon…the registrar at the local registry office was out rent collecting, and anyway forty-eight hours' notice was necessary prior to the ceremony. A telephone call to the soldier's C.O. explaining the situation was sufficient to give the man another hour, but 3 o'clock was the deadline. Another phone call was made, this time to the Catholic minister, who, after conversation with the bishop, carried out the ceremony just in time to return the soldier to his unit without being A.W.O.L.

So began married life for one Anglo-American couple—'A life perforated with hellos and goodbyes'. It was the same story for thousands. Men were posted, trained, or flew missions, and finally joined the invasion of Europe. For the G.I. brides there were classes run by the Red Cross and booklets telling them what to expect in their new lives. Then they settled down to what was likely to prove a long, frustrating and somewhat worrisome wait for the time when it was peace again and they would be able to set sail for their husbands' native land—and check out these glowing descriptions of the 'new country' for themselves.

The Regensburg—Schweinfurt Africa Shuttle Mission

Narrated by William Arnold van Steenwyk 94th Bomb Group

It was August 17, 1943 and the Photo Lab phone usually rang to inform us that we were to install our aerial cameras in the designated planes for the coming mission, this time however, it was Major Leonard on the line and he wanted me to come to the S-2 Office immediately.

William Arnold van Steenwyk

The time was around midnight so I biked over to the Intelligence office and Major Leonard showed me orders that had come down from Divi-

sion Headquarters…all Photo personnel who had aerial gunnery training were to be included in the roster of the coming mission.

I was the N.C.O. in charge of the Photo Section and hadn't flown any
missions as my primary duties were to run the photo lab designate the
duty roster, work with the photo officer and try and keep the guys
happy. I had been the one N.C.O. in photo when the cadre was
formed in Tucson, arriving there after graduating from gunnery school
in Las Vegas so this opportunity, flying as an aerial photographer-gun-
ner was going to be a new experience.

I had to hurriedly get checked out on the P.O.W. briefing and other
last minute "must do" instructions. We were to bring toilet articles,
winter flying gear, underwear, socks and mess kits and radio equipment, etc.

Breakfast was to be at 1 a.m. A big topic of conversation was the "fresh
eggs being served but the main conversation was trying to figure out
where we were headed and for how long?

At briefing we saw the ball of yarn on the map that dropped all the way
down to the follor…where Africa would be and then the questions
began. "Why are we going there?" "All the way without fighter support?" "What kind of target is so important?" and so on. And then
briefing began.

We learned that the target was Regensburg, Germany, a manufacturing
plant for the ME-109. We were told that this plan furnished over 30%
of all the Luftwaffe Messer-schmidts, and if we could knock it out we
could significantly cut down the fighter action. After bombing we were
to proceed to North Africa by way of Austria, Brenner Pass, Italy, Cor-
sica, Sicily, flying over the Mediterranean and then landing on the
northern African coast.

The plan was this. Our group the Regensburg flight was the 4th combat wing, consisting of 7 Bomb Groups. The Schweinfurt flight, called the first wing, with 12 Bomb Groups.

The first wing would leave the English coast about in the same time frame as the 4th wing, both wings would converge around Leige, Germany, fly as one huge task force and then the first wing would make a 90 degree left turn and head up to their target Schweinfurt and the 4th wing would continue to fly south towards our target, Regensburg.

The planners of this mission figured that this would confuse the Germans and it would split their fighter forces. Now we come to the element that could foul up the whole mission -and it did—the weather!

Take off time had been scheduled for 5:50 a.m. Parts of England were clear but EVERY B-17 Base was covered by cloud cover, so the waiting began. At 6:40 there was some improvement at Bury St. Edmunds but not much.

Finally, it was decided that if this section of the plan was to land in Africa, it would have to take off soon or it would be difficult to land in a strange environment without the use of daylight.

The First Division could not take off but Col. Le May with his constant practice missions and instrument training for his pilots could get his men airborne,. The Schweinfurt Force was socked in and it would be hours before they could take off so the surprise element of the mission was ruined and the Fourth Division would have the entire Luftwaffe on their backs all the way to Italy were there was supposedly another small force waiting.

We were driven to our designated planes. I was scheduled to fly with a ship called "Dear Mom" with Lt. Nayovitx and Lt. Jack Smith as co-pilot. This ship had been installed with our one (and only) k-17 camera which took a 12x12 with good definition.

As I was getting set up in the radio room, getting my gear hooked up and checking out the camera, I was informed that they didn't have enough oxygen for an "extra man". So I had to leave and find another camera ship near by and it turned out to be "Little Minnie II" being flown by Lt. Sweeley a 332nd pilot.

They welcomed me aboard with no problems. This ship was also equipped with a camera but a much smaller version taking a picture about 5x7. I got all of my gear settled down in the radio room. The aerial camera was mounted in a well underneath a trap door in the fore part of the room.

Take off time was finally set for 7:30. We broke through the overcast at around a thousand feet and started the long slow process of climbing and forming into the proper elements for the beginning of the mission over the English Channel.

This being my first mission everything was exciting and new and we crossed the Channel with no problem and then about ten minutes inside the European coast the Germans hit with their force of about 100 fighters. As we neared Antwerp a couple of B-17's headed home with enemy fighters chasing them.

I looked through the radio room window and saw Lt. Smith in "Dear Mom" tucked in closely to our left. We waved to each other and shortly after that Lt. Sweeley swerved upwards to our left with evasive action.

I fell over the radio desk and frantically checked to see if I was still plugged in with oxygen, radio and heated suit and then when things settled back down I looked out of the window again. It was "Dear Mom" on fire pulling out of formation to the left with a direct hit to the cockpit area.

There was a big explosion, where the tail section separated and pieces were scattered all over the sky. Lt. Nayovitz, Lt Smith and the other two officers and both turret gunners were killed from the burst of cannon fire. T/Sgt. A. Mc Donnell, the radio operator was badly injured and was blown out of the plane. He managed to land but was severely injured and was taken prisoner.

S/Sgt. B.C. Geyer escaped after the plane broke in two. He avoided capture and was returned to the 94th, received the DFC, and later a cluster for evading capture. He was a crack shot, shooting down 3 enemy planes in his first 10 missions. Well, hey now—we are just over Belgium, the plane I'm supposed to be in has been shot down in flames, we still have at least another 7 hours to go and at this point I'm not too sure about my future.

We didn't have any left cover now and looking back I could see the groups behind us really taking a beating. I could see other B-17's on fire, pulling out of formation, some trailing smoke and still trying to hang in with their crippled condition.

Through all this I failed to see any P-47's that were supposed to have flying with us but my vantage point wasn't the greatest in the radio room. The 94th, with it's good tight formation flying discouraged a lot of enemy fighters. They were going after the groups ahead of us and behind us.

Looking up ahead I could see another B-17 on fire . I checked my watch and it was now around 11a.m. I could see about 15 fighters lining up for a pass at the guys directly behind us and about 10 minutes later looking back I could see three B-17's on fire.

We had another hour to go before reaching the target area and it was without a doubt the longest hour I have ever lived through. As we neared the target area with Col. Le May leading the Division and Col.

Moore and Col. Castle also leading their respective units I opened up the camera bay doors.

Flak had damaged one of the doors and I had a problem with it. As I looked down through the camera well, I could see the target area. The previous elements of the formation had clobbered the target very extensively and the last unit before us had dropped incendiaries so the entire area was covered with smoke. It had been mentioned at briefing that if the target area was abscured when we approached, perhaps a second run should be made.

The lead bombardier couldn't find an opening and so the 94th made another run. Hey there was a lot of grumbling and swearing going on in a lot of planes that instant but we made another pass, dropping the bombs dead center in the middle of the smoked area.

Later recon photos showed that they were very effective. About now I was lying on my stomach in the radio room one hand on my intervolometer taking pictures as the bombs were released and following them into the target trying to get as many shots as I could of the group's bombs going in.

At this time the ball turret pulled around to the front and fired a burst of shots directly underneath me. The vibration that bounced up on me felt like I had been hit and when I wiped my faced with my gloved hand, which was a brown leather glove I looked and saw something wet...and with a good imagination and panic playing its role, I assumed that it was blood.

I kept on taking pictures, waiting for some sort of pain to set in and again wiped my face with the same results! Finally I figured out that the moisture was from condensation from my oxygen mask. What a scare.

Now, being relieved I closed the camera doors and hatch and looked out of the windows and noted that we were having a field day in aircraft recognition. There were ME-110's, ME-210"s, ME- 109's, an FW-190's and in the distance a JU-88 was lobbing cannon shells into the formation.

The two engine fighters were also involved. They'd climb up and then come in on either side of the unit- one of them must have made a direct pass through because one minute I was standing looking out of the window taking pictures with my K-20 camera and the next minute I was on the floor. Lt. Sweeley made a dive during avasive action that upended me. He probably saved his ship with this action...he was a GREAT pilot.

After evading fighters all the way to the Alps, the forward unit of the wing circled a lake waiting for stragglers to catch up (I think it was called Lake Garda.) and we were some of the stragglers.

After the planes were all in a tight formation again, ready to take on a new grow up of fighters that were supposed to be in the area but never showed up, we headed out over the Brenner Pass, down over Italy, Sardinia, Sicily and over the Mediterranean. We still had nearly five hours of flying time left to go and more than 900 miles of enemy land and sea to cover before reaching the coast of North Africa.

We saw five B-17s ditch in the sea. By the time we reached Africa there were 24 B-17s missing out of the 146 dispatched and 122 over the target. Of the 230 B-17s sent to Schweinfurt, 184 bombed the primary target, 36 planes were missing. A total of 60 B-17s and their crews were either missing or killed in action.

After flying lower and lower and getting shorter and shorter on gas, we finally landed at a levelled off piece of land at Bertoux. After living through eleven and a half hours of pure terror for this GI, and six hours on oxygen, I could literally kiss that sandy, muddy African soil when we landed.

After checking out my cameras, we had chow using our mess kits. The bread was terrific, unlike the English French style bread, this was soft and white, not unlike angel food cake—Spam and pickles and white bread, with canned fruit Cocktail on the side—after 11 hours it was feast! We were served by Italian POWs who were happy to be "out" of the war.

After I took care of cameras, and met up with the other Group Photo guys. I got back to "Little Minnie II" around 2:00 am. The guys were sleeping on the wing and inside the plane. I was lucky to be able to sleep in the radio room. During the night some ground crews came around and pumped some gas from 50 gallons drums using hands pumps—giving us just enough to get to our next destination, the Telergma Depot.

We had the same chow for breakfast as we had the night before. The bread was still delicious. Later a chow truck came around with something more substantial, but I filled up more bread and beans (I skipped the sardine-onion-salad fare). The lima beans were great.

We had many little Arab visitors, and when I took the pictures of the entire group in front of one of the B-17s on Sunday, a lot of them were included in the photo. They were good little guys but had to be watched.

We had a little shower the next day, a muddy, sandy mixture, but everything soon dried off again and we continued on the trip to Telergma. Now the work began, cleaning guns, loading up gas with hand pumps, loading bombs, and preparing the planes for the return bombing trip home.

Some of us visited the nearby village, others went to Constantine.

A truck was provided for a swimming party in some filthy, dirty muddy river. I took some motion pictures and still shots of this great event. By this time a lot of us were already victims of dysentery. I lost several pounds the week we were there. We also had a nice supply of watermelons, which we were eating when the sand storm arrived.

At Telergma we were furnished cots so we could sleep under the plane and wings, and someone lowered the flaps on "Little Minnie II" so that we could have a little more shade in the morning.

The morning we were preparing our planes for the return trip home, the flaps were going to be reset to their original position. Apparently the wrong lever was engaged and the landing gear collapsed. The plane broke its back over the ball turret, and it was impossible to move, so it was stripped of all of its good equipment for planes in need, and by morning it was a skeleton.

"Little Minnie II" and her final destiny.

Most of Sweeley's crew ("Little Minnie II") were sent to Marrakech to await transportation home. I went back to Bury St. Edmunds with Capt. Kirk's crew on the "Shackeroo", who ended up leading the flight after the wing leader had to abort. But that's another story.

William Arnold van Steenwyk died in September 2001.

The story was mailed to the Author by William Arnold's daughter, Nikkii Lynn van Steenwyk.

A Time To Remember

Narrated by Raoul deMars, 96th Bomb Group.

The day started at 5:00 a.m. when the duty clerks made the rounds and woke up the crews scheduled for a mission that day. I was the co-pilot of a B-17 in the 96th Bomb Group, 339th Bomb Squadron, 3rd Air Division, 8th Air Force, based on one of the multitude Air Bases which dotted the English countryside. Our base was located at Sneatherton Heath, which was a rail stop in the countryside of Suffolk County. We were about 30 miles from Bury Saint Edmunds and approximately 60 miles N.N.E. from London.

Breakfast was great. As on all mission days, you could have as many "fresh" eggs as you wanted, plus bacon, ham or sausage (or all of these), and even steak and potatoes if you so desired. Days when you weren't scheduled for a mission it was dried eggs, etc.

The Crew.

Back row L to R:
S/SGT C. L. Segalla Engineer, SGT R. A. Lauer Waist Gunner, S/SGT S.
T. Mrozek Ball Turret Gunner, S/SGT A. C. Esler Radio Operator, SGT E.
E. Morgan Tail Gunner & SGT J. A. Hamlin Waist Gunner.
Front row L to R:
2nd LT R. A. deMars Co-Pilot, 2nd LT K. E. Bethe Pilot, 2nd LT H. J.
Juskowitz Navigator & 2nd LT R. D. Smith Bombardier.

Breakfast over, we went to the Briefing Room, a fairly large room with
the whole of one end taken up with a huge map of Europe, including
England. This map was covered with a curtain and it was a very dramatic moment when the Briefing Officer drew back the curtain and
revealed what was to be the "Target for Today".

"Today's" target was Poznan, Poland, about 160 miles due east of Big
"B"—Berlin. The lines drawn in grease pencil on the Plexiglas cover of
the map elicited a lot of "Oh my God, how damn far is that?", and
"Hell, we'll never make it back" comments from the crews.

After a few "at ease" calls from the C.O., we were given the gist of what the long lines meant. Instead of flying over the North Sea (Denmark and the Baltic Sea), and being subjected to very little anti aircraft fire and fighter attacks, we were routed over land, across the northernmost tip of France, Belgium and the long haul across Germany, past Berlin and on to Poznan. This was an attempt at diversion, to make them think we were going to some other target.

Weather was to be our ally, with a lot of clouds under us most of the way and clearing up slightly when we reached Poznan. If it were undercast at Poznan and our pathfinder (Radar) Aircraft couldn't make out the primary target, we were to fly to our secondary target, Stettin, Poland, on the Oder River about 40 miles inland from the Baltic Sea.

I'm not sure how many groups were in the force assigned to bomb Poznan, but our plane was to be part of a composite group, made up for planes from several different Squadron and Groups within the 3rd Air Division.

A note of explanation: A Squadron consisted of four flights of three planes each, with spare crews and planes. A group was made up of three squadrons and so on up the chain of command thru Wing, Division and numbered Air Force.

The route we were to fly and the other factors controlling the mission, assembly, climb to altitude, rendezvous with other Groups, air speed, etc. gave us an estimated time in flight, from take off to landing at home base, of just under 12 hours. This was stretching it just a bit, and making allowance for a very small fuel reserve.

We, the whole Poznan bomber force, were forced to maintain a slower than normal air speed to conserve fuel. This meant that any time we were over anti aircraft batteries they would have a longer period of time to zero in on us, and it also meant that many of the fighter planes which came up and attacked us on our way to Poznan had ample time to return their bases, refuel, rearm and then come back up and press their sustained attacks again on our way home from the target.

We only knew one other crew in the composite Group, LT Joe Ziegler and his co-pilot Joe Gold and the rest of the crew.

On the first leg of the flight we ran into a few scattered areas where there was concentrated flak, but our main concern was the incessant fighter attacks which dove right thru the B-17 formation and it appeared that some of them were committed to crashing a B-17 to take it down. This caused several of the pilots to take drastic evasive action. Three of our B-17s were shot down, and the one flying my left wing got a direct hit in the Bomb Bay and just disintegrated. We didn't have time to worry about it, or anything, but that was the slot Joe Ziegler had been flying.

Over Poznan the Pathfinders could not pick up the targets so we were routed to Stettin. On the way to our secondary target we had more vicious fighter attacks, and the closer we got to Stettin, the heavier the flak. We lost #3 engine over the target, and shortly after "Bombs Away" and before we had the Bomb Bay doors all the way closed, we got a near miss just below the plane, which sprung the doors and did some minor structural damage so the doors wouldn't close completely. The extra drag, and only three engines, made it impossible for us to keep up with the formation and we started falling behind.

By the time we were flying over Northern Germany, headed for home via Denmark and the North Sea, Bethe, the Pilot and I decided we would be better off at a lower altitude as we would be able to maneuver better in the denser air (we were about 28,000 feet then), and if we went down to tree top level there would be less chance of ground observers or fighters spotting us. We started to let down as fast as we could, given the condition of the aircraft, when we spotted more fighters coming at us.

They made several passes at us and it was on one of those passes that I got hit. They also knocked out #2 engine and hit an oil line on our #4 engine. That left us with one good engine #1 and #4, which was not much good, as it started to overheat almost immediately due to loss of oil. We had managed to partially feather #2 engine when it went out, but #3 could not be feathered, so it just kept on windmilling, causing even more drag. We knew we would never make to England and decided to head for Sweden, which was neutral.

About that time I was beginning to feel kind of weak and the pain was really getting to me. Apparently the fighters had either run out of armament or were too low on fuel to press in for the kill, as they just peeled off and left. Maybe they saw the smoke from the oil leak on #4 and figured we were done for. Our crew, on this flight, had five Nazi fighters shot down and confirmed.

Bethe decided that I was in no condition to keep flying Co-pilot, so he ordered me back to the radio room to have Johnny put some proper bandages and some sulfa powder on my wounds and possible give me a shot of morphine for the pain. Up until this point I just had a pressure bandage over my eye, which I was holding in place with my hand.

The plane was extremely hard to hold on course, which we had calcu-lated to be toward Sweden. I say calculated because the 20 mm shell which exploded on entry over my head and wounded me had also wiped out the only compass we had left, the magnetic compass. We were flying on only the #1 engine now, the #4 engine having gotten so hot from lack od oil that it froze, and steadily loosing altitude, having come down from 28,000 feet to just a few hundred.

The crew had jettisoned everything possible, all 50 caliber machine guns, all remaining ammo, all ten parachutes, as several of them had been rendered useless by enemy fire, and every crew member elected to "ride it down all the way", though the risk of a crash landing was very great, shot up as the plane was. Anything that wasn't fastened down got thrown out, and I can still see our Bombardier scrambling around on his hands and knees in the nose picking up waxed paper discs about three inches in diameter (used in the sextant) and throwing them out. We didn't know until after we had landed that he had left the ammo belts for his nose turret in and had 800 rounds (400 each) left when we crashed. Could have killed him at the time, but it hadn't made much difference.

When I went back to the radio room I had to go thru the Bomb Bay on the catwalk and I could see what the near miss had done to the Bomb Bay doors. They were very nearly closed except in the front, which were sprung open about three or four inches. I lay down on the floor in the radio room and Johnny (an ex-medic who had volunteered for gunnery school) took charge. His main duty was waist gunner, but we had not been bothered by any fighters for some time and the guns had been jettisoned, so he could tend to me.

He cleaned out the wound as best he could with cold water from a canteen and poured sulfa powder in and all around the wound. Then he bandaged it and tried to give me a shot of morphine for the pain. There were at least six first-aid kits per plane and each had a small tube (with needle attached) of morphine. Johnny tried the first two kits and had no luck, one tube had leaked and had no morphine, while the other one wouldn't work when the needle broke off at the tube as he tried to open it. He quickly gathered all the other first aid kits and tried again. One more had a broken needle and another had leaked dry. Two kits had no tubes of morphine in them (probably stolen), so I didn't get a shot. I'm glad that they weren't all that reliable, because had he been able to give me the shot, I would have been out cold when we crash landed, and being unable to run with the rest of the crew, would probably have spent the rest of the war in a POW camp.

Tony Segalla, our engineer and top turret gunner, got into the co-pilot's seat as soon as I went back to the radio room. He had to help

Bethe hold the plane on course by pushing the left rudder pedal as hard as he could with both feet. The #1 engine was the only one still going and with both #3 and #4 creating so much drag by windmilling, the pressure to try and turn right was very difficult to overcome. From where I was sitting on the floor of the radio room I could look out of the waist windows and by raising up a little I could see that we were very low. About that time Bethe called over the intercom to brace ourselves, we were going to touch down.

Ten, maybe only five seconds before we touched down I felt a shudder go thru the plane and thought for sure it was going to break up. We all must have been doing something right though, as the shudder was the result of striking a telephone pole about six or eight feet from the wing tip, which slewed the plane around enough to prevent it from crashing through a farm house which had been directly in our path. At that low altitude and that slow a speed there was no way Bethe and Tony together could have turned the aircraft without dropping a wing and cartwheeling, instead of landing level straight ahead.

Bethe did a superb job of landing that plane—a lesser pilot could have killed us all. When we touched down the weakened plane opened up just ahead of the radio room and acted like a plow. Dirt was forced up into the radio room so much that it lifted us, Johnny, Al Esler and me, about three feet. All we had to do to get out was take one step up thru the open hatch and jump onto the wing and down to the ground.

I will never know where they all came from, but within minutes after the plane came to rest there must have been at least six or eight people there, all trying to talk at once, and all trying to tell us what to do. We couldn't understand the language and as more people showed up, a man who identified himself as a Canadian who was working with the underground, came and told us what we should do.

The B-17F #42-3535 on the fields of Taastrup, Sealand, Denmark.
German soldiers to the left.

We were to cross a ditch between the field we had landed in and the one next to it, which had been plowed. Then we were to run about 300 yards to a small stand of trees, which were back across the ditch. We ran, I mean ran as we were told, and as we went down the plowed field, Johan Nissen came behind us with a harrow and wiped out our tracks. The trees were very dense and with so much undergrowth that we had to crawl on our hands and knees. When we got to the center of the woods, at least as close to the center as we could judge, we just lay down and stayed quiet. This little stand of trees and underbrush could not have been more than a couple of hundred feet in diameter. There were a few spots in the middle where some of the crew could sit up, but most had to lie down. Mr. Nissen came past with the harrow and told us to stay quiet as they could hear the Nazis coming. He gave us a pass-word, , which I wish I could remember but I can't, and said he would be back after dark when the Germans were gone and tell us what their (the underground) plans were for us.

Very shortly we heard the Nazis over by the plane questioning the Danes. We couldn't understand them but were sure they were trying to find out what happened to us. We found out later that the Danes told them we were gone when they got there. They even told them they had heard another plane and maybe it had picked us up.

It wasn't very long before the Nazis, who were all older non-combat types of the occupation army, were at the edge of the woods, looking for some clue as to whether or not we were in there. About this time the Bombardier got out his pocketknife and started to cut a small branch off the tree he was lying under, as it was brushing his face. The whole damn tree was shaking, no noise, just movement, but if all the Nazis hadn't been poking around the edges they would surely have seen it waving. Tony reached over and grabbed his wrist to make him stop. He really got the point across, because the Bombardier complained of a sore wrist for days. Looking back on it, none of us were surprised that he would do such a stupid thing; after all, hadn't he been throwing out paper discs to lighten the aircraft and then left 400 rounds in each of his nose guns?

The Nazis finally got tired of poking around the edges and left. I don't blame them for not entering the woods—I don't think I would have if there was a possibility of there being ten armed men in there. We stayed as still and quiet as possible until dark when it was safe to move around a little. It was getting colder with darkness, and lying on the ground wasn't helping any. I thought I would freeze. I started shivering and Stan Mrozak and Hy our Navigator crawled over and lay as close to me as they could to warm me up. They thought I was going into shock, but I wasn't, I was just cold (I think). We took off all of our insignia and all identification except our dog tags and buried it. (It may still be there).

It seems like an eternity and we were beginning to speculate as to what could have happened that would stop the Danes from coming back. Nissen and two other men came to us about midnight and led us to his farm, where we went up into a hayloft. was a welcome change—hay to lie on and a lot warmer than the cold ground. Soon we were brought something to eat and drink, and though I can't remember what it was, I do remember thinking it was the best food I had ever eaten. It had only been 24 hours since breakfast the day before, but what a long 24 hours.

They told they were sure that the Nazis would be conducting a building by building search of the area in the morning, so we would have to be moved before daylight.

Plans had been made to move us in a truck, piled with straw, but as yet they didn't know where. They told us to try and rest for a few hours and they would be back for us before dawn. We were all too nervous and scared to sleep, especially our Navigator, Hy. The fact that he was Jewish caused him great concern, as it was well known how the Nazis treated the Jews. We still had our side arms and Hy vowed they would not capture him alive.

In a short while that seemed endless to us we heard a truck stop in front of the barn and Mr. Nissen called for us to come down, and hurry. We all went out by the truck and were told then that we would be taken to Copenhagen. We were to be staying in an apartment on the top floor of the apartment building which, I think was ten or twelve stories high. We climbed into the back of the truck and were covered with straw. I don't know how far we were from Copenhagen, but it couldn't have been far as it seemed to be a short trip under the straw.

The truck stopped several times and each time I thought it was Nazi patrols wanting to search, but it must have been only stop signs as we immediately started again each time. Finally the truck stopped and we heard the door open and the driver (I never did know his name), told us to get down from the truck, one at a time. The truck was parked on the side of the street next to an alley and they guided us, one by one, into an elevator which was being held on the basement level. When we were all in the elevator they took us to the top floor and went into the apartment of one "Tom"—Robert Jensen and his wife. He was very active in the underground and was later caught by the Gestapo and killed.

I don't remember for sure whether we stayed in the apartment for two, three or four days, but I do remember we were treated like royalty. We had to be very quiet, walk around in our stocking feet, talk in whispers only and only go to the toilet before they left in the morning or after they came home in the evening.

Robert Jensen—code name "TOM"

A Silver Star for gallantry in action was awarded posthumously by the War Department to the following-named individual:
Robert Jensen, Danish civilian, organized and maintained a maritime escape and supply route between Denmark and Sweden from March to July 1944 carrying out many gallant self-imposed missions at great risk to his life and that of his family until he was apprehended and killed by the Gestapo. At the cost of his life, Mr. Jensen rendered outstanding services to the Danish resistance movement and the allied war effort.

Food for a mob like that was sure to be a problem, or so we thought. They brought hot meals for us in the evening and we had ample supplies of sandwiches and drinks during the day. I don't know where they found it, but they *even* brought us a small American flag on a stand and American cigarettes. We all crowded around the radio and listened to the BBC (British Broadcasting Corp.) news of the war. We also listened to the English broadcast of "Lord Haw Haw" from Berlin Radio. Lord Haw Haw, as he was called, was British and had gone over to the

Nazi cause. He broadcast propaganda beamed at Allied troops and obviously had quite a few spies in England.

To digress a bit, I recall one night several weeks before being shot down when the crowd at the Officer's Club was larger than usual, as the next day was a "stand down" and no mission was scheduled. It was time for the Berlin Radio and Lord Haw Haw, so nearly everybody got quiet so we could hear. Well, he gave his usual spiel about how well the Axis were doing and how badly the Allies were doing and what terrible losses the Air Force was sustaining. We didn't believe it all but it did have a sobering effect. Then something that left most of those present in a total disbelief. He said "A bit of advise for you chaps of the 96th Bomb Group. I know you don't have anything on for tomorrow, but if you want to be on time for your next mission, the clock over the bar should be reset. It is now five minutes slow". All eyes went to the clock, then wristwatches and back to the clock. Sure as hell, it was five minutes slow. How much else did they know? Scary!

As I have said, I am not sure how long we stayed in the apartment in Copenhagen. You could figure it out from the date on the Visa from Sweden which is in the scrap book, as that day was the day after we left Copenhagen. On the evening we were to leave Copenhagen, they told us we should be ready on a moment's notice as they were not positive about exactly what time the truck would be there to pick us up. Nazi patrols had a habit of arbitrarily stopping any truck to inspect the cargo and the driver's papers, so we had to expect that this might happen. It didn't, and when the truck arrived sometime after dark we all went down in the elevator to the same building entrance we had used before.

We were sent out to the truck one at a time and each of us put in what must have been tanks for carrying fish. They were about 2 ½ feet wide, 3 ½ feet deep and 3 ½ feet long. They were made of fairly heavy gage steel and each one had a cover. There was no fish odor but I couldn't think of anything else they could have been used for and when we arrived at our next stop on "The Underground Railroad", it more or less confirmed our suspicions; it was a small fishing village on the coast of Denmark, across from Sweden.

We were taken to an Inn of some sort where they once more fed us. They also had a Doctor there who checked my wound, cleaned it up again and put on new bandages. The Doctor had the highest praise for the job Johnny had done cleaning, treating and bandaging me up. He (the Doctor) did not speak English, and I had the devil of a time convincing him that I had a tetanus shot not more than six weeks ago and didn't need one now.

We sat around waiting for the rest of the night until just before dawn. We were to be put on board a fishing boat which was to rendezvous with another fishing boat from Sweden.

Finally it was time to leave and we were all taken outside, down a short street and told to crouch down behind a kind of sea wall about three feet high. Don't make a sound. We heard footsteps and peering over the wall could see, a few feet away, a Nazi soldier walking on patrol. He went a short way past our position, did an about face and marched back the way he had come.

When he was out of sight two of us at a time went over the wall and ran to the boat, where we were put into the small cabin. Each time the German patrol marched to the other end of his beat, two more of our crew made it to the boat. Five times, and each time the tension was so high as to be almost unbearable. It must have been far worse for those poor Danes than it was for us, for if they had been caught they would have been shot, whereas we would only have been taken prisoner.

Almost immediately, the "crew" of the boat came down the street, talking and laughing as if this was just another fishing day. They walked over to the boat, and even stopped on the way to give the German patrol a light. It seems he had run out of matches very soon after going on duty. The boat crew came aboard and without any fanfare set out for the rendezvous. This was a very ticklish operation as Denmark was an occupied country and Sweden was neutral, and the territorial waters of each country met in a well defined line between the two.

German patrol boats were operating in the area and would fire on any Danish boat going into Swedish waters or stop and search any Swedish boat in Danish waters, but the rigid discipline of the Nazi armed forces worked in our favor. Their patrols were so regular you could set your watch by them, and the Danes and Swedes had the rendezvous timed to coincide with a period of time when there would be no patrols in the area. They shoved off the dock and we were on our way to Sweden and safety. It seemed an eternity before they cut the engine back to idle, and we thought we must be close to the Swedish boat but it was a patrol boat checking our boat. They just wanted to know what boat it was and make sure it was authorized to be out. The skipper of our boat knew and was known by all the patrol boat crews so they didn't bother to come aboard, or even get very close. We were all glad they didn't or we were all set to go over the side and hold on to a handrail that had been added to the side of the boat just below the water line. It was not yet full daylight, and the skipper told us later that had it been light the patrol probably would not have questioned them at all.

We started moving again and before long we were out of sight of the patrol boat. We changed course and before very long we spotted the Swedish boat, apparently just sitting waiting for us. The skipper pulled alongside and we were told to GO. As fast as we could we jumped into the Swedish boat and hid below the rail. In a matter of seconds the two boats separated and we were in Swedish territorial waters and safe.

I don't' remember how long it took us to get to Malmoe, but that made no difference, we were safe.

As soon as we landed we were met by the American Consulate, who arranged for the Swedish Visas for each of us. Almost immediately they took me to a hospital to check out how serious my eye wound was. Bethe and the rest of the crew were taken to temporary quarters, as they were to go to Stockholm the next day. When I got to the hospital they cleaned me up and I was admitted. The Chief of Surgery told me (thru an interpreter) that they would have to operate on my eye to remove shell fragments in the eyeball and to repair the damage done to my eyelids. Also some stitches had to be taken in a small laceration in my right cheek just below the eye. (This was were a shell fragment had entered and gone down thru the roof of my mouth and broke my upper plate, which the also fixed).

Bethe and the rest of the crew came by to tell me they were leaving for Stockholm around noon and told me where they would be staying. They didn't know and, because of security, couldn't find out when there would be a flight to England, so they didn't know whether or not I would get out of the hospital in time to catch up with them.

They operated on my eye the next day and that was a weird experience. The doctor used a local anesthetic and I could see everything he did. It was kind of scary lying there and watching the instruments get closer and closer, but there was no pain at all and all I could feel was a slight pressure as he took the pieces of 20 mm out of my eyeball and sewed up my eyelid and cheek.

It didn't take very long and I was pleasantly surprised that there was relatively little pain as the anesthetic wore off, just a slight discomfort. The doctor that did the surgery told me there was very little damage to the eyeball and if there was any change in my vision it would be almost unnoticeable. He also told me that the first-aid (Johnny's cleaning, sulfa powder and bandaging) had in all probability saved the eye from infection and possibly loss of the eye. Thanks again, Johnny.

The doctor told me he didn't think there would be any complications but was going to keep me for a couple of days to make sure. He was great. He came to visit me several times a day and we had some interesting talks. He told me there were only a few of the staff at the hospital who spoke English and he enjoyed talking to an American. I told him it was a mutual feeling, as it was difficult to communicate with the nurses in sign language. He also told me a bit about Sweden and socialized society. For instance, the Chief Surgeon at the hospital was not earning as much as I was as a 2nd LT. Taxes were very high also, but their standard of living was also very high. He seemed to have few complaints about the system.

I don't remember how many days I was in the hospital at Malmoe. On the day I was released LT King from the Air Attache's Office picked me up and took me to the train for my trip to Stockholm. Some train. I went first-class coach and it was really first-class; huge windows and swivel recliner at each window. There was a dine car on the train, and the waiters all spoke English, as well as French and German and, of course Swedish. One of them told me, when I asked, that most people in any way employed in the tourist endeavors; transportation, lodging, restaurants, etc. spoke several languages. It was about 300 to 350 miles from Malmoe to Stockholm and we made very good time. It seemed to me that the train was going very fast, though it was one of the smoothest train rides I had ever had. (The trains in Japan are much more crowded, but very fast and give just as a smooth ride).

Bethe and the rest of the crew met me at the station and took me back to the hotel where we were staying; the Continental. It was a very nice hotel and I really enjoyed the three or four days I spent there.

They took me shopping for clothes the next day, which the Air Force paid for, and I got everything from skin out; underwear, socks, two shirts, shoes, necktie, suit and a topcoat. I also got shaving gear, including a mug and a brush. The clothes I turned over to the Air Force when I got back to our base but I still have the shaving brush, which is pure badger bristle and cost US Dollars 9.00 even then. I don't know why it was so expensive.

It was just luck, fate or something that the rest of the crew was still in Stockholm. They had left on a flight for Scotland the day before I got there, but foul weather and unexpected head winds over the North Sea forced the plane to turn back.

The flight was re-scheduled and we were taken out to the airport late in the afternoon. The plane we were to be going in was a B-24 Bomber, which had been modified to carry people instead of bombs. A platform had been built in the Bomb Bay with four benches the length of the bay; one on each side and two back to back in the middle. The Bomb Bay doors on the B-24 opened by rolling up along the inside of the fuselage (like a roll top desk), and we got in thru a trap door in the platform. Our crew were not the only passengers, as there were a lot of Jewish refugees who had made their way thru Denmark to Sweden, and also quite a few Norwegians. Norway was occupied by the Nazis and for some reason they were far more lenient with the Danes than the Norwegians. We took off just before dark, and there were so many passengers in the plane that a few of them had to move to the nose of the plane so it could keep the nose wheel on the ground to taxi to take-off position. By holding the brakes on and using about half throttle the pilot could hold the nose down while the passengers could make their way back to the rear of the plane.

When we were airborne we immediately started climbing, as we had to get high enough to clear the mountains in Norway. We also had to take a longer than "as the crow flies" route to avoid anti-aircraft guns and the fighters based in Norway. It was cold—there was no heat in the Bomb Bay and a frail old man from Norway (he told us he was 78) was in a very bad way. Several of us gave him some of our extra clothes but he couldn't seem to get warm at all. His fingernails started to turn blue and we were afraid he was going to die.

Again Bethe proved his worth —he figured that the plane crew would have hot coffee so he crawled up to the pilot's compartment, told them of the old man's predicament, and came back with a thermos full of hot coffee. We gave some to the poor fellow and in a matter of minutes he was O.K. He stopped shaking and the color in his hands came back. The rest of the coffee was given to several other people who seemed to be in the greatest need for it.

After we landed, the pilot told us that he would personally see to it that any future flight would have the hot coffee available. He couldn't promise crème and sugar, as they were rationed, but the important thing was the hot drink. I think it saved the old man's life.

We landed at a field in Scotland and our crew was the first ones out of the plane. I stood beside the plane and counted them as they came out, and there were 78 passengers and a crew of four, including our crew of ten. That made 82 people on that B-24. I still find it hard to believe. We were taken in hand by boys of G-2 (Intelligence—it was still the Army Air Corps then) and delivered to 63 Brook Street, London for "de-briefing". We figured it wouldn't take long and we were anxious to get out and explore London. What a surprise we were in for. We were restricted to the premises "until further notice" and informed that the de-briefing would start in the morning. It lasted for several days; they interrogated us individually, in two's and three's and then as a complete crew. We were rather unique, being one of the very first crews who escaped from enemy territory as a complete crew during the war. They wanted to know about everything, and I mean everything we saw or heard while in Denmark.

One thing that made us feel that we had a pretty good intelligence force was this; when we told them about the crash landing, and the Canadian who was there with the Danes, they said "oh yes, that would be "so and so" naming him. I can't remember his name now, but we knew it then.

After the first few days our restriction was lifted and we were given passes to go out of town—London. The whole crew went together and were seeing the sights when one of the crew (I don't remember which one) let out a yell, "it can't be". Almost simultaneously we heard a yell from up the street. We all turned to look and all hell broke loose. It was Joe Ziegler's crew—every last one of them, safe and sound. We were so sure that theirs had been the plane on my left wing which got the direct hit and exploded. What happened was that in some of the violent maneuvering to avoid the German fighters, several planes in the group had rejoined formation in different positions. Joe's crew saw us drop behind, and when we didn't make it home, they were sure we were either dead or captured. Needless to say we were twenty happy guys and had quite a celebration that night.

After a few sight seeing tours we were sent back to our base to get our personal belongings before being returned to the States. As escapees or evades we were placed in what was called category "R", which meant we were restricted from any more combat flying. Having been in enemy territory, if we were shot down and captured we could have been shot as spies. Good news—we all wanted to go home. Lady luck had smiled on us so many times in the past little while and nobody can have good luck forever.

We chose to fly a war-weary B-17 back to the States for modification and our first stop was Prestwick, Scotland, where we were to pick up the B-17, and took off for Reykjavik, Iceland, which was the only stop we would make before landing at La Guardia in New York. The ground crew asked us if we had any scotch (I guess every war-weary crew that came through had the same idea) and told us we would have all our baggage checked by customs when we landed and would have to pay duty on each bottle. They also told us that the plane would be parked in a special area reserved for the Air Corps.

Well, before we took off from Reykjavik, we hid bottles of scotch all over that plane. The majority of it was wrapped in our wool socks and placed in between the braces of the partially lowered flaps. Then the flaps were raised completely and we were ready to go. Not being able to lower the flaps 30 degrees (which was standard take-off procedure) we held the brakes until we had almost full power on and the plane just kind of leaped down the runway. No problems. We were airborne with a third of the runway left.

Erik Dyreborg: Raoul deMars and his crew was the first American crew that evaded and escaped as a crew.

The Long Walk Back From The Last Mission

Narrated by Robert R. Kerr 303rd Bomb Group

"MISSING IN ACTION" APRIL 29, 1944

2nd LT. ROBERT R. KERR, O-815165

8th AIR FORCE, 1st BOMB DIVISION

303rd BOMB GROUP, 427th SQUADRON, MOLESWORTH, ENGLAND

Target for the day: Berlin

Crew Members on board B-17G, A/C # 42-31241, "Spirit of Wanette," for above date:

Pilot	2nd LT Howard J. Bohle	POW
Co-Pilot	2nd LT Robert R. Kerr	EVD
Navigator	2nd LT John K. Brown	POW
Bombardier	2nd LT Joseph J. Nevills	POW
Flight Eng.	SSgt Laurence W. Rice	POW
Radio Ope.	SSgt Henry J. Jensen	KIA
Ball Turret	Sgt John A. Derschan	KIA
Waist	Sgt Frank (NMI) Gorgon	KIA
Waist	Sgt Paul 3. Mulhearn	KIA

| Tail Gunner | SSgt Michael Musache | KIA |

(sub. for Cpl Charley F. Brock, who was hospitalized that day.)

The day started early, with a 0400 wake-up, breakfast at 0430, and briefing at 0630. It was to be maximum effort, a "thousand plane" mission to Berlin.

Good fighter support was expected, both en route to the target and on the return flight home. Intense enemy action was expected, from both ground fire (flak) and by fighter defences.

Meteorology forecast no adverse weather, but some lower cloud cover en route, and possibly over target area.
The Crew.

Back row, L to R: Henry Jensen, L. Rice, C. Brock, P. Mulhearn & J. Derschan
Front row, L to R: H. Bohle, Robert Kerr, J. Brown & J. Nevils

We were told that our position in the formation was to be on the left wing of lead plane in the division, with deputy lead plane flying on the leader's right wing. This seemed to be a desirable position for us, until one reflects as to just where enemy guns would be concentrating their firepower.

Takeoff and form-up of the group, and then the division was without incident. The formation climbed to altitude en route, so that by the time we crossed the coast into enemy territory we were at the designated cruise altitude of 22,000 feet.
Enemy action was minimal until we reached the IP (Initial Point; start of the bomb run).

Anti-aircraft fire (flak) became quite intense, and several minutes into the bomb run our plane received a direct hit in the right wing, immediately behind the number three engine, by what appeared to be an 88 mm anti-aircraft shell.
Fortunately the Germans did not use either contact or proximity fusing on their shells, but rather chose to utilize altitude setting (or sensing) shells, for the shell that struck our plane went completely through the wing and exploded some distance above us.

It did considerable damage to the wing, the most serious being the destruction of two main fuel tanks, plus damage to the number three engine, such that it became necessary to feather that engine at once.

With the loss of one engine it became impossible to maintain position in the formation, even after salvoing (dropping) our bomb load, so we gradually fell behind until finally we were all alone.

It seemed most prudent to reduce speed, sacrificing speed for maintaining altitude. At this point it became obvious we could not expect to successfully return to our home base, or even to England, due to severe loss of fuel.

Consequently, it was unanimously agreed that our best hope of survival was to head for neutral territory, either Switzerland or Sweden.

Sweden appeared to offer the best hope for safety, since the rugged terrain in Switzerland offered fewer possible landing places.

Accordingly a course was taken that Navigator Jake Brown felt would take us to Sweden. At the time we were above a solid cloud cover, so exact position could not be determined with any degree of accuracy. We knew our line of flight would probably take us over Rostock, a heavily defended seaport on the German coast of the Baltic Sea, but there was not much alternative, given our options at this point.

Several friendly P-51 fighters picked us up and flew escort for a short time, then broke off and headed for home.

We continued on without incident for some time until Brown told us that he was just not sure of our position, since we were still above a solid overcast, and he was not confident of the validity of wind forecasts we had received at the morning briefing, particularly as we were now well north of the planned track.

He reminded us that we could be in trouble if we overflew Sweden and wound up in Occupied Norway, so we elected to start a let down, with ultimate goal of getting below the clouds and verifying our position. We had descended to about 18,000 feet, just above the top of the cloud cover, when Sgt Musache, the tail gunner, called on the intercom that an aircraft was approaching from 6 o'clock (directly to our rear).

He was told to hold his fire until aircraft could be positively identified, as we knew it was customary for the Swedish Air Force to send up fighters to challenge foreign aircraft, and such aircraft were to signify intention to land by lowering landing gear.

Almost immediately Sgt Musache called that the plane, a German Focke Wulf 190, was firing on us, and he was returning fire. It became obvious that the fighter had been sent up to verify what had been seen on German radar, for after the enemy fighter had made a pass at us, the flak guns opened fire, with accurate results, for we received several direct hits almost simultaneously.

Flying in the pilot's seat, I looked out the left side window and saw the accessory section of the number two engine get blown away, then the number four engine caught fire, and a hit in the tail section locked the controls (and apparently killed Sgt Musache) so that the decision to abandon the aircraft was mandatory.

I hit the alarm bell and prepared to bail out!

We were wearing flak vests and flak helmets, so they were quickly taken off. Our parachutes were British chest type, consisting of separate harness, worn while airborne, and 'chute pack, which was kept under our seats (pilot and co-pilot).
I grabbed the 'chute pack and snapped it on the harness and headed for the escape hatch, immediately beneath the flight deck.

Pilot Bohle was experiencing some difficulty exiting the right seat, so I helped him down, then followed him out the hatch. I believed I was the last survivor to leave the plane, as it spiraled down trailing thick smoke.

As I went out of the escape hatch head first in the prescribed manner, my sunglasses were swept from my eyes by the slipstream, and I remember thinking I should have removed them before jumping.

Almost at once I was tumbling through the clouds, for what seemed an eternity but I'm sure was only minutes, wondering just how far down the clouds extended.

I finally decided to pull the ripcord, thinking to delay might bring me too close to the ground for safety. The 'chute opened, then seconds later I broke out of the clouds, and to my dismay I was still about seven thousand feet in the air, directly over water.

Several other parachutes were seen, including that of the attacking German fighter pilot. (Their chutes were easily identified by the darker color material used.) Apparently our gunners had scored a disabling hit on his aircraft as he made his pass on us.

The chutes of other crewmembers could be seen below me, quite scattered out, but I could not tell which member was which. As I descended I managed to tear up all papers in my flight suit; target maps, etc.

Fortunately I was able to manouver by vigorously pulling on the 'chute risers so that I floated over land, finally coming down in a freshly plowed field for a relatively soft landing.

A farmhouse was close by, and a young lad standing by the house had watched me descend and land.
No other persons were seen, so after gathering up my 'chute I walked over to the boy and attempted to find out where I was, and if there were any Germans in the area.

Unfortunately he did not understand English and I could not make out anything he was saying. By pantomime (my goose stepping, etc.) I thought he indicated which way the Germans might be, so I took off in the opposite direction.

I stuffed the 'chute in a ditch, then proceeded to walk along a hedge row, toward a road in the distance.

As I got closer to the road I saw a man approaching from the road. He was not in uniform, but still I was somewhat reluctant to trust him. He made signs of wanting to be friendly, and I figured that, since there was only one of him, I could at least see what he was up to.

He could speak English, enough to let me know he was a local farmer, that I was in Denmark on the Isle of Falster, and that I should accompany him. We walked quite a ways and came to his home, where he invited me in.

Robert R. Kerr 1944

I told him I was reluctant to enter his home, as it would put him and his family in jeopardy, should the Germans discover he had provided shelter to an American airman.

He insisted, so I decided to briefly accept his hospitality. His name was Jes Frederiksen, he was married, and had a young daughter small enough to be in a highchair. They asked if I would like something to eat, and of course I said yes, as it was now about one thirty in the afternoon, nine hours since breakfast!

First he wanted to know if I would like a Schnapps, as it must have been obvious I was under stress. When I said yes, he poured what appeared to be a shot glass full of a clear liquid and gave it to me to drink. I was not aware that the accepted way of consuming Schnapps was by sipping slowly, so I took it like a shot—"down the hatch".

It was literally breathtaking! It acted on me like spinach always was depicted as reacting on Popeye; i.e. going out to all the extremities, to the very finger tips. They were surprised, then amused at my reactions, but then prepared a sumptuous meal; fresh eggs, Danish ham, toast and coffee.

After eating, Frederiksen said he would take me to a secluded place on the farm where I should remain hidden until dark. They prepared sandwiches for me to take, placed them in a basket, together with two bottles of Carlsberg pilsner beer, then he led me to a remote corner of the fields, where there was dense undergrowth of bushes. He told me to crawl into the center of the patch, and that he would come for me at dusk.

I burrowed into the brush and lay as still as possible. I could hear in the distance what I was sure were search parties looking for me, and over-head German aircraft could be heard flying low altitude search patterns. Needless to say I remained very quiet, although I periodically experienced the "shakes", as one would with severe chills.

Just before dark I heard Frederiksen approaching, being very careful to identify himself to me. He had a complete change of outer clothing, except for shoes. He explained that he had no shoes that would fit me. I changed, leaving all my military clothes in the woods. (He assured me he would return in a day or two and dispose of them.)

He had two bicycles for us to ride, and he explained that we were to ride to some friends who were expecting us.
We rode for what I estimated was 10 to 12 kilometers (6 to 7 miles), passing two separate German patrols en route, finally arriving at a crossroads with several houses.

We went to one of them, the home of a young schoolteacher and his wife, where I was invited in and welcomed. After some brief conversation we retired, as by this time it was rather late. I was put up in the upstairs guest room, in a great, soft feather bed, where I seemed to sink almost out of sight.

I had no trouble sleeping, and when I came down in the morning I found a small American flag in the center of the dining room table.

A neighbor lady, who then later came over to meet and talk to me, had brought it in that morning. She had lived in the U.S. for many years and had returned to Denmark to live following the death of her husband. Of course she was eager to talk to me and learn what all I could tell her about the U.S. and the war.

Additionally, she served as an excellent interpreter, for while my hosts could speak elemental English, they were quite limited in their understanding of the "American" English the neighbor and I spoke. After a delicious breakfast they informed me of the efforts already being made on my behalf by the Danish Underground to move me to Sweden.

It at first appeared that I would be taken to the village of Stubbekobing on the island's north coast, there to be put in the care of a fisherman who would take me to Sweden, for a substantial fee of course.

This plan was abandoned because they reasoned that if the fisherman, whose loyalty they were unsure of, would agree to this dangerous undertaking, might he not then accept additional money from the enemy and turn me over to the Germans.

It was finally decided to send a coded message to the Underground in Copenhagen about me, which they did by telephone, telling them they had obtained "some American cigarettes".

Late in the afternoon a woman arrived from Copenhagen to accompany me on the train ride to the city. In the meantime my hosts had obtained a new pair of shoes for me, as I obviously could not get on the train wearing my GI high shoes, as they would be an obvious giveaway.

A first class train ticket was purchased for me, and we went to the station, at the town of Eskilstrup I believe, to catch the evening train to Copenhagen.

My instructions were to follow the woman, not to walk beside her. If either of us were stopped or challenged, we would not acknowledge knowing the other person.

The electric train arrived on time and we boarded.

It was then I discovered the train had originated in Germany, for the car we entered contained mostly German soldiers, apparently returning to duty from leave. The railroad car was divided into a Coach, or Third Class, section, and First Class compartments.

We had First Class tickets, but had to walk down the isle, through the Coach section, to get to the compartments. Walking that aisle between the many German GIs was without a doubt the most nerve-wracking part of the whole experience, for I was certain they would see me as an American.

No one paid any attention to me, for I'm sure the last thing they expected to see getting on the train was a U.S. Airman!

Upon arriving at a compartment we took our seats, my guide sitting across from me. I had a newspaper and pretended to read it but did not understand much of the Danish I was "reading".
After a bit the conductor collected tickets but asked no questions, then I feigned sleep for the rest of the trip. Some time after nine o'clock p.m. the train stopped in the southern suburbs of Copenhagen, and my guide got off so I followed.

We passed two men standing under a light on the platform with their coat collars turned up, like something sort of a spy novel. As we walked past the two, they intercepted me and then took me to another track, where we caught a local train.

I never saw my woman guide again.

We rode the train to the suburbs north of the city, getting off at a station that seemed to be about thirty kilometers from the city limits. We walked a short distance to what turned out to be the home of Elo and Sigrid Greiffenberg, at Nojsomhedsvej 22, Copenhagen, Denmark, with whom I would be spending the next week or so. They were a middle aged couple and very active in the Danish underground. They owned and operated what was known as a "green-grocery" market in the main part of the city, selling fruits and vegetables.

He was Danish but she was from Oslo, Norway, and they often kidded one another as to which country was best, much as Americans are doing concerning different parts of the U.S.

We got along just fine, especially considering their limited English. We often played cards, and many times their friends and fellow underground activists stopped by to visit.

During such visits they described some of the activities they were involved in, particularly publishing an underground newspaper. The Germans had recently found the printing presses, so a new facility had to be found.

One of the activists was named Ida Rasmussen, and she and her fiancé were quite concerned that the Gestapo was getting too close to them for comfort.

I learned later that the Gestapo arrested him, but do not know what happened to him.

We always included discussions concerning plans being considered for getting me to Sweden, and it soon became evident that the timing of any plan was of paramount importance.

We were alerted several times that a move was imminent, but conditions apparently were not just right.

Then on the ninth of May we received word to be ready to go, and late in the evening two escorts arrived to accompany me to the city.

We rode the train to a station in the outskirts of the city, and then met a taxi that had been arranged for. The taxi, an old model Ford, was powered by a gas created by an on-board generator, mounted on the rear, which I believe used charcoal as fuel. It was a poor substitute for gasoline, for the taxi was so underpowered it could barely make it up the slightest grade.

We were dropped off near the university, then made our way to the home of a professor. I was told we had to wait until it was considered safe to proceed.

We had supper and engaged in a most interesting conversation concerning the existing conditions in Denmark, the activities of the underground, and much more.

One of the gentlemen I met was Robert Jensen. He was said to be the owner of a radio manufacturing company, supplying radios to the Germans, but using proceeds to fund the Underground activities.

Finally, just after mid-night, it was decided to proceed, so we again boarded the taxi and were driven to a boat yard on the waterfront, where I was guided to a small fishing boat moored at a dock.

A small group of people was gathered near the boat, and I soon learned they were to accompany us on our journey. The group consisted of both Danish and Norwegian members of the underground who had been identified by the Germans as activists, and thus they were destined to be arrested, prosecuted and probably executed.

They were instructed to get into the compartments on either side of the front (normally used to store the days catch of fish) which they reluctantly did, as the odor was quite fishy, then the covers were put in place.

I was invited by the captain to join him in the cockpit, which also contained the engine, and told to lie down, out of sight, beside the engine. I immediately recognized the engine as a four cylinder Model T Ford engine of somewhat ancient vintage. The engine exhaust was directed into a length of stovepipe, which protruded above the cabin roof, and when the engine was started it was obvious there was no muffler. In fact I was sure the noise it made would be heard all over the country!

We got underway at about five or six o'clock in the morning and, although the sun was not up yet, it was quite light out We proceeded cautiously out into the bay, stopping every few minutes so the captain could observe.

The strategy, as had been explained to me previously, was to make the run while the German patrol boats were in port for the change of shifts.

At last the captain accelerated the boat and we were out into open water. While we were getting on board and waiting to get underway I was cold and shivering, but now, with the engine running at what must have been it's full power, I was quite warm, and getting warmer.

Shortly thereafter the captain indicated it was all right to stand up, as we were well out in the channel between Denmark and Sweden. A short while later the engine was stopped and the boat was anchored.
A short distance away was a warship, which turned out to be a Swedish destroyer. We were out of sight of land, midway between Denmark and Sweden.

The captain explained that now we would wait for a boat to come out from Malmo, Sweden, for if he were to take us all the way into Malmo his boat would be confiscated.

It was a bright, sunny morning, and all the refugees had come on deck from the fish storage holds, happy to take advantage of the fresh sea air and sunshine.

After some time a boat approached from the east and hailed us.
Upon being recognized it came along side and we quickly transferred over to it and got under way. This boat was considerably larger than the first one, and I later learned they were both owned by the same man, Robert Jensen, whom I had met earlier that night.

Finally the Malmo harbor came into view, and as we proceeded into the entrance we were hailed by a patrol boat, that then came alongside.

A uniformed man came aboard and asked if there was an American on board. I identified myself, and he said to come with him. As I boarded the patrol boat the officer said, in English, "Welcome to Sweden".

We went directly to a dock where I was placed in a police car and taken to the Police Station. After questioning they gave me a lunch, then a doctor checked me over. Following this I was placed in a cell and told to wait.

Being in a jail cell was another new experience for me, but I don't believe that it was a bad experience, as it was immaculate, light and airy—but still a cell.

At last in mid-afternoon I was given some papers, released and told that a taxi would take me to the American Consul. I was dropped off at the door and walked up the stairs to the Office of the United States Consul. As I looked up the stairway there was a large United States Flag displayed, without a doubt the most welcome sight I had seen in a long time!

After welcoming me, the Consul, whose name I can not remember, told me that I would be taking the overnight train to Stockholm, and in the morning would be reporting in to the American Embassy there.

In the meantime he invited me to his home in Malmo, and we went there in his small car, which I saw was fueled by a gas that came from two long cylindrical tanks mounted on the car's roof. He explained that the gas was acetylene, and, while barely adequate to propel the car, was one of the few gasoline substitutes available to the Swedish civilians.

After a pleasant dinner, during which he brought me up to date on the status of the war, he drove me to the train station, bought my ticket, then made sure that I was in the right car and compartment. The accommodation was in a "Bad Vagen", or sleeping car, and turned out to be very comfortable.

The train locomotive was electric, hence clean and quiet. Departure was at about nine or ten o'clock, and we arrived in Stockholm around seven in the morning. The bed was comfortable and I slept soundly throughout the trip, as I was exhausted by the previous twenty-four hours activities.

An employee of the U.S. Embassy met me and took me first to the Hotel Continental, which was located opposite the central railway station, where I had a room assigned (#302) then to breakfast.

Next we went to the Embassy, where I was introduced to the Ambassador, then to the Military Air Attaché, Lieut.Colonel Felix M. Hardison, to whom I was told I would be reporting for the duration of my stay in Sweden.

To my surprise one of the first things done was to give me my April pay, which I would have received on April 30th at Molesworth, had we made it back.

Payment was made in Swedish Kroner, and at the prevailing exchange rate (four Kr to one $, as I recall) gave me quite a stack of strange looking currency.

It was then decided that I needed clothing and some personal items, as up to now I had been traveling rather lightly, so I was taken to the Nordiske Company, the largest department store in Stockholm, and outfitted head to toe, from the skin out.

A shaving kit and a small, inexpensive suitcase were purchased for the planned trip back to Britain, although it remained to be seen just how or when that would be accomplished.

I was told that it would be necessary for me to report in to the embassy office every morning, Monday through Friday, to receive such information or instructions as there may be for me. Otherwise I was free to sightsee around Stockholm, or just to relax.

Sweden was of course a neutral country, so it was quite a change from both England and Denmark; no real evidence of a war, such as the blackout at night, or rationing. There also were embassies there for our enemies, including Germany and Japan.

I recall going to lunch with fellows from our embassy and we might find men from either the German or Japanese Embassy sitting at an adjoining table. We knew that they all understood English, maybe even studied in the U.S. or England, so we would make it a point to discuss our opinion of them in no uncertain or flattering terms; it at least made us feel good.

Stockholm is a lovely city, and I enjoyed seeing as much of it as I could, usually by riding the streetcars that covered the principal streets very well.

After a week or so I was informed that a plan to evacuate me had been developed that sounded quite interesting.

Sweden was recognized as a major source of precision ball bearings, a very critical item to the war industry, and had been a supplier to Germany for some time. What wasn't generally known was that they also furnished bearings to England as well, and the method of getting them from Sweden to England was quite unique.

An unarmed RAF Mosquito bomber, piloted by a member of the Free Fighting Polish Air Force (really!), would fly into Stockholm by first climbing to high altitude (typically 25,000 feet) over England, then make an ultra high speed descending approach over Norway (which was occupied by the Germans), thus eluding both the fighter and anti-aircraft fire.

After loading the plane to the maximum with ball bearings, the pilot would take off, climb to altitude while over Sweden, then make a high speed descending departure, again over Norway, leveling out low over the North Sea and proceeding on to land in Scotland.

Using this technique, no planes or crews were lost, insofar as I know. I was told that I could expect to be a passenger on one of these flights, and to be ready when notified. The opportunity to use this means of leaving Sweden never materialized, so another plan was advanced.

This involved use of a larger aircraft, such as a "heavy" bomber, capable of carrying a number of persons. The reason for this was that quite a few members of the Norwegian and Danish Underground had made their way to Stockholm and it was imperative that they be evacuated as soon as possible.

The aircraft used would be unarmed and would not have sufficient oxygen for any extra passengers (these planes were not pressurized). Thus the strategy planned was to depart in the middle of a night when weather conditions over Norway were just right for creation of heavy ground fog, a situation that would keep German fighter aircraft on the ground.

Several times I was alerted for departure, then cancelled at the last minute.

Finally on May 26th word came that we were going, and about midnight I was driven out to the Stockholm Airport. It should be noted that the nights were rather short in Stockholm at this time of the year, so our "window of opportunity" was rather narrow; hence time was of the essence. The aircraft turned out to be an American B-24 Bomber, but had British markings, identifying it as British Overseas Airways, or some such subterfuge.

The crew was American Army Air Force, and included a rather famous pioneer airman, Col. Berndt Balchen. Col. Balchen was a veteran arctic pilot, who had been with Admiral Byrd on many Arctic Expeditions, and was responsible for much of the airport development on Greenland, during and after the war.

A most interesting gentleman, and I only wish I could have been able to talk at greater length with him.

The bomb bays of the B-24 had been modified by installing seats lengthwise along both sides, and by the time I arrived nearly all seats were taken by Norwegians and Danes.

The crew advised me that there was no room for me on the flight deck until after takeoff, then the navigator could go forward into the nose when the landing gear was raised. So I seated myself next to the door leading from the bomb bay to the flight deck and tried to be relaxed, for it was quite apparent that very few, if any, of the other passengers in the bomb bay had ever been in an aircraft before.

This was made more obvious when the engines were stared and the plane began to taxi. The pilot applied the brakes to slow the plane down, at which point the hydraulic pump, located just above my head, was automatically actuated, resulting in a intense high pitched squeal for the short time it operated.
I was certain that many of the passengers would have jumped out at this point if they were not restrained by seat belts.

We got off the ground without incident, climbed to intended altitude and proceeded on course. I took my place on the flight deck when advised there was room, and looking out the window discovered that it was a clear night; no ground fog, as was hoped.

The Flight Engineer went back to the tail position, normally occupied by a tail gunner, to observe, watching for any kind of enemy action. Of course the plane had no guns of any kind, with the possible exception of the Very pistol, a device used to fire colored signal flares, so we could only hope that we would not be detected. Sometime later, when we were well past the mid-point of overflying Norway, the Flight Engineer advised the pilot on the intercom that he thought he detected some ground fire from anti-aircraft guns, so immediately the pilot initiated evasive action, which I'm sure must have seemed like a wild roller coaster ride to the passengers in the bomb bay.

No further incidents were experienced, and, just as it started to get light, we crossed the coast and were out over the North Sea. The pilot descended until we were just above the water and continued at a minimum altitude until reaching the area near the Scottish coast where it was felt the threat of enemy action was minimal.

At about six o'clock A. M. we landed at Leuchars Fife Royal Naval Air-Station, located quite near Edinburgh.

As we made our approach to land, just to the north we could see the famous Saint Andrews golf course, but it was obvious that no one was playing the course that early in the day.

It certainly was a good feeling to set foot on British soil once again, for there had been times not too long ago when I wondered if it would ever be possible.

After clearing through British Customs, just as though we were some tourists, I was put aboard a small U.S. twin engine plane for the flight to London.

En route we flew over Loch Lomond, a pretty highland lake well known in song and verse. On arrival in London I was taken directly to a United States Special Reception Center, 63 Brook SL, London W.1, located just off Grosverner Square, in the city center.

I was told that I was under a form of quarantine and thus confined to the premises until such time as I could be positively identified, to preclude someone coming into the country by assuming my identity.

The next day, May 29th , an officer from my squadron, Lt. Shirley W. Estes, came to London and certified that he knew and had been associated with me, thus identifying me to the satisfaction of G-2, Army Intelligence, and a paper so stating was drawn up and a copy given to me.

I was still in civilian clothes, but with this form I was allowed to leave the Center and see some of London. I was told that my personal effects were being held at my squadron, having just missed being sent to the U.S., which was the usual procedure when personnel were Missing in Action.

It seems that upon my arrival in Sweden the word was passed to Army Air Corps Eighth Air Force Headquarters, my unit was notified and a hold put on my things.

On June 4th I traveled to Molesworth, site of my unit, retrieved my things, and got back into uniform. I stayed at the squadron until returning to the Reception Center in London on June 7th.

Having been on the base on June 6th , which of course was D-Day, I witnessed an incredible sight, as the 303rd Bomb Group flew almost continuous missions, albeit short missions, in support of the Invasion.

I had to decline several offers to accompany crews on missions, as I had been instructed that under no circumstances was I to fly over enemy territory, the reason being that should I again be shot down and fall into enemy hands, I would be treated as a spy, since my previous evasion had afforded me opportunities to observe certain German military activities.

Back in London I was asked to report on some of the things I had in fact seen while traveling about in occupied Denmark, and to that end was sent to be interrogated at RAF Intelligence Headquarters.

The office I was directed to was located in an old building in central London, several levels below the street. A senior RAF officer questioned me at length on what I had been able to observe, but mid-way through the session we were interrupted by a young WAF (Women's Air Force) carrying a tray with our morning tea. All work stopped for tea time while we engaged in idle chit- chat, then we resumed our serious intelligence discussions. It was a most interesting experience, indicative of the British attitudes toward values and priorities.

The next day I learned I was to return to the U.S. and received copies of orders authorizing the travel.

That evening I boarded a train bound for Glasgow, Scotland and was given a bedroom accommodation. The room was quite comfortable and contained an actual bed, rather than a bunk, which was what I expected. The train was a fast express, and I slept through most of the night. At about five a.m. on June 9th I was awakened by the conductor stating we would be arriving at our destination in about forty-five minutes. He had brought a cup of tea, which he placed on a fold-down shelf above the bed; quite a civil way to awakened.

On arrival at the station I was met and driven to the Prestwick Airdrome, from which we would depart later in the morning. The designated aircraft was a U.S. Army Air Corps C-54 (Douglas DC-4) operated by MAC (the Army Air Corps Military Airlift Command). Departure was on time, and our route over the North Atlantic included refueling stops at Reykjavik, Iceland and Gander Newfoundland, before arriving at the final destination, Washington National Army Air Field, Washington, D.C.

I was temporarily assigned to the Pentagon "for the purpose of interrogation", presumably for the same type of information I had previously given the RAF in London. Toward that end the next day I was driven to Fort Belvoir, Virginia to meet with Army Intelligence.

Following the briefing I was driven back to the Pentagon, where I learned that I was to report next to Fort Sheridan, just north of Chicago for reassignment.

This was quite fortuitous, as I hoped to be able to spend some time in the greater Chicago area.

Upon reporting at Fort Sheridan June 14th I received orders to report to the AAF Personnel Distribution Station at Miami Beach, Fla., for processing and reassignment. A delay enroute of 23 days was authorized, so I was to report on-or-about July 14th. These orders had the effect of giving me three weeks leave, which were most welcome and spent visiting with family and friends.

Looking for Robert Kerr's Danish helpers

Narrated by Erik Dyreborg:

In April 2001 Nelson Liddle "found" Robert R. Kerr. Robert told us that he had been in Denmark in 1979 and 1995, trying to find some of his helpers but he didn't succeed.

After having received Robert's story, the one you have just read, I started my research and tried to find / locate some of Robert's helpers.

I contacted the local Historic Association (very near to the place where Robert landed) and a gentleman called me and we agreed to meet. Meanwhile, this gentleman had done his research and upon my arrival, he had to tell me that all of Robert's helpers had died, with the exception of one—maybe?

The only one, possibly still alive, was the widow of Jes Frederiksen, the very first of Robert's helpers. We found out that she was still alive and that she lived only 20 miles away, I decided to give her a call and if possible pay her a visit.

She got very excited about the subject of my call and asked me to come over to her place right away. Karin is 85 years young, and I mean young. She has a very good memory and she talks fast.

She received me as the guest of honour, in the typical Danish way, with coffee and cake served in the finest room in her house.

There we sat down for two whole hours, talking about Robert and what happened back in April 1944.

Karin even gave me her private photo album from 1944 and 1945, enabling me to scan the photos I needed.

Karin also told me that she and her husband had tried very hard to locate Robert after the war but they did not succeed and after several attempts they gave it up.

Before I left Karin, I gave her Robert's adr. as well as my own adr. and phone number. I drove back to Copenhagen with a pleasant feeling of having done some good.

Karin called me that same evening and told me that she had written a long letter to Robert and how pleased and excited she was of what happened to her that day. She even said: "After I have met with you Mr. Dyreborg, my life has become so exciting".

I did a lecture at the local Historic assn. in May 2001 about Robert, his evasion and escape, which also Karin attended. The people from the assn. told me, that normally there would be around 30 people attending lectures—85 people showed up. It was a good and successful evening in spite of both the over head projectors broke down.

The 35 Missions

Narrated by James L. Litchford 305th Bomb Group.

We finished our overseas flying training at Pyote, Texas latter part of April 1944 and after three days pass home reported to Kearney, Nebraska for getting a plane to start overseas to U.K.

The Crew.

Back row L to R: James Litchford Engineer 19, Joseph Mead Waist
Gunner 20 KIA, Roman Lekawski Radio Operator 25, Ken Larsen
Armoror 20, Richard Fisher Ball Turret Gunner 20 and Norman Auger
Tail Gunner 19.
Front row L to R: Richard Henley Pilot 24, Robert Coverstone Co-pilot 21
KIA, Harry Nichols Navigator 22 & Reynolds Saunders Bombardier 21

They were flying new planes in from Seattle, Washington so we got a shiny new one with very few hours on it.

When it became to depart from Kearney, we had 77 planes leave near 9 p.m. at night—destination Bangor, Maine. But 30 minutes out of Kearney one engine had an oil line leak. We returned to Kearney to get it repaired and left within 2 hours but due to heavy thunder storms over western part of New York, we only made it to Gremer Field at Manchester, New Hampshire. Stayed there for 24 hours, checked plane out etc. and flew on to Gander New Foundland. Stayed five days and all 77 planes took off, destination Nutts Corner, Ireland, where we arrived in 11 ½ hours.

That was the last we saw of that shiny new B-17. We took a ferry and train to a training area in northern England called "The Wash". After a few days there, we were transported to Chelveston Air Base near Northampton England, were assigned to barracks and were soon to begin flying bombing missions over Germany, France, Austria etc. These missions began May 7, 1944 and mine continued to January 13, 1945 when I had attained the 35 missions.

I was assigned to 305th Bomb Group, 422nd Bomb Squadron, our Bomb Group also had 364th, 365th and 366th Squadrons. We normally put up 12 planes per squadron plus four alternative planes. That was if anyone developed engine trouble or other reasons to abort the mission before a certain point in the mission, then one of the four could move up and take that plane's spot. Otherwise the four returned to base.

If we had any flak damage, engine trouble etc., on a mission, after we returned and these problems were repaired, the Pilot, Co-pilot, Navigator, Radio Operator and Engineer had to take the plane up for check out to see if all was OK to make another mission. So all together I made 35 Bombing missions and 44 practice missions due to after repair and around England.

On two occasions on bombing missions we had a solenoid malfunction due to flak over targets and after Bombs Away the bomb bay doors would not close, so it was the Engineer's job to crank them shut manually—188 turns while on walk around oxygen bottle.

We lost our Co-Pilot who was flying with another crew. Their plane and another from the 306th Bomb Group collided while landing. Both planes and 20 crew men were lost October 20, 1944. Our Co-Pilot is buried at Cambridge, England.

Later we lost a Waist Gunner. He was also flying with another crew on CHAFF RUN and German FW 190s shot down 10 out of 12 planes that day in late December 1944. Normally these CHAFF RUNs were considered "Milk Runs" but "Jerry" was waiting on these few planes dropping chaff-ahead of large groups of bombers.

Our Waist Gunner Joe Mead was buried in Germany, then returned with that lost crew to a Cemetery at Jefferson Barracks, near St. Louis, Missouri.

My last and 35th Mission was to Karlsruhe, Germany on January 13 1945.

Close Calls!

On my second mission I was getting out of the top turret when my cord to my heated suit caught on the bicycle gun grip, causing the turret to rotate. I was caught half in and half out of the turret. Luckily the bombardier came by and saw my plight and flipped the switch, stopping the turret. I was bruised pretty bad, but soon recovered.

After this I refused to wear my heated suit.

Another time I had bent down to get to a fuse panel (I was the engineer). While I was bent over, a flak burst destroyed the turret bubble, where my head would be if I had not been looking for the fuse panel. So I didn't hear so well for a while. After I got home the VA furnished me with hearing aids.

Dean and three friends took the train one time to see me at Chelveston and while there I got my Pilot to allow them to go up with us on a check-out trip around our base—and they all got AIR SICK!

US Base, Warrington, England late summer 1944. James Litchford (R)
visiting his child hood friend Dean Beard.
(You're supposed to notice the "fancy" curtains in the windows)

Late January 1945 I was sent to Scotland where we boarded the English Liner "Queen Mary". Before leaving Scotland on "Queen Mary", we—1,700 able bodied men—helped load 525 wounded on stretchers from ferry boats of Air Corp., onto the ship. Several of these men were seriously injured—we carried them to the various decks. This loading took the better part of 5 days.

Then we left Clyde River on "Queen Mary" February 2, 1945 and on February 7, 1945, late in the evening, we saw the Statue of Liberty in New York—quite a sight for a 20 year old Tech. SGT from Texas.

A WAC band played music for us when we arrived at Camp Kilmer, New Jersey at 2 am. After that we were sent to the mess hall to ask for any thing we wanted to eat, especially fresh eggs. While this was going on our papers were being processed and we were put on respective troop trains to our different locations in the States. As for me it took three days by train to Amarillo, Texas and I was only 50 miles from home.

I went to my parents home (I wanted to surprise them). As I knocked on the door, I was greeted with a house full of ladies having a baby shower for my sister to be—I had not been told about this while I was overseas. I enjoyed that surprise—that sister is 57 years old now. I have no brothers but five younger sisters.

After my leave I went to Santa Ana, California, where I arrived March 13, 1945. I stayed at a Rest Center until early June 1945. They fed us well and as a golf player in my high school days—the service furnished clubs at any golf course in California.

I was hoping to go on B-29s to the Pacific but the Air Corp. said "we are not going to need as many of you "fly-boys" now that the war was going well in Europe." So the Army came up with a "point" system that was compiled with your months in service, months overseas, and points for various decorations.

I had four battle stars as well as an air medal plus five oak leaf clusters. You had to have 85 points for discharge and mine counted 93, so I said, "I'm ready to go home."

I was transported to El Pas, Texas where I was honorably discharged June 12, 1945. I returned home at an age of 20—in Texas you weren't old enough to buy a beer or vote!!

The Final Mission

Narrated by Robert B. Clay 351st Bomb Group

Prologue

By Tom Clay , son of Robert B. Clay.

On April 23, 1999 retired Lieutenant Colonel Robert B. Clay sat in his room of the hotel that was hosting the 54th Anniversary Convention of POW's held captive in Stalag Luft III during World War II. The war that changed the entire world had also created a generation of American heroes, the last of the breed of men and women that engaged in a truly worldwide conflict between good and evil. Their upbringing during the Great Depression in the United States had proved to be a necessary ingredient in developing the character and stamina needed to lead their country and its Allies to victory.

This POW reunion was just like past annual conferences where the aging men reunite to share a common story, relive wartime experiences, and ruminate over the decreasing number of attendees. They represented the surviving prisoners from Stalag Luft III, a prison camp for downed airmen operated by the Luftwaffe. During the war these men were stationed at one of many airfields somewhere in England, North Africa, or Italy. Robert Clay was stationed in Polebrook, England where the 351st Bomb Group launched their offensive attack on Hitler's Third Reich from across the English Channel.

After the War, the 351st Bomb Group Association began the publication of a newsletter called *The Polebrook Post*. Its intention was to preserve the comradeship established in service and commemorate members who sacrificed their lives in defence of the country. Daniel Surprise, former POW, and waist gunner on Clay's final mission over Berlin, came to visit him while he was in Kansas City during conference. He carried with him the recent edition (March 1999) of *The Polebrook Post* to Clay's hotel room where the two old crewmates had planned to meet. Surprise had something he wanted to show his former captain. After a quick and cordial greeting Surprise asked Clay if he'd seen the recent edition of the *Post*. Clay responded that he had received it, but hadn't yet found time to look at it very closely. Surprise opened his copy and showed Clay the editorial section that contained a photograph of a crashed B-17. Clay nonchalantly glanced at the photo and replied, "If you've seen one crashed plane, you've seen them all." Surprised encouraged him to take a closer look. Clay studied the photo for a moment and noticed the plane had the familiar triangle J insignia on its tail, that being the insignia of the 351st Bomb Group. As Clay stared at the photograph of the B-17 wreckage a dark and long forgotten memory became sharply into view. He recognized the rolling farmland. He recognized the cottage tucked away in the woods. A flood of emotion filled his being as he realized that it was his plane, "Stormy Weather", that he was staring at.

Tears stung the eyes of this old pilot as he thought how miraculous it was to see this scene after so many long forgotten years.

For 40 years after the end of the war Clay had not even spoken of his experience. He didn't wish to relive the anger and the bitterness that the war had caused him so many years ago. Only in the last decade had this 82 year old veteran decided that all those events were far enough in the past that it was as if he was talking about a different time, a different world, a different person. Time, however, had healed the wounds that had scarred his mind with an indelible memory of the tragedies of war. He slowly began to share his war-time experiences. Now before him, in a lonely hotel room in Kansas City, was a kind of tangible evidence that substantiated all those stories that he had verbally related to his children, grandchildren and hundreds of school children for the past 10 years.

Robert B. Clay never imagined that the discovery of the photo and subsequent correspondence with eyewitnesses to the crash would be the beginning of the final chapter in his story. His wartime experience, like those of many others, instill in the current generation a poignant sense of awe and respect for a past generation, whose sacrifice and valour we can only read and dream about.

This story, told by Robert B. Clay, is about his crew and their experiences flying missions over Europe during WWII, and their tragic crash and subsequent capture behind enemy lines.

Robert B. Clay 1944 & his first crew. Back row L to R: Robert B. Clay Pilot, James W. Emerson Co-pilot, James W. Riley Waist Gunner Daniel Surprise Waist Gunner, Marshal R. Pullen Navigator & Stanley A. Walaszek Bombardier. Front row L to R: Frank H. Belsinger Radio Operator, Michael De Marie Ball Turret Gunner, Charles B. Jilcott Eng / Top Turret Gunner & Franklin L. Travis Tail Gunner.

To England

Our first stop was at Scott Field where we traded our B-17F for a brand new B-17G (with the nose turret), which I appropriately named the "Clay Pigeon." Heading east we circled Niagara Falls and spent a couple of days at Bangor, Maine, then on to Gander Labrador. We spent several days there waiting for good weather to fly over the North Atlantic. The night we took off, over 100 planes headed East at two-minute intervals. Our bomb bay contained a 500 gallon gas tank on one side and hundreds of cartons of cigarettes on the other side. The extra gasoline was needed for the 12 hour transatlantic flight. The cigarettes were given to the personnel in the military who smoked, which looking back, seemed to have been just about everyone. Two habits were formed by most men who joined the service, smoking, and cursing.

A few hours into the 10-hour flight, I noted a huge cloud ahead, so I decided to fly over it. I called the crew on interphone and told them to go on oxygen. A few minutes later, the waist gunner called back and said he could not find his oxygen mask. I angrily told him to stick the oxygen hose in his mouth and not go to sleep, or "you might wake up dead." I never heard another word from him until we landed at the designated airport in Ireland without incident.

The next day we flew to central England and found out that half of the double strength 401st Group was being sent to established a single strength (the 351st Bomb Group) making it easier for the 401st to begin operations. Since I was a sore thumb to the 401st, because I out-ranked most of the squadron command personnel (who were still 2nd Lts.), they were happy to transfer me over to the 351st, stationed at Polebrook. I and seven other crews were assigned to the 509th Squadron.

We had just settled in with the 351st when we were alerted to fly a combat mission. Custom decreed that I was to fly "Tail End Charlie" (more about that later). As I was climbing up to the assembly point, my left outboard gas tank (in the wing behind the #1 engine) was siphoning fuel out of the tank air vent. This was a fairly common occurrence and could be stopped by momentarily interrupting the flow either by slowing the plane (to reduce the partial vacuum above the wing); pulling the nose up sharply (to put more g's on the gas being sucked up through the overflow/air vent); or waiting until the tank was more or less empty, etc. After about 15 minutes of trying to stop the flow of gas and noting the significant loss by the #1 fuel gauge, I decided to return to the base at Polebrook. Upon landing, I was surprised to be met by an irate Group CO and the 509th Squadron CO. They were upset that even before my first mission I had acquired "battle fatigue." They complained that the 401st BG had transferred all the misfits to the 351st Bomb Group. They were going to send the plane up right now and see if it still siphoned gas.

While I was being chewed out, a staff car pulled up and told them the mission had been scrubbed and the planes were on the way back. I never heard another word about the incident.

A couple of days later, I completed my first combat mission to Solingen in the Ruhr Valley of Germany. Ironically, that first mission was, in many ways, my worst mission.

Combat

First Mission—Tail End Charlie.

At this point in the war, theoretically, every crew would complete 25 missions and not return, but in reality about one fourth of the crews were lost on their first few missions, principally because of flying "Tail End Charlie" (TEC) and lack of experience; another one fourth were lost during the remaining 25 and about half finished up and went home. Flying TEC you were more vulnerable to be attacked from the rear by German fighters. The tighter the formation the more protected each plane was because of the coverage of all the 50 caliber guns on each plane.

The high and low Squadron leaders fly on the Group leader, the second flight leader flies on the Squadron leader and TEC flies on the second flight leader on the outside of the 18-plane formations. Many factors, i.e., throttle changes, turbulence, anxiety, etc., produce an accordion effect on the formation with TEC coping with the whiplash effect of being in last place. It can be compared to the stop and go on an overcrowded freeway, except you can't stop.

Here is a typical oscillation: As TEC, I am closing in on my flight leader, so I ease back the throttles—I'm still gaining so I pull the throttles all the way back—I'm still gaining because he had de-throttled before I did, so I pull the nose up—I'm still gaining so there is nothing to do but pull the nose up until I can no longer see my flight leader—as the nose starts to mush down, my flight leader comes into view 100 yards ahead and accelerating away—so full throttle. This sequence can happen over and over every few minutes. The only way to break the chain is to drop back and smooth out the oscillations—maybe that's why many new replacement crews never survived their first few missions.

In the fall of 1943 I flew in the "Tail End Charlie" position. We encountered enemy fighters and flak. Endless flak, the only time I remember seeing colored flak—red, yellow, and green. I swear the lead navigator led us down the Ruhr Valley. On the way back, we could see a jagged hole in the middle of the right wing, where an 88mm AA shell passed through without exploding. (The right wing was replaced.) After six hours of hell, I landed but was so exhausted that I could barely walk. That night as I recalled events of the "nightmare" mission, I concluded that I probably would not last five missions, let alone the 25 missions required to complete my tour. Because I was a 1st Lt. (among mostly 2nd Lts.), after about four missions I was advanced from Tail End Charlie to a flight leader (i.e., the lead plane of a three-plane V formation). At that time I vowed that if I ever became a leader, I would not be a "throttle jockey."

The typical formation was 18 aircraft in a single squadron in a bomber stream. Bomber raids started as small intimate affairs. Usually moderate altitudes with a modest number of bombers, striking simple targets along the coast. As the numbers of available bombers increased the raids became larger and more daring. Some of the largest raids employed 1000 bombers to strike targets in Germany. This bomber stream could be as long as 100 miles and as wide as 1 mile. At 180 mph over target an air raid could last from 35-45 minutes.

Each squadron in the bomber stream was composed of 3 flights of 6 aircraft each. Each flight had two elements of 3 aircraft each. In this formation the lead flight flew at the designated altitude. The planes in an element were separated by 50 feet horizontally, and each element was also separated by 50 feet. The high flight was 50' behind and to the 50 feet right of the lead flight. The low flight was 50 feet behind and to the 50 feet left of the lead flight.

This deployment of aircraft made it nearly impossible for a single fighter to get hits on multiple aircraft in a single pass through a squadron. Secondly, it also spread the attacking force out making it difficult for it to concentrate its fire. Thirdly, this opened up the gunners field of fire increasing their effectiveness.

The Interim

On December 31, 1943 our group was assigned to lead the wing to Bordeaux France to bomb a German submarine pen. Our 351st CO, Col. Hatcher, flew the lead ship along with the group bombardier and group navigator. As a result of Col. Hatcher's plane being downed, and the subsequent reshuffling of personnel, I was moved up to Squadron Operations Officer for the 509th Bomb Squadron. I proceeded to designate my crew and Lt. Brooksby's crew as "lead crews." A lead crew would fly a mission only when our squadron was assigned to lead the Group (18 planes) or the Wing (54 planes). At the same time I replaced Walaszek with Hap Arnold and made him the Squadron Bombardier. Since a lead crew only flew a mission once every two or three weeks, I had to give my plane, the "Clay Pigeon," to a new replacement crew (Lt. Neuberg, who inherited the "Clay Pigeon"). About five missions later my old plane was shot down and I never heard what happened to the crew.

In the meantime, the lead ships required the ability to bomb by radar if necessary because of cloud under cast. Consequently, these lead planes were maintained at Wing Headquarters and flown to each group the afternoon before a scheduled mission.

The various subdivisions of a Bomb Squadron such as armament, engineering, etc., exist only for support of flying missions. The Squadron Operations Officer schedules and controls the assignment of crews and planes when a mission is scheduled. The 509th Squadron had about 20 crews and B-17's and on my 12th mission I led the Wing over Germany. My co-pilot was Lt. Col. Cobb, a Wing staff officer. He told me at briefing to lead the best I could and if he had any suggestions he would let me know.

Take off and assembly were uneventful. At 28,000 feet over Germany, clouds covered our primary target and secondary target. In the distance, I could see a large break in the under cast. We were approximately 10,000 ft. above the clouds and as we approached the opening it was like a slow motion uncovering of the landscape. At first we could only see green fields and trees. Then, buildings began to increase in number. (Most of the roofs in Germany are covered with red tile.) The near field of view showed increasing red across the full width of the cloud opening. Suddenly it dawned on me that we were almost over a very large city, which meant anti-aircraft (AA) guns. I knew we should not risk AA damage unless we were on a bomb run, so I started the gentle left turn necessary to maintain the 54-plane formation.

Within about 50 seconds about 100 bursts (called a box barrage) of black flak appeared off to the right, at our altitude and just where we would have been if we had flown straight ahead. So far, so good. Gentle turns are the only evasive action, which can keep a wing in good formation. Should I start a right turn, or hold the left turn? Ordinarily, evasive action involves a turn one way, then a turn back the other way. I knew that it took the Germans two minutes to follow the formation by radar, and then set the time for the AA shells to detonate at the selected altitude, and finally the flight time for the shell reach our altitude. I reasoned that the Germans would assume I would zigzag, so I kept turning left. Another barrage of flak appeared off to the right. I kept turning left and the flak kept blossoming on my right. After a 180-degree turn I went back the direction I had come from. Behind me the sky was black with flak, but not one plane had been hit. My evasive actions proved successful and I felt a sense of personal victory for having outguessed those jokers below!

Soon we saw a column of smoke erupting through the clouds and we dropped all 54 x 4 tons (216 tons) of bombs into the smoke column. Ironically, I heard later that Lt. Col. Cobb received a commendation for leading a successful mission under adverse conditions without losing any aircraft.

With 16 of 25 missions completed, the spring of 1944 found me in good spirits. The Allies were controlling the skies; we now had P-51 fighter cover in and out of targets deep into Germany; most of my friends which had been transferred with me from the 401st BG were finishing up and going home; the weather was much nicer; I had recently been promoted to Captain; and I felt that my chances of going home were very good. The new replacement crews needed to fly 35 missions to complete a tour of duty because of decreasing losses on bombing missions.

Several years ago I had softened my initial attitude of "I want to forget my entire war experience" to the point that I had written up my 17th and final mission.

Final Mission

I'm sure that each member of our crew would write widely differing accounts of our final mission because each individual sees the world through a different pair of eyes.

On the 23rd of May 1944, the group was alerted for a mission the following morning. Since the 509th Squadron was to lead the 351st Group, I assigned crew and myself to the lead ship, which had been flown over from Wing HQ that afternoon. It was equipped with a newly improved Norden bombsight, which included an auto-leveling gyro, which markedly increased the accuracy of a bomb strike. My bombardier, Lt. "Hap" Arnold, told me it was worth about $50,000.

This was to be my 17th mission, but I was not worried about it because the 8th Air Force loss ratio of one in 25 missions (i.e. theoretically on a pilot's 25th mission, he would be shot down) flown in 1943 when I had arrived had decreased to one in 30 and was approaching one in 35 missions flown. In addition, I had survived several potentially disastrous predicaments with luck and good management and, like everyone who continually faces danger, I was resigned to my fate with little apprehension to interfere with my ability to cope with any situation.

About midnight on May 23, 1944 I was awakened by my phone ringing—it was Lt. Wimmer, an assistant operations officer from another squadron asking if he could fly the tail gun position in my plane (the group lead ship utilized a pilot in the tail gun position to keep the pilot assessed of events and conditions which were beyond the sight of his lead pilot position). I explained to him I was not pleased to be awakened and besides, I already had assigned a pilot from my squadron.

Wimmer persisted, saying he wanted to get his 25 missions in and go home, so I relented and told him okay, for I knew most pilots did not relish getting in a mission as a tail gunner.

The next morning (May 24, 1944), I discovered my copilot, Lt. Emerson, was grounded, so my crew now consisted of myself, pilot; Lt. Hatten, copilot; Lt. Pullen, navigator; Lt. Arnold, bombardier; Sgt. Jilcott, flight engineer; Sgt. Belsinger, radio operator, Sgts. Surprise and Travis, waist gunners; Sgt. DeMarie, ball turret gunner, and Lt. Wimmer, tail gunner.

In the briefing room when the curtains were pulled back showing the red line out over the North Sea then into Big B (Berlin), no common groan was heard as had occurred in January of 1944 when the first Big B raid was unveiled. We had been there several times during the intervening five months and we all knew it was a tough target, but not a particularly dangerous one because we now had P-51 cover all the way.

Nothing unusual happened as we assembled and headed east over the North Sea on a course that would minimize the time we would be over enemy territory. Two things of note as we turned right over the German coast: First, we enjoyed a 100 mph tail wind, and second, the IP (initial point of the bomb run) was on the same beeline as the route to the target.

About three minutes from bombs away, the oil pressure on #3 (left ~~right~~ inboard) engine started down, so I feathered the prop. Ordinarily I would have aborted and let the deputy leader (a wing man) take over, but I was afraid the time was too short for the deputy bombardier to successfully synchronize on the target so I simply upped the manifold pressure to about 40 inches on the good engines to maintain the prescribed airspeed.

After bombs away, I aborted, cut the manifold pressure to 34 inches and made a 180-degree turn and headed back toward the coast, thus avoiding the extra distance to the rendezvous point.

The best evasive action at that time was to vary altitude because the German antiaircraft artillery shells did not have proximity fuses, rather their flak exploded after a preset time. Because diving and climbing pulled the formation apart, the only evasive action allowed by the lead ship was gentle horizontal turns. So it was sort of exhilarating to fly back across Berlin alone, doing altitude evasive action with flak bursting on all sides and all altitudes.

After clearing the Berlin area, I settled into a 110 mph gas-saving slow descent. The 100-mph tailwind going in was now a headwind going out. The bomber formations above and to the right gradually passed us up. By the time we reached the North Sea coastline, we were alone except for a P-51, which dove down and dipped his wing, then headed west. Up until now, I felt no particular worry about our predicament. However, I did feel almost naked and alone at 20,000 feet over the enemy coast. Suddenly, the #4 engine (right outboard) started to run away and pushing the feathering button had no effect.

Now, the situation was serious. With 100-mph headwind we were almost standing still with respect to the coastline far below. Months before, the crew had voted to never ditch in the North Sea, if there was any possible alternative. With that in mind, I turned parallel to the coastline, hoping we could make it to Holland or France before going down.

My mind was racing to figure out some options when I recalled that even though Sweden was officially neutral, some bombers that had made it to Sweden somehow were flown back to England.

Without a word, I made a 180-degree turn and asked Lt. Pullen for the heading to Sweden. Now we had a 100-mph tailwind and I felt better.

At about 18,000 feet we ran into clouds so I went on instruments. Now that fighter attacks were improbable, I ordered the men to throw everything possible overboard—flak suits, guns, ammo, etc. Lt. Arnold asked if that meant his new self-erecting Norden bombsight. "Especially that," I said. One of the gunners asked if he could shoot his ammo. When I asked why, he answered, "We were told to shoot bursts of five seconds or less to prevent the guns from overheating and jamming and I'd like to see how long it takes for that to happen." So I said "OK." I could feel the familiar faint chatter of the 50-caliber for about 20 seconds before it stopped. Later, he told me that the barrel was smoking and too hot to handle before it jammed.

A few minutes later, at about 13,000 feet, in a straight-ahead slow letdown, the plane was surrounded and racked with black balls of flak. We were out of it in a few seconds with no apparent direct hits. Later I determined that we had flown over Flensburg, a German city near the Danish border. Within two or three minutes the #3 engine (right inboard), damaged from the flak, started losing oil pressure, so I feathered it.

There we were at 12,000 feet, on instruments, with both inboards feathered and the right outboard wind milling. The situation was now critical. Where would we be when we broke out of the clouds? No time to worry about that, because I noticed a conflict in the instrument readings. The tiny plane on the blind flying artificial horizon looked okay, but the airspeed was increasing at a steady rate.

For a few seconds I couldn't understand what was happening; then in a flash I understood the problem. Earlier in the year, I had held a series of engineering classes for pilots and I remembered that the two inboard engines ran each vacuum pump for the pilot's blind flying gyro instruments, and now both inboards were feathered. So the airspeed indicator was right and the flight instruments were wrong.

When a plane starts to dive, the natural instinct is to pull back on the wheel, but if you are in a turn the plane rapidly rolls over and goes into a vertical dive. Overcoming my instincts, I held the wheel, as nearly as I could, to a straight-ahead wings level position. The airspeed crawled up to 200 . . . 240 . . . 260 (the red line). I had never pushed a B-17 to that limit. Meantime, as the airspeed had gone up, the noise increased in intensity and pitch. The controls became tighter and tighter. I strained my eyes into the white void ahead hoping we would break out of the clouds in time to avoid a crash. The full view came in a flash—ocean straight ahead. We were in a 45-degree dive with wings approximately vertical. I rolled out and zoomed back up to the cloud base about 4000 ft. above the water. Ahead was water and behind was land. I had no choice but to make the 180-degree turn back to the land.

Passing over the seashore I gave the order to bail out. Arnold and Pullen crawled out of the nose and went rearward. A minute later I told Hatten to check the rear of the plane. He returned and said all were gone. By that time we were at about 2000 feet with the left outboard pulling a manifold pressure of 44 inches of mercury at 2300 rpm and the plane requiring strong left rudder and wheel to keep from flipping over to the right. I told Hatten to hurry and bail out and that I was going to crash land because I couldn't cut the outboard engine at 90 mph without stalling out and crashing, and if I simply let go of the controls, the plane would wheel over and dive in. He answered, "If it's all right with you, I would rather crash land than bail out." I said, "Okay, buckle up."

We had descended so fast that the thick bulletproof windshields were cold enough that frost had formed on the inside, so we could not see straight ahead. So we opened the side windows and peered around the edge of the windshield. The terrain below consisted of rolling wooded hills with flat farm clearings and houses about every quarter mile in all directions.

With my side window open, I circled left for a half turn looking for a suitable spot, but there was none and we kept losing altitude. We were soon flying in a wooded gully between two wooded hills, when straight ahead was a dirt road fill between the hills on either side. I aimed for the top of the road and, just as we passed over, the right wing stalled out and struck the road. I dimly recall grinding and banging noises and streaks of light as we were jerked around.

Suddenly all was quiet. I could hear birds chirping and the gentle hiss of escaping oxygen. For a moment I wondered if this was Heaven, but when I could focus my eyes, I looked over at Hatten. His entire face was dripping with blood and I knew we had survived.

The nose of the ship was headed directly back toward the road we had struck with the tail next to Hatten's side window. The control cable had pulled the pilot wheel solidly against my chest.

Somehow I managed to make my way out of my seat and up through the open side window. Hatten could see only dimly, so I helped him out of the plane and led him about 30 yards away.

"Stormy Weather"—photo taken late afternoon Wednesday May 24 1944.

I went back to burn the plane (it was required by regulations to destroy your aircraft in the event of a crash landing) as best I could with the 80 gallons of fuel remaining in the left wing tank. The baseball size incendiary charges behind the pilot's seat designed for just such an occasion were not there. Silently, I cursed Wing for providing such an inadequate plane. (I had noted before takeoff that the engines had over 200 combat hours, which was the usual time to change them with rebuilt engines.)

I was determined to try and burn the remains of the crash anyway. So I reached in the cockpit and grabbed the Very Pistol and some shells. (A Very Pistol, sometimes called a flare pistol, was used to shoot various colored flares through the roof of the cockpit to instruct the formation without breaking radio silence.)

I took the gas cap off the left outboard tank, stepped back and aimed the pistol at the opening. The double red flare bounced off the wing and zoomed up over the same road that had caught the right wing. Until then I had been only dimly aware of a group of five or ten adults and children on the road. As the flare swished over their heads, they ran screaming in both directions.

Now I was really upset with the situation. I was going to burn the remains of that wrecked plane even if it killed me. I loaded another shell into the pistol, stuck the barrel of the pistol into the gas fill spout, closed my eyes and pulled the trigger.

I could hear the flare sizzling about inside the tank, so I opened my eye and a blue one-foot-high flame curled lazily out of the opening. I unconsciously stuck the Very Pistol under my belt and started leading Hatten up to the nearest farm house, leaving the object of my frustrations to its own fate.

A kind old man with a Red Cross armband met us outside the back door. I motioned to Hatten and then to the house. Surprisingly, he told me in English that this was Denmark, which was occupied by the Germans, and he could not help me because of reprisals. So I asked him if I could wash the blood from my copilot's face and he reluctantly led us into the kitchen where his wife had a pan of water ready. I was washing Hatten's face trying to determine the seriousness of the laceration when the family started a verbal commotion. I glanced out a window and spotted a well-fed German solider, Tommy gun ready, sneaking up on the house. He kicked open the door and yelled at me loudly in German while swinging the gun menacingly. The old man told me to drop my pistol to the floor, which (after realizing it was under my belt) I did, quickly. Later, I thought what irony if, after the struggle to survive, a Very Pistol with a spent cartridge would have been the reason for my death.

C'est la guerre (such is war), we were now POWs.

One Year Behind The Wire

Captured.

By late afternoon of May 24th, 1944, a German Army truck had picked up all of my crew members, who had parachuted out, and arrived at the house where Hatten and I had been held captive by a German solider.

All had survived our final mission with only scratches and bruises, except Hatten, who had sustained a long laceration across his forehead between his eyes and hairline.
We were driven to a German naval base on the east coast of Denmark where Hatten's wound was sewn up like a potato sack (i.e., stitches through both sides of the wound, then over the top to the next stitch, etc.), which healed to a long welt across his forehead.

The next day our crew was put on a train with four or five guards armed with fixed bayonets and transferred to Dulag Luft at Frankfurt on the Rhine for solitary confinement and interrogation. My new quarters for the next two weeks were an eight-foot-square underground dungeon surrounded by concrete and steel bars with a small frosted windows about 10 feet above my bed of wooden slats. The only lights were in the hallway. If I needed a rest room, a guard would unlock my cell and escort me to the john. Three times a day, a bowl of soup and a cup of water were pushed through the bars.

After four or five days of no outside noise, no outside sunshine or view, I began to think it was all a big stupid joke. It was spring outdoors, and I was wasting away in a dungeon. On the seventh day I was led upstairs for interrogation. I was ready to state myname, rank and serial number. The first question the German interrogator asked was, "Captain Clay, do you think 1st Lieutenant Newman Van Tassel can take your place as operations officer?" .

The implications of that query stunned me mentally because Van Tassel was my assistant operations officer, and I had no idea they knew so much about the details of our supposedly confidential Group organization.

He next took a liquor bottle off the shelf and offered me a drink. I said, "I don't drink liquor." He said, "We are now stuck with cheap liquor. Your Colonel Hatcher finished off the last of the good whiskey year." I glanced around the room. On one wall was a detailed layout of the 351st air base at Polebrook showing labeled areas such as revetments, buildings, hanger, etc., stamped "SECRET." I could see their psychology—since they knew so much, anything I would say wouldn't matter.

I pled ignorance to most of their questions, i.e., Where was the IP (Initial Point for the beginning of the bomb run)? Why five officers aboard? What about the Black Widow night fighter? Why didn't I bail out? When was the invasion coming? etc. A few minutes later I was dismissed with the reminder that "For you, da var is offer."

A couple of days later I was taken upstairs again and interrogated this time by a young man who spoke English with a southern accent. I asked him about that and he told me he was born and raised in Texas and was visiting relatives in Germany when the war broke out and the Nazis would not let him out of Germany. At the end of the meeting, someone brought in a young, good-looking blonde girl. The Texan introduced me to "Greta" and, pointing through a window to a small, brightly painted house about 50 yards away, said, "See that bungalow, if you would care to, you can spend a couple of days with Greta over there. She doesn't speak any English, but she sure is a lot of fun." I said no thanks and was hustled back to my dungeon cell. I had figured out that they wanted me to feel obligated to be cooperative, or even worse, even blackmail me with photos.

About two days later a little obnoxious German came down to my cell and started to ask questions from outside the bars. When he got around to the invasion question, I suddenly thought, "You have invaded my territory in this dark hole, you ratty little Joker, and I'm going to feed you all the garbage I can think of."

During the previous month I had led two, six-plane, night fake invasion missions whereby we were part of a thousand plane effort that would fly directly across the English Channel, turn right about two miles from the French coast, fly about 10 minutes, turn right and fly back across the Channel, turn right and fly back up the English coast to our original position. They called it the invasion box pattern, which we would repeat about 10 times. By the 10th time around most of my squadron had dropped out of formation and I could see the dim blue night formation lights (the blue light on the every plane that helped the pilots see the other planes in order to help them stay in formation during night missions) passing me, going in all different directions. The 8th Air Force never said how many bombers we lost on those missions (which did not count as combat), but I knew it was dangerous and stupid but part of our psychological warfare. I really thought they would not invade at such an obvious place as across the Channel.

With that background, I told the arrogant little joker that we were going to invade across the Channel and that we were going to invade real soon. I explained that we were going to invade with one million men and that the Germans were "kaput". To cap it off, I told him that if his leaders were smart, they would give up before it was too late.

About five days later when I was allowed outside into the sunshine, the other officer crewmen were lying on the grass asking where had I been and why I was so late coming out and had I heard about the invasion on the 6th of June?

I counted back the days since I had sounded off to the ratty little German and figured it had been two days before D-Day. I suddenly felt guilty wondering if it had affected the outcome of the invasion. I have since learned that my pretentious talk had made no difference.

During interrogation at Dulag Luft the Germans took whatever GI equipment they wanted, i.e., flying boots, warm clothing, hats, and insignia, even GI hack watches. Bombardier "Hap" Arnold wore a Rolex instead of a GI hack watch and the Germans took his Rolex. When he argued that his watch was not GI and not subject to confiscation, they still would not give it back. He then said "Okay, Buster, after the war, I'm coming back and look you guys up" and the head interrogator answered, "Ve vill see who iss da victor."

Stalag Luft III

That afternoon we were herded on board a "40 and 8" box car (40 men or 8 mules) and began our journey from Frankfurt to Sagan, Germany (Stalag Luft III) located on the Polish border about 100 miles southeast of Berlin.

Much has been written about the conditions in the "40 & 8s". When 60 men are crowded into one for long periods of time conditions were extremely miserable. There was no hole to see out or urinate through. No room to lie down. If half the POWs were sitting, the other half had to stand up and if someone had the "GI's," we all suffered the consequences. The train would stop for about 10 minutes every 6 or 8 hours and sometimes we would get a drink of water. Once the train stopped unexpec-tedly because of an air raid and the engineer released all his steam (so it wouldn't blow up in case we were strafed). In my mind, I can still see hundreds of Kriegies squatting along side the railroad tracks reliving themselves then enjoying the 30-minute delay to build steam pressure back up, in the mean time stretching our legs and basking in the sunshine.

The next day we arrived at Stalag Luft III (Prison of Flyers #3) and marched into the West Compound. The five officers from our crew were assigned an unoccupied room together with three other Air Force officers. Since I was the ranking man, I automatically became the room commander. Each room was about 20 feet by 20 feet with four triple deck bunks. From time to time during the summer, other new POW's were assigned until all the bunks were filled. Each bunk had wooden slats across the bottom with a sack of wood shavings for a mattress. The wood shavings gradually changed to sawdust with usage and sifted through the burlap cover onto the bunk below.

The compound was new, with single story barrack-type pre-fabricated buildings, atop several three-foot-high concrete pillar-like foundations running the length of the building so that the "ferrets" (unarmed guards) could patrol under as well as alongside and through the buildings. Each ferret carried a long steel rod (similar to a short fishing rod), which he periodically plunged into the ground in search of tunnels dug by the Kriegies (short for Kriegsgefangenen, i.e., war prisoners).

Because we had been "shook down" of all our flying gear at Dulag Luft, when we arrived at Stalag Luft III, we were issued a GI helmet liner, two GI blankets, an Eisenhower jacket (a waist length, light-weight jacket), a pair of cheap shoes, a large bowl, and eating utensils (a large aluminum spoon and fork, and a regular case knife). Everyone sharpened his knife on a concrete step or a rock.

The Germans were always giving us a bad time. For example, the Christmas of 1944 they promised us a bottle of beer, only to tell us later that there was none because the Allied "Terror Fliegers" had bombed the beer factory. Several times they would say "No Red Cross parcels this week because your bombers blew up a trainload of Red Cross parcels." Another memorable harassment was that morning and night the Germans would line us up for Appel (French for roll call) to count us. Soon after I arrived, 2000-plus U.S. Air Force Officers assembled on a rainy morning and the count showed two Kriegies missing. (They had escaped during the night). The Germans kept recounting then decided to keep us in formation while they searched all the buildings in the compound. The end result was that we stood for six hours in the rain with no protection from the elements. We could not even break ranks to visit the latrine.

In turn, whenever possible, we gave them a bad time. Soon after I arrived in Stalag Luft III, arriving POW's told us there would be no more attempts to escape or evade because we had successfully invaded France and were winning the war, so it was safer to stay together. Another reason was because, just before I was shot down, the English compound at Stalag Luft III had made a mass escape of about 70 English POW's, and all but three were rounded up and massacred. This tragedy is accurately portrayed in the popular movie entitled "The Great Escape."

The fact that we should no longer attempt to escape was no reason we couldn't give them a bad time. For example, there was one day that a truck loaded with coal briquettes got mired in the mud outside our barracks. It was raining cats and dogs but the guards came into our barracks and ordered every one out to push the truck out of the mud hole. The 100-plus Kriegies could have picked the truck up, but with not a word spoken we all began to rock the truck back and forth while pushing downward rather than forward. In about a minute, the wheels were mired to the axles both front and rear! The goons (Germans) gave up and brought in a big tractor the next day to pull the truck out of the mud hole.

Another example of the fun we had was that on one day we decided to get even with a particularly obnoxious ferret. The floor in each room of the barracks consisted of prefabricated sections looking similar to 4'x4' pallets. There were cracks between the sections as well as cracks between boards in each section. To clean the floor we would throw buckets of water on the floor and simply sweep the floor, which allowed the muddy water to leak through the cracks. One day this troublemaker ferret was probing the ground under our barracks. A lookout gave a pre-arranged signal as the ferret reached the middle of the long concrete supporting wall foundation, and everyone in their rooms began to flood the floors with water. A half-minute later the ferret emerged from his inspection soaked to the skin with dirty water. It was a good thing he had no gun because he was angry enough to shoot all of us.

The reason the ferrets were unarmed is because they were continuously walking through the compound and it would have been easy for a group of prisoners to overtake a single ferret and take his gun.

The British compound at Stalag Luft III was about 60 feet to the south of our West Compound (four barbed wire fences away). The British occupied the first compound built (in 1939) and one English pilot had been a POW since before the start of World War II. (He had crash-landed in the North Sea and was picked up by a German boat two days before war was declared, but was still in Germany when English declared war on Germany.) Over the years the British had built a clandestine radio, which could receive the BBC news. They would summarize the news on a slip of paper, fasten it to a small rock and at a prearranged time there would be Englishmen exercising and swinging their arms near the fence and if there were no ferrets in view, the rock would come sailing over the fence to be picked up by one of us in the West Compound. The Compound was well organized and operated just as any other military unit. The Security leaders would arrange to read the news summary in each barracks during the same day.

The main memory I have is that the German newspapers (furnished by the Germans) told how Hitler was winning the war, while the BBC news broadcast that the Allies were also winning the same war. However, Kriegies who could read German, kept a map of Germany on a bulletin board up to date showing the East and West Fronts. The newspapers told how Germany was conducting a "Victorious Retreat."

Past Times

At Polebrook, in England, the small talk between crews and friends involved dances, parties, and weekends in London usually involving girls, with little mention of food, because it was adequate and plentiful. However, in Stalag Luft III, the opposite was the case. The Germans gave us daily a large serving of soupy stew consisting of a little meat and mostly vegetables (Brussels sprouts, cabbage, carrots, potatoes, etc.) plus a fifth of a one-kilo loaf of black bread, which was said to contain some sawdust.

Some pre-med flying officers in camp calculated that the diet furnished by the Germans was about 1200 calories per day, which I can verify is a starvation diet. The thing that made life livable and hopeful was the food in the Red Cross parcels, which the Germans gave out sparingly and irregularly according to their fancy. (A Red Cross parcel weighed about 10 pounds, contained concentrated food which added up to about 30,000 calories, plus six or eight packs of cigarettes). It was a good week when each of us received a half parcel, and a bad week when we received none. After the war was over, I read that even though only one in ten Red Cross parcels reached the POWs, our government claimed it was well worth the cost and effort because it saved many POW lives.

In our room we pooled our food and shared equally not only the rations, but the household duties of cooking, washing dishes, etc. The person who served the food into each bowl had last choice to choose a bowl of the divided food.

After the second day in Stalag Luft III the number one subject became FOOD. During a good week, I could trade a package of cigarettes for a chocolate bar, but during a bad week I would simply give my cigarettes to a buddy who smoked but who prized food more than smoking.

When lights were turned off at 9:00 at night, a favorite pastime was lying in our bunks taking turns telling what we were going to do when we returned home. Nine times out of ten it was about food. One hungry prisoner would say, "When I get home I'm going to keep my pockets filled with candy bars, so whenever I feel like it I can just reach in and eat as many as I want." Another might say, "Every morning I'll have my wife cook three eggs with ham and plenty of toast covered with melted butter." I don't remember once hearing about drinking at a bar or cavorting with the girls.

The British compound had been in operation since 1939 and had accumulated a fairly large library, which they shared with us. About once each week our room would get a book to read. I used to read most of them but after two or three months the words because so blurred that I stopped reading. I had developed double vision along a line parallel to my two eyes which was mainly caused by a dietary deficiency of some kind.

In the summer months we were allowed to bathe as often as we wished.

The temperatures in the summer time reached near 90 degrees. There were spigots placed around the camp that were used out in the open for washing and bathing. In the winter months the temperatures would drop to below freezing. We were given one warm shower per month in the winter.

Staying warm in the wintertime was a miserable challenge at best. We were issued 2 thin GI blankets, which were made of wool. Most prisoners would fashion a type of sleeping bag from them by folding them over to form a couple of layers and then safety-pin them together . This was sufficient to keep us somewhat warm enough to sleep during the nights when the temperatures didn't drop too low.

I never suffered any serious health problem as a POW, but I did develop a chronic case of athlete's foot. My sister recalls the problem when I arrived home in June 1945 with the phrase "I never saw such awful looking feet in my life." To me, it never seemed like a big deal, but it did take months to clear up.

People ask, "How was it in POW camp?" One answer is that one year then seemed like five years now, mainly because of the uncertainty of the future and the hope of earlier liberation. Another is that even if we were not tortured, we were treated much worse than the Allies treated the German POWs. It turns out that each Stalag had its "death march."

Christmas

The Christmas of 1944 was one I shall never forget. Some time before Christmas, the Red Cross had sent our compound of 2500 U.S. airmen food parcels and other various gifts, one of which was a small wind-up phonograph, along with several 78-rpm phonograph records. By the time it arrived at my room in our barracks, the needles were so worn that nothing legible came from the speaker. Nobody wanted it in our building.

Having been born and raised on a farm in Willard, Utah, I had a background of solving endless problems. So I decided to grind a new point on one of the worn out needles. I did this by simultaneously rotating and rubbing it gently on a rock until it looked like the ones used on our old phonograph at home.

Sure enough, the needle produced loud and clear music from the recordings. My favorite song was one that I had never heard before. It was "I'll Be Home for Christmas" sung by Bing Crosby. It gave me new hope that it was an omen for a miracle to somehow take me home by Christmas time.

But it was not to be. The morning of December 25th dawned cold and wintry and still locked up in Stalag Luft III.

We marched out of Stalag Luft III at midnight on 30 January 1945 because the Russian cannon fire from the East was growing louder each day. Christmas at home was finally realized in June 1945.

When I hear Bing sing that favorite carol at Christmas, I still feel the same nostalgic emotional rush I felt just before that Christmas in 1944.

Anecdotes of Stalag Luft III

Our compound was built on forestland. About 20 feet in any direction was a stump of a tree about two feet tall and the size of a telephone pole. As a supplement to the meager allotment of coal briquettes for cooking and heating, a Kriegie could dig up a stump and drag it to a supervised area for cutting with an axe and splitting with wedges. The only catch was, we had no equipment for digging up the stumps, except the empty cans from the Red Cross parcels. During the summer of 1944 I decided to make a one-man project of harvesting a stump. I scooped dirt all day long for one week. I found out that big cans are better than small cans; some roots went out 20 feet before I could break them off and the taproot went down four feet. It took one more day to split and chop the wood into usable pieces for our little stove.

The coal briquettes that we used for fuel for cooking and keeping warm were about the size of a bar of soap and consisted of fine (slack) coal pressed together with a small amount of a tar-like binder. It was difficult to make a fire hot enough to burn the coal completely, because as a briquette heated up it fell apart into a pile of slack coal particles. Consequently, about half of the coal wound up on the compound dump. I noticed that some of the unburned particles were up to 1/4" in cross section and these larger particles burned much better than the fine powder portion. So I constructed a comb to rake out the larger particles from the fines and ashes.

Making the comb was fairly easy. The ends of a tin can from a Red Cross parcel were cut out by a small, hinged can opener (similar to a backpacker's can opener) found in some Red Cross parcels. Then, using a narrow crack in the floor as support, my sharpened case knife could cut through the rim of the can then split it endwise. Straightening it out into a flat sheet furnished the basic component for making large pans or pots, etc. In this case I cut the strip in two in the long direction leaving the rim on one side for a rigid handle. I next slit that side into strips about 3/16" wide by 1" long. Rotating each strip 90 degrees produced the needed comb. To prevent copy -catting, I would visit the garbage dump when no one was around and in 10 minutes I could fill a small pan with a couple of pounds of coarse coal that burned much better than the briquettes.

During the fall of 1944 another Kriegie and I fashioned a high jump standard from some sticks we found at the dump. Even now I recall the sun setting and I was jumping higher than I ever did before or after. It seemed dreamlike as I cleared the bar set even with my chin. It amazed me how losing 30 pounds or so made such a difference.

Leaving Stalag Luft III

Once arriving at Stalag Luft III, our building CO had admonished us to keep in shape to walk out of Stalag Luft III if necessary. Consequently, most of us walked around the inside of the West Compound (about ½ mile) several times a day.

The only maverick was a guy by the name of Arragona, a second-generation Italian Second Lieutenant. When most of us were ready to walk, I would try and roust everybody out.

Usually Arragona would be lying on his bunk and he would say, "Go ahead, you eager beavers, because I'll be walking past while you're lying alongside the road." Arragona had been shot down and had evaded for some time. He had stolen clothes off a clothesline and discarded his uniform, even his dog tags. He had a dark complexion and a large hooked nose. When he was captured, the Krauts thought he was a Jew and put him in a Jewish prison. After two or three weeks, the Germans decided he was an Air Force officer and sent him to Stalag Luft III, then to my room. When he told us how terrible he was treated, we all figured he was full of stories, but now I think maybe he was put in a concentration camp. More about him later.

Late in January 1945 the distant cannon fire to the East became louder each day. We all surmised it was the Russian Front pressing westward.

At 10:00 p.m. on January 30th word came to be ready to walk out at midnight during one of the worst blizzards of the year. We each put our necessities on our two blankets, rolled them into a cylinder, tied the two ends together, threw the bedrolls over our heads, onto our shoulders, and we were ready.

It was an eerie feeling with snow about a foot deep and snowflakes swirling about our head. Marching out through the gate, which had confined us continuously for about eight months, left me with an eerie feeling.

The road out went past a row of long storage buildings. On a concrete dock in front of a well-lighted building were pallets of U.S. Red Cross parcels and piles of German black bread for us to take all we wanted. I looked inside the building and I could see pallets of parcels stacked to the ceiling. I guessed there were thousands of pallets each with about 100 parcels.

And to think that the Germans had been telling us we could only receive a half parcel each occasionally because the "Terror Fliegers" were bombing and strafing all the trains. Later when I told others about all the parcels the Germans were hoarding, they were skeptical. However, at the 50th POW reunion in 1995, I saw a picture of what I had seen. I took a picture of my wife Mildred, pointing to a man about halfway up the mountain of Red Cross parcels.

Our West Compound was one of five (Central, East, West, North and South), each with about 2500 Kriegies.

Consequently, over 10,000 of us moved out that night. The South Compound moved out first and then we followed. It turned out that we would walk 50 minutes, and then rest for 10 minutes. I had picked up one Red Cross parcel while others grabbed two or three. At the first rest stop, I opened my parcel and packed most of the items in my bedroll, leaving the rest behind.

Walking in the wet, freezing weather was miserable. My shoes were the cheap worn out pair that the Red Cross had issued. I had worn holes in the soles and my attempts to repair them with cardboard from a Red Cross parcel box proved feeble in the winter conditions.

About 4:00 a.m. that morning along a lonely stretch of road, which was cut through heavy forest, a shot rang out. Immediately the guards began firing in all directions and everyone dove into the borrow pit alongside the road. The entire scene seemed unreal with the blizzard swirling around us. Soon the firing stopped and a minute or two later some of the Kriegies started to crawl back onto the road and rifle fire started up again. This time we waited until the guards ordered us back on the road. It would have been a cinch to evade at the time, but nobody did.

Years later, I read that a guard had accidentally fired a shot and the others thought it might be a Russian patrol (the front lines were only a few miles away).

We arrived at a small town the next morning and were told to get some sleep. Kriegies were everywhere, but "Hap" Arnold and I found an old shed where we could get out of the weather. That night we started marching again. During the ten minute rest stops that second night, most of the excess black bread and Red Cross food taken by the naive but hungry Kriegies had been discarded. However, they were not wasted because peasants lined the route waiting to pick up anything thrown away.

While many have described it as a "death march," I personally know of only one Kriegie who did not make it. He was from another room in our barracks and marched out with a sore throat. He was put in a horse-drawn wagon after the first day out, but died en route to our planned layover destination about 50 miles northwest of Stalag Luft III.

At dawn of the second night of our frantic march, we arrived at a town with a huge warm building full of large tanks and specialized vessels made of clay for the chemical industry. It turned out to be a one-block square building for drying large chemical vessels prior to being fired into ceramics. Arragona, the dissident back in Stalag Luft III who belittled the walking workouts, came around begging for help. He had thrown away all his food during the evacuation march so I gave him a half loaf of black bread and two cans from my Red Cross parcel.

For two days we alternately ate and slept, at which time the more able Kriegies were marched out. My toes had been frostbitten and developed large blood blisters so I, and a couple of thousand others remained behind.

We were crowded into the despised "40 & 8" rail cars and two days later we arrived at a deserted prison camp just outside Nuremberg known as Stalag Luft XIIID. I surmised it had been filled with Italian POW's because of all the Italian tin cans at the dumpsite.

Stalag Luft XIIID—Nuremberg

Life in Stalag Luft XIIID was much worse than at Stalag Luft III because the camp was an old camp and consequently infected with several types of vermin. While there we received no Red Cross parcels during the two-month stay. We were often being herded into air raid trenches both day and night, and we had too little fuel to keep warm during February and March of 1945. We burned bed slats, tables, and etc. to stay warm.

The most memorable event was the total destruction of Nuremberg during February 1945. The first day the Americans had a maximum effort (1000-plus bombers) and soon Nuremberg was enveloped in smoke and dust. That night, the British came over en masse (three or four planes a minute for several hours). Every two or three minutes a pathfinder (radar equipped planes) would drop a parachute flare which would light up several square miles of the city like daylight. The following planes would drop their bombs on the flare. Being only two or three miles away provided fireworks like I have never seen before or since. We were supposed to keep our windows shuttered, but we disregarded that order. I can clearly see in my mind's eye the following panorama: A two-mile-long by two-mile-high stage filled with swinging searchlight beams, continuous bursts of flak, salvos of bombs shaking the earth, bombers on fire slicing downward, intermittent flares lighting the entire stage bright as daylight. I was transfixed by the enormity of the sights and sounds. Suddenly a brilliant flash followed immediately by a blast of air that smashed the partly opened shutters into our faces and sent us reeling backward amid the noise of everything being knocked off shelves and tables. A stray British bomb had landed at the edge of our camp killing a guard in a watch tower and collapsing a couple of barracks but not killing any POW's.

The next day another maximum effort by the 8th Air Force finished off Nuremberg. From my viewpoint it appeared that the only visible target was a huge cloud of smoke and dust to drop bombs into.

From Nuremberg to Moosburg

About mid-March of 1945, the faint booming of artillery indicated that the Western Front was slowly moving eastward. The battle sounds grew closer day by day until the order came to evacuate Stalag Luft XIIID and head southeast to avoid liberation.

In contrast to the apprehension when we were marched out of Stalag Luft III, we all welcomed the chance to leave the vermin-infested buildings behind. The weather was spring-like and I knew we were winning the war because we were told no "40 & 8" rail cars were available.

The 100-plus mile trek from Nuremberg to Moosburg was especially memorable. Our guards were agreeable old men who admitted, "Deutschland was kaput." They were more like grandfathers than guards. Since we were younger and stronger than the guards we often carried their knapsacks and rifles.

The weather was so pleasant and it felt so good to be "free" that the entire march was a lark. In one little town we went through, the people thought we were the conquering army. They threw flowers at us and some came forward to give us food. It kept the guards busy, trying to keep the people away from us. Sometime during the march, word went around that President Roosevelt was dead. We knew he had been elected to a fourth term, but it was a great shock to try and comprehend his death.

We marched through several small towns on our way to Moosburg. A typical little town of about 1000 people would have a boarded up Shell gas station at the edge of town and a boarded up Woolworth store in the middle of town. This started me to think that the Germans were more like Americans than the English. The entire war suddenly appeared to be a big crazy mistake and I felt like a born-again conscientious objector. I had joined the Army as a cadet several months before December 7, 1941, planning to learn to fly, then renounce my commission. But before that could happen, I was caught up in the wave of national patriotism following that infamous day the Japanese bombed Pearl Harbor. I was glad that I would not have to drop bombs on the Germans any more. The brainwashing I received between 1941 and 1944 that we should rid the world of Japanese and Germans had been replaced by my pre-war feeling of good will toward mankind.

In one town we spotted a "40 & 8" on a side track prominently marked "Red Cross." We talked the guards into checking it out. They opened it up. Hallelujah! It was full of American Red Cross parcels. Needless to say, we spent the rest of that day and night gorging ourselves.

About the middle of April we finally arrived at Moosburg (Stalag VIIA) in southern Germany. I was happy to be reunited with the members of my crew whom I had not seen since we were separated early in February. I was surprised to learn that the 80,000-plus Allied officers at Moosburg constituted bargaining power for any negotiations Hitler might have with the Allies. Rumor had it that we would all march to Burchtesgarten in the Alps if necessary. Many of the POW's were high

Berchtesgaden

ranking officers from France, Russia, etc. One memorable fellow walked around every day stark naked talking to himself and yelling unintelligibly. I was told he was a Russian general.

Moosburg

Moosburg was a city of tents, each housing about 10 bedrolls, laid on the ground. When new POW's came in, we would simply move our beds closer together.

Security was getting more lax every day, so one dark night "Hap" Arnold and I decided on an adventure. There was no guard at a well-used hole in the barbed wire so we slipped out and headed for some buildings. We carefully opened a door to the first building and could see it led into a dimly lit hall the full length of the building. We opened and entered the first hallway door and it was very dark inside. Just then we heard a door slam and two men, conversing, in German, walked down the hall past our closed door and left the building. I fumbled about in the darkness and felt a heavy wool blanket. I started to wad it up and felt that part of it was stiff with a dried residue (I'll always think it was dried blood). We searched further until we each found a good blanket, then decided to return to camp while we were still ahead of the game. Heading back toward the hole in the fence, stumbling in the darkness, I heard a splash. I said, "What was that?" Hap replied, "I fell into a ditch of water, help me out." I cautiously helped him out and discovered he was still clutching his dripping blanket. His teeth were chattering so I wrapped my dry blanket over his shoulders and we continued. At the hole in the fence I could make out a guard with a rifle. I figured with Hap half frozen I needed to bluff my way back into the prison camp. The guard could speak English so I told him I was bringing back my buddy who had tried to escape without my permission. The guard let us back inside, warning us that we could be shot if we left camp again.

Toward the end of April, occasional cannon fire was heard from a northwest direction. Everyone knew the end was near and apparently we were not going to march out again as rumored.

Liberation

The 28th of April 1945 dawned clear and warm. About mid-morning we could see several tanks coming toward us from the rolling hills to the northwest. In a few minutes we could make out five Sherman tanks bearing down on us. When at about 200 yards, some of the guards opened fire with their rifles. The tanks stopped and answered back with 50 caliber machine guns as all the POW's hit the ground. The skirmish was over in 30 seconds, when the guards threw down their rifles.

The two lead tanks drove through the prison gate and were immediately surrounded by thousands of celebrating Kriegies, shouting, jumping up and down with arms flying. The GI's in the tanks started throwing out K-rations and cigarettes. The tumult started to die down when someone pointed toward the small town of Moosburg about 1/3 mile to the south. From a flagpole on the highest building flew a large stars and stripes flag. That was a moment to remember. We were all swept up simultaneously to an emotional climax. The tanks could not move because of the surrounding crush of the wild ex-POWs.

After about 30 minutes things started to calm down and someone asked what they were going to do with the 40-odd guards who had been rounded up. The tank commander answered, "We do not take prisoners," inferring that they simply killed the enemy, then kept going. A Kriegie spokesman said, "Let us keep them as POW's until the foot soldiers arrive," and the tank commander said, "Okay." An hour after the spearhead tank column moved off to the east, the Kriegie leaders told the guards to "get lost." They had been treating us humanely and now we had the chance to return the favor. This was no occasion for reprisals.

So now we were free, but instructed to stay put until after the war was over so that an orderly evacuation of the 80,000 men could be achieved. We were not confined to the POW camp so, after a couple of days of staying put, Hap Arnold and I decided to walk around the town of Moosburg (population 4-5000). Some of the Allied POW's were more familiar with the spoils of war than we were, because as we walked up and down the residential area every house had a sign posted on the front door stating "KEEP OUT—THIS HOUSE IS OCCU-PIED BY LIEUTENANT JOHN DOE R.A.F." or a similar message.

A few Kriegies left Moosburg and headed west by hitching rides but my crew all waited another couple of weeks before being trucked to an airfield east of Moosburg.

Prior to boarding a C-47, we were thoroughly dusted with a new de-lousing powder called DDT. On the trip west to Camp Lucky Strike in France, the pilot of the transport plane let me and the other pilots fly the plane for a few minutes.
After deplaning, we all enjoyed two consecutive showers with GI soap and were issued new uniforms. That system worked, because body ver-min did not torment me again.

A week of rehab (i.e., soft food, vitamins, exercise, etc.) at Camp Lucky Strike was followed by an ocean trip to the U.S. aboard a Victory ship. My bunk was #10 (about 25 feet up) in the bow of the ship. All I remember is that I was nauseated every time I raised my head from my pillow, and the anchor kept banging against the outside of the ship about 10 feet from my head.

We landed at Camp Miles Standish, New Jersey, and after we regained our land legs, Hap Arnold and I wandered around the camp. Discover-ing a small PX, we went inside to buy something to eat and were informed by the girl behind the counter that this was a sub-PX which allowed sales only to Italian and German non-com POW's. I was already bitter about the entire sequence of POW life, delayed repatriation, and the long ship ride home, and this only added fuel to my bitterness.

Post War

I decided to forget the entire five years of my life from 1941 through 1945 and never think of it again. That was 50 years ago and it took about 40 years to overcome my phobia.

Ten years ago, at the urging of my navigator, Marshal Pullen, I began attending POW reunions and 351st Bomb Group reunions, along with some members of my crew.

After the war I had put GI clothing, papers, letters, pictures, etc., into two footlockers and never opened them. My daughter Karen went through everything pertaining to my military history and decided if I would help her, she would compile a detailed book and memorabilia for our posterity so they could better remember and understand World War II from a first-person viewpoint. These memoirs are the result of those efforts.

Bitterness

Many people have asked me why I was so bitter when I came home after World War II. Recently (2001) I decided to remember and analyze my feelings which quite naturally can be described under the headings of physical and mental.

<u>Physical</u>

In roughly chronological order:

- Approximately 13 days in solitary confinement in a 6 by 8 foot underground cell at Frankfurt, Germany (Dulag Luft) on the Rhine, underfed and interrogated 3 times. Learning that the Germans knew in detail, information which I understood to be confidential or even secret.

- 3 day trip from Frankfurt to Stalag Luft III in "40 and 8" box cars which were so crowded that of the 60 odd POWs only one half had room to sit down while the other half were forced to stand.

- Living behind barbed wire from the middle of June 1944 to the end of January 1945 in Stalag Luft III and subsisting on 1200 calories per day consisting of a bowl of soup with one third loaf of the worst black bread, with promises of Red Cross parcels of food which were seldom ever kept by the Germans.

- 2 olive drab GI blankets for sleeping on a burlap bag filled with wood shavings; a GI helmet liner, and Eisenhower jacket and light weight pants and shirt (the Germans took all of the good flying clothes during interrogation.)

- Once a month warm showers in winter and bucket baths in summer.

- I developed double vision due to diet deficiency, so I could barely read.

- Marched out of Stalag Luft III at midnight during a blizzard on the last day of January 1945. The Germans offered us all the Red Cross parcels we wanted from a warehouse filled with thousands of pallets which fell into the hands of the advancing Russians.

- Marched 50 miles during 2 nights and one day before finding a warm building for the 10,000-odd POWs of Stalag Luft III. During the march I wore out 3 sets of cardboard shoe insoles, which I made from Red Cross parcel boxes. This provided little help in proctecting my feet in my worn out shoes.

- After two days about 9000 POWs marched out leaving about 1000 not able to go. My feet suffered from frost bite, blood blisters and athletes food so I was one of the 1000 who stayed behind for 2 more days then crammed in "40 and 8" box cars headed for the old POW Stalag XIIID just outside of Nuremberg Germany.

- At Stalag XIIID conditions were much worse than Stalag Luft III. The bunks were vermin infested. There was no fuel for heat except the wood from our own building which was trashed by the time we marched out on the first of April, 1945 to avoid being liberated by the advancing US Army.

- We marched the 100 miles from the Stalag XIIID at Nuremberg to the Stalag at Moosburg. During the 1 week march we lived off the land because everyone knew the Germans were "kaput".

- At Moosburg I was reunited with the 4 other officers from my crew.

- Liberated by Patton's tanks the end of April 1945. But remained for another 2 weeks before being flown to France.

- Too seasick to eat during the 8 day boat ride home to Camp Miles Standish.

- Tried to buy food at a small PX at Miles Standish but was refused service because we were "not German or Italian POWs".

Mental

- In prison but not guilty of any crime.

- Guilt for causing my crew to become POWs.

- Wondering what happened to the enlisted men of our crew.

- Uncertainty of the future for 1 year.

- The deceit and treatment by the Germans.

- Seeing our silver bombers only 5 miles (up) away.

- Finding out that my money, radio, camera etc, from my room in England, was not returned to me.

- No credit for my final (17th) mission because I did not return to my base in England (credited after my complaint).

- A wasted year of my life plus the lives of 10,000 fellow officers.

- Time to decide how stupid wars are.

In May 2001, the 57th anniversary of the crash landing, local Danish people had arranged for a ceremony on the site of the crash landing on the Island of Als in the south west of Denmark.

L to R: Robert B. Clay, Frank Hatten, Charles Jilcott & Daniel Surprise.
R. B. Clay making his speech.

The ceremony took place in Denmark at the site of the crash 57 years after. More than 1,500 people attended the ceremony.

The Final Mission

Narrated by Frank Hatten 351st Bomb Group.

I married Fannie Adelle (Dell) Swaney on June 16, 1943 in Douglas, Arizona. Six days later (June 22, 1943) I received my commission as 2nd Lieutenant and pilot.

Transferred to Roswell, New Mexico to start training in B-17s. Had option to take 5 days off for honeymoon if I chose B-24s, but chose B-17s because they had a better reputation for maintenance.

Transferred to Moses Lake, Washington to start training with my crew. My wife went with me. We heard that the base would close for the winter and I would be transferred to Florida for further training. I bought my wife a ticket to her home in Ranger, Texas, and then I also bought a ticket for her to fly to Florida, so she could be with me before I left for England.

After finishing my training with my crew, we got orders to fly through South America to North Africa (Casablanca) and then on to England. On the last leg my navigator suddenly realized he had made a mistake and we were too far west of England, so then we started descending east to get our bearings and found a field there to land.

After we landed, I left the airplane and my crew and I were transferred to the 351st Bomb Group at Polebrook. We got another plane there, and it had the name "My Gal Sal" on it, and each crew member added their wife or girlfriend's name nearby.

We were required to fly 25 missions before we could rotate back to the States, so I did everything I could to get my missions in as soon as possible. On each mission if the squadron leader had weather problems and had to return to base, each pilot could decide to join an empty space in any other formation going on another mission. Twice during my first ten missions I joined another group and got credit.

Frank Hatten , Polebrook. In front of "My Gal Sal" which he piloted.

On my tenth mission my plane was shot up a lot—my navigator, David Ruth, even caught a piece of flak through the nose cone in his hands, but quickly dropped it! We were able to fly back to the base and landed safely. After that I got a new airplane and had flown five missions in it before Captain Clay wanted me to fly with him that day and be checked out as a squadron leader.

We were going to fly in my plane, but when he saw I had the new nose cone, he didn't want to fly in it (something about that type of nosecone wasn't satisfactory), so he went back into Operations and changed planes, and his crew and I moved over into his old airplane, which was due for maintenance. But his crew forgot to move his parachute back into his old plane.

My original crew, with co-pilot George Reish and navigator David Ruth finished their remaining 10 missions flying my plane, "My Gal Sal," and went home.

The mission that day was Berlin. [same story as Captain Clay's about the loss of engines, etc.]
After we bailed out the crew Capt. Clay told me I could bail out. I told him that he didn't have a parachute, so I would stay with him since four eyes could see more than two, and I would help him find a place to land the plane. As we got lower—maybe 300-400 ft.—I saw a ploughed field ahead which I thought we could ease into without putting down our wheels.

He saw what he thought would be a smooth, grassy field to the left, however, he didn't see a raised road and one telephone pole, which we hit with the tip of our right wing, and it actually helped because we just had one engine left (#1 on the left), and it tilted up higher after hitting the post, and our right wing hit the road near the top and we bounced on over, leaving #3 and 4 engines on the hillside and landing with our rear tail hitting the ground first and splitting our plane at the radio compartment, and we were stopped looking up at the other side of the causeway (it was steeper on that side). He was not injured, but I had a cut above my left eye and some blood squirting down on my face.

[Same as Captain Clay's story from here, including help from the couple at the cottage.]

We were picked up within the hour by a German officer and taken to a doctor's office. He checked the cut above my eye but did not think I needed any stitches. I had leaned over to keep the blood from dripping on my jacket, but he slapped me upright. I noticed his two orderlies were more nervous than I was, working with him—their hands were shaking!

We were taken to a small jail and locked up for the night. The next morning Capt. Clay and I were put on a train and the guards took us to be interrogated.

Memories from prison camp: Stalag Luft III at Sagan (eastern edge of Germany, now part of Poland)

We were put in the west camp for officers—the "Great Escape" happened in the center or main camp in March before we arrived in late May. I was around twentieth on the list for escaping from the tunnel we were digging, but we were having trouble getting rid of the dirt we dug up, and one of the officers prevailed on the camp commandant to let us build a swimming pool, which gave us a place to dump our pockets of dirt.

The barracks were set up like the German system, so we had one room of four airman in each barracks. The airman were supposed to serve the officers, like the German system, but we never asked them for any service!

There wasn't a doctor to check the injury above my eye, so I sat out in the sun to let the sun kill the germs and help heal the cut. Among the 2000 in our camp, some of our officers had been chiropractors in civilian life and could help many of the crew members who had gotten hurt as they landed in their parachutes.

We started with four double-bunks for eight officers in each room. Later they tripled the bunks so each room held twelve officers. Usually each room had one or two volunteer to do the cooking and serving what food we obtained each day from the Germans, and our Red Cross parcels. The only thing we got from the Germans was potatoes. The Red Cross parcels came about once a week, and they had cans of food and maybe two packs of cigarettes. It was one box per person each week. Since I didn't smoke, I gave my cigarettes away provided they gave me the empty packages so I could use the paper to make a notepad by attaching the paper to some metal from one the cans from the Red Cross parcels.

I also made a cup and a small eating tray from some of the cans. In the notepad I kept record of names and addresses of officers I met, details about the places we had been, some of the camp slang, and notes about letters from home. One officer received a letter from his wife that said, if you stay a little longer, I will be able to finish paying for the car! Another one got a "Dear John" letter that she was divorcing him and marrying an old friend. The Salvation Army also provided some musical instruments, which some of our officers could play or train others to play. It gave us some good music to listen to.

Near the end of January 1945 we got news that our camp would be closed since the Russians were getting close. The Germans were closing all the prison camps in that area and moving all the prisoners southwest. Either the 28th or 29th of January we were told around 10:00 p.m. that we had to pack up and march out. Fortunately, the week before I had received a package from my wife (the only one out of all she had sent that actually arrived) which contained two pairs of long underwear. I kept one and gave one pair to a friend. We left the camp before midnight and marched through the snow all night and part of the next day until about 4:00 p.m.

We arrived at an old factory in a small town and all of our prisoners were put in the building to sleep the rest of the day. I was on the second floor where there were warm bricks we could get down between. The next day we marched to a railroad station near another town. Some of us stayed overnight in a haystack in a big barn. The next morning we were put in boxcars on a train. They had just taken the cows out of the boxcars and it wasn't very clean inside. The train started out toward Munich and by that evening we were at Moosberg in a big camp with other POWs from many other camps.

Some prisoners had radios they had received in gifts from home. We were listening to all the news about General Patton's advance from the time he had passed through a town named Hatten (later found it on a map, north of Strasbourg) on the German border, where there was a big tank battle. General Patton freed our camp on April 29, 1945.

The guards had agreed in advance to surrender, but they had arranged with General Patton's troops that they could fire a few shots into the air to make out like they were defending the camp. I saw General Patton when he came into camp. He went into the big tent where the injured and sick were located, shook hands with some, told everyone that they were now free, then he left the camp and headed toward Berlin for the end of the war.

After the German guards left, our MPs took over to protect us. However, a friend and I decided to take a trip under the fence and we told the guard we would be back in 3-4 hours and he said OK. We went down the road and stopped at a house. We told the housewife that the war was over and we were now free, but we hadn't had a home-cooked meal in a long time and would she cook us some eggs. Then her husband and another man came in, my friend could speak German, so he told them that we were now free and would not hurt anyone anymore. They were nice to us, and after we ate some food we left the house and went down through a small village and into an empty store. We looked around, and then we went back to the camp.

Two or three days later we were put on cargo planes and taken to a holding camp near Paris. We were to stay there until they had a ship available to take us home. While we were waiting, some of our group went into Paris to celebrate and drink beer. Since I didn't drink, I didn't want to go. Two or three days later we were loaded on a big ship to go back to the United States.

The letter

Transcript of a letter from Lt. Frank Hatten to his sister, Sallie, and her husband Adra and family (Bob, Eddie, Eloise, Jane, and Betty), in Breckenridge, Texas, written May 30, 1945, when he was still en route by ship to the U.S. after being liberated. He was only able to talk to his wife, Dell, on the phone after arriving in NYC.

Dear Sallie, Adra & Family,

Well, at last I'm on my way home. This time last year I was entering a P.W. Camp for what I thought was a short stay, but they had the thing better guarded than I expected! O, well, I've got lots of time now to tell you about my adventures. We were allowed 3 letter-forms and four post cards a month, so I wrote Dell and Mother as often as possible. However, I'll bet few letters got home, and even then they were pretty old. Last letter I had from Dell was dated Nov. 24th., so I'm 6 months behind on home news.

As of the last letter everything seemed to be O.K. at home, and I hope nothing has changed. Of course I'm "sweating" out Roy, Ray, Warner and John [his brothers in the service]. Guess they are all out in the Pacific. However John might have gone to England. Roy hinted that in one of his letters.

Hope you two and all the kids are fine and still in the old grocery business. Guess Bob and Eddie are working—especially carrying the baskets for ladies with pretty daughters!! Is Eloise helping Sallie with Jane and the baby? Really be happy when I can see all of you again.

How is Dell? Guess she is now a graduate of T.U. [University of Texas]. Good thing she had something to keep her busy while I was away. At least it helped.

We were liberated on Sunday, April 29th., after a 2 hr. 45 minute battle raged over us. The 3rd Army drove into Moosberg, which is near Landshut and north of Munich, and eliminated a group of S.S. The S.S. had a fight with our guards, because our guards wouldn't let them (or help them) exterminate any of us. They did kill about 600 Poles, but only 3 or 4 in our camp were injured and that was during the battle. There were about 30,000 in Stalag VII A, 10,000 being American, of which about 8000 were

Air Corp Officers. In the area of our camp there were about 70,000 more P.W.'s so you can see how the Germans had moved us into a compact area.

On Monday a Sherman tank drove down the main street of the camp and was covered with ex-kriegies (that's us.). Also an American General came in and looked us over. The next day or so saw a procession of Generals and Senators. General Patton came in with a 3, 2, and 1-star General at his heels. He wore his two pistols and his newly acquired 4th star, and was covered with decorations. He went thru one barracks and one tent, and then gave us a talk and complimented us on our high morale.

I haven't seen any Brekenridge boys but I've met one each from Cisco and Ranger that I knew in civilian life, and husbands of an Olden and a Ranger girl. There is also a Capt. from Strawn, but I haven't seen him yet. Our section of the State was pretty well represented in P.W. camps. I'm traveling with a group of Texas boys now. We will land in New York about Sunday and then go to Ft. Sam Houston for our leave. Saves us travel money to be near home when we get leaves. I think it will be 60 days but I'm not sure yet.

Our ship is the U.S.S. LeJeune, a former German luxury liner and supply ship to the Graf Spree that was skuttled by its crew near Brazil. The food is excellent and we eat all we can hold. At last we can buy all the candy, gum, mints, P.X. supplies, etc. that we want. Sure is wonderful to be an American. Naturally several boys have made themselves sick on candy, but guess it's their privilege. However, because one ate too much and died at the camp near LeHarve, we had to wait until we got aboard ship to get any.

I'll tell you about lots of things when I get home—such as—combat missions, capture by Germans, prison camps, march from Sagan in blinding snow blizzard, trip overseas, and lots of minor adventures. Tune in this time next week!!

Say, better get a place fixed to keep Dell and I a couple of days. I'm used to sleeping in barns, on straw mattresses, on floors or on the ground, so you see I'm not hard to please.

Hope all the folks are fine and that mother has not been worrying too much.

She was right in her dream about me. I did get a hole in my eye lid and eye brow that took 4 stitches to patch up, but you can't tell it much now. I managed to get the picture the Germans took of me when I was captured, and it shows the injury. Same picture!! It will make you laugh.

Just managed to get a fountain pen—only $1.—, so I can write easier now.

I don't have much idea what my future with the Air Corp will be. Guess I'll wait until after my leave to find out. While I'm home I'd like to talk over possibilities with you for after the war, Adra. That is, if I have to stay in until it's over. If I get out sooner, then we might be able to plan something more definite.

Well, guess I had better sign off. Tell Bob and Eddie that grocer men can do anything. I saw plenty of big, husky boys turn blue and pass out the second night of our march from Stalag Luft III at Sagan. Even two or three former All-Americans fell out in barns for the sick, & lame [here he crossed out: "and lazy"]. It sure isn't the size of a man that counts [Frank was 5'7"]. The old spirit will beat physical ability.

Hope to see you soon.

Your brother and Uncle,
Frank

In New York I called Dell and told her I would be home as soon as the train could take us.

The Final Mission

Narrated by Charles B. Jilcott 351st Bomb Group

Enlisting

I, Charles B. Jilcott, Sr., M/Sgt., USAF, retired, was born on a farm near Roxobel, North Carolina, December 15, 1923. I attended the Roxobel-Kelford School and graduated in the spring of 1941. After graduation I obtained a job with the Seaboard Airline Railroad as a brake mechanic, located in Portsmouth, Virginia.

During a visit home, December 7, 1941, I had stopped in Roxobel to get gasoline for my return trip to Portsmouth, when the radio station gave us the news of the Japanese attack on Pearl Harbor. As I returned to Portsmouth, I gave some thought to enlisting in the army. Upon my arrival I called Clyde Bryant, the only boy with me in our high school graduation class, and we began our plans to enlist. I wasn't quite eighteen, lacking 8 days. We gave it quite some thought, and about two months later decided to enlist in the army.

Believe it or not, when we attempted to enlist we were informed we would have to wait a while, because the draft and volunteers had too many men to accept us at that time. They gave us a date to report. We were accepted in June and sent to Ft. Lee in Virginia, and issued our clothing and many vaccinations. We were transferred to St. Petersburg, Florida for basic training.

We were there only a short time when Clyde was sent some place that I have forgotten. I was sent to Kessler Field, AFB in Biloxi, Mississippi, to begin training for aircraft mechanic and to complete my basic training. Those were long days, basic training in the morning before school and in the afternoon after school. I completed this school in the fall of 1942.

A small group of us were transferred to Boeing Aircraft Co. in Seattle to study the B-17 Bombers. We completed that course in early 1943 and then transferred to Indian Springs, Nevada for bomber gunnery training. After completing this training we were transferred to Ephrates, Washington, to be assigned to flight crews.

Sgt. Frank Belsinger and I were selected by a pilot and we became the first crew of the 401st Bomb Group (H), 614th Bomb Sqd. (H) (H is for heavy bombers) and sent to Spokane Army Air Force Base to complete the crew and begin crew training. It required some time to complete construction of the total aircraft and putting together crews for the group. While waiting for the necessary men and aircraft, we went to train in Florida for jungle training. This gave us the thought that we would be going into Pacific Theater for combat. After completing this training, we returned to Spokane to complete our group.

During this training my aircraft needed some rather complicated maintenance so we took it to the Depot of Maintenance, Fairchild Army Air Force Base, just a short distance from Spokane. During this time of maintenance, I met Ruth Elizabeth Klemz, age 16. She was training for aircraft maintenance. She was a lovely girl and we went together regularly.

Shortly after this our group was completed and was transferred to Great Falls, Montana. The Group Command and Squadron were based at Great Falls and the remaining Squadron were assigned to different bases in Montana.

Our Sqd. (614th) was assigned to Glasgow AFB in Glasgow, Montana. During this time I called Ruth and proposed. She accepted. I now had to see my Sqd. Commander for permission to get married.

At that time you had to have permission from your commander to marry. So I called the for an appointment to see Capt. Eveland. I had flown with him many hours, but in the Army at that time you still had to have an appointment to discuss anything personal. When I met him, he gave me things to think about and he told me if I still wanted to get married I had his permission.

A couple of days later, I got a 5-day pass and went to Spokane. Ruth and I were married on June 20, 1943. She was able to come to Glasgow sometime later.

Also, at this time Lt. Clay came to Glasgow and was assigned to our crew. He replaced Capt. Eveland, because a commander could not have a crew. Lt. Clay was a pilot trainer in Florida. He had many hours of flight instruction and experience, which was unusual at that time. We all felt very fortunate that he was to be our pilot.

After completing our training in Montana, we were sent to Scott Field, Illinois for a new aircraft to be flown to England. We took the route to Bangor, Maine, then to Gander, Labrador, Canada, and then on to Iceland. Here our crew was transferred from the 401st BG to the 351st 509th Bomb Sqd. Col. Hatcher was commander of the 351st and Lt. Col. Ledoux was our Sqd. Commander.

About this time Ruth wrote to me and said we were having a baby. It was an exciting time in my life, having a baby and flying combat missions.

War Experience

Our first mission, December 1, 1943, was to Solingen, Germany in the Ruhr Valley. We lost both of our wing planes to German fighters, ME109Fs five minutes after entering the Ruhr Valley. Our crew made it back with limited damage to the plane. The future of flying combat didn't look too good at that point since we had 24 more to go. But, then you could look at it another way, which was, they couldn't all be that rough.

I was on my 20th mission before I went down with my crew after being shot up over Berlin on May 24, 1944. We went down on the island of Als, in Denmark and were taken prisoner by the German Army. We were sent by train to the prisoner interrogation to be questioned by the German Intelligence. We were there about 11 days. The reason for such a heavy interrogation was due to the fact that we had 5 officers on our flight. Regular crews had on 4 officers. They were sure we were some special crew. I had been questioned many times and all I ever gave was name, rank, and serial number. After my final questioning I was relieved, and as I saluted and was going out the door, the officer called for me to come back a moment. When I turned and stood at attention he asked me if I wished he would send a telegram to Ruth to let her know I was okay since she was expecting a baby. Now that was a surprise! I wondered how he knew about her. I said I would appreciate this.

On June 22, 1944 Ruth Jilcott got the following telegram:

> REPORT JUST RECEIVE THROUGH THE INTERNATIONAL RED CROSS STATES THAT YOUR HUSBAND TECHNICAL SERGEANT CHARLES B. JILCOTTIS A PRISONER OF WAR OF THE GERMAN GOVERNMENT LETTER OF INFORMATION FOLLOWS FROM PROVOST MARSHALL GENERAL

It is hard to believe, but Ruth got a telegram from Sweden. It did not state the Germans sent it. She still has it to this day. It was a couple of months later before she received one from the military saying I was a POW.

After the interrogation was completed, the enlisted crew was sent to Stalag Luft 4. I was assigned in compound "B". All the other of our crew was assigned in Compound "A". Our prison was just a little distance from Danzig, Poland. There I stayed with nothing to do except think about Ruth, our baby, food and warmth.

I think it was about February 1, 1945 that the Russians were getting very near our prison and we were to leave. We were loaded into boxcars with very near a hundred in each, maybe more. There was not enough room for sitting down so we had to stand until quite a few men would just fall down. We were given no food or water. We would get water by sucking in from the cracks in the wood siding of the boxcars as there was a lot of snow on the roof of the cars and body heat from the all the men helped it melt and run down the sides of the car. We were in this boxcar seven days, I think. When we arrived at Nuremberg, we were told to get out. It was unbelievable how difficult it was. Upon opening the door our eyes were blinded because we had total darkness for seven days. Also not having any food left us hardly enough strength to get out.

On arrival at the prison #17 there was nothing that resembled a building. The walls were all gone and the floors almost gone. Most of the roofs in tatters. The officers on the other side of the fence had some buildings that were in fair condition. We were there when the Army Air Force and the British bombed Nuremberg continually for 48 hours. The city, which was about one mile from us, was burning from end to end. When the bombing ended we saw thousands of people being buried behind Hitler Stadium, which was just across the railroad from our camp. Machines were used to dig deep trenches. Trucks loaded with bodies would dump them in the trenches and then they were covered creating a mass grave site.

We were marched out of Nuremberg to go to Moosburg, about 100 miles. After we had arrived in Moosburg and were there for a few days there was a terrific amount of gun fire just over the hill from our camp. The bullets were flying everywhere. A few minutes later tanks came rolling over the hill. A few minutes after that General Patton was in our prison. We were free men!

We were sent to Camp Lucky Strike to regain our weight and health before we could go home. It took about a month for me to gain the weight necessary to be released to the U.S. During my stay at this camp I got a telegram from Ruth saying we had a son, Charles, Jr. born April 18, 1944. He was a little over a year old when I first saw him and he was quite a boy. I was indeed a proud father.

The Final Mission

Narrated by Daniel Harvey Surprise 351ˢᵗ Bomb Group

I was born November 20, 1924 on a small farm in Ness County, Kansas.

I started school at the age of six in 1930 and quit school in 1939 and joined the Civilian Conservation Corp, or the CCCs. It was here I had my first taste of military life and I liked it.

My brother, Walter L. Jr. and I were sworn into the U.S. Army at Leavenworth, KS. We were sent to St. Petersburg, Florida for basic training. In about two weeks, we were moved to Clearwater, Florida. Due to prior military training, our training was curtailed and we were sent to Harlington, Texas.

Because of our small physical stature, we were chosen for aerial gunnery school which lasted six weeks. We were the first two brothers to graduate, so we got a lot of newspaper publicity.

Daniel H. Surprise 1943.

Then we were sent to Amarillo, Texas for aircraft maintenance training. Six months later we graduated and were sent to Salt Lake City, Utah for further indoctrination and training. We were then sent to

Ephrata, Washington, where I was assigned as a tail gunner on a B-17 crew commanded by Vernon K. Cammack for crew training. After that I was assigned to the 401st Bomb Group for combat training in Glasgow, Montana.

A decision was made to give me radio training, but after two days in radio school I went to the operations officer and told him I would rather be grounded than take radio training. As a result, I was assigned to Captain Clay's crew as a waist gunner.

We completed our combat training and in the fall of 1943 we headed for combat in England and went through St. Louis, MO and picked up a new B-17. We flew to Newfoundland and then to the British Isles. We were reassigned to the 351st Bomb Group at Polebrook, England in exchange for a combat experienced crew which was assigned in our stead to the 401st Bomb Group.

On our first combat mission we aborted due to fuel siphoning and this fact was recorded on a poster in the Operations briefing building showing the date, target, pilot, and problem. I called this the "embarrassment board". This may have influenced a later event, but that I will never know for sure.

I never recorded the individual targets for the missions I flew.

One mission which I remember, on December 1, 1943, was to fly to Solingen, Germany which is in the Ruhr Valley. The target was a ball bearing manufacturing plant and it was heavily defended with both flak (anti aircraft guns) and fighter aircraft.

The mission was rated a huge success and to my knowledge the 351st never returned to that target. The next noteworthy target was Frankfurt, Germany.

On February 11, 1944 both Sgt. Riley and myself were flown as replacements on other crews for this mission. The two airplanes we were on were hit and both became crippled. The one I was in was in front, coming back to the base. The pilot of my plane called for fighter escort and two fighter planes arrived and the pilots waved at us. We could see the other cripple being hit by German fighters. We asked our pilot to send one of the fighters back to help the other cripple, but he refused. He said the other pilot should have called for fighter escort.

Although I did not realize it at the time, this was the plane that Sgt. Riley was on. I, on the other hand, returned back to base safely.

After our return, the crew gathered and discussed the situation and agreed to go to Capt. Clay and tell him we did not want to fly as replacements any longer. We agreed that we wanted to fly as a crew and asked that we be allowed to do this with him or Lt. Emerson as the pilot. Captain Clay agreed with our request, but explained that he was a lead pilot (pilot of the aircraft leading the bomber formation) and ultimately we would be slower putting in our 25 missions which were the quota required to return stateside. The crew said, "we want to fly with you."

Another incident happened when we were returning from a mission during which we had a runaway prop that wouldn't feather (meaning the pitch could not be changed so it would run with it until it broke off). A British fighter came out as we approached the White Cliffs of Dover to lead us to an emergency field. We missed finding the runway in the grass on the first pass so the British pilot said he would roll over on the next pass, which he did so we were able to land safely. The British put us up overnight and the next day we returned to our base without our airplane since it needed the maintenance men to change the prop before it could be airborne again.

The next mission that sticks out in my mind was the final flight where we were assigned as lead crew on a Berlin mission May 24, 1944.

Typically we were assigned to a particular plane but ours had been requisitioned and we now were assigned "Stormy Weather". We took off and the formation came together over the North Sea and then headed for Germany.

It is my belief that when we had just passed onto Germany proper, there was a discussion or comments made that the oil pressure on one engine was fluctuating, or fluxing, a little but we flew on toward the target where we held our lead position until our bombs were dropped on the target.

We turned to the right and the first engine was feathered and we headed back to base. We lost the second engine (due to loss of oil pressure) and when the third engine gave up the ghost over the North Sea, we dumped all the excess weight we could (ammo, guns, the Norden bomb sight, flak suits) and then headed back toward Sweden.

Once over land we could see German fighters taking off and the word was given for us to bail out! I was the last to bail out. Captain Clay and Lt. Hatten remained and crash landed the plane.

When my parachute opened, I noticed the silence and saw that I was drifting toward water. I also noticed a German boat loaded with troops heading our way. I could see people on bicycles and when I would dump the chute (grabbing the lines to change direction) I could see them stop and turn their bikes around to correct for the change I had made by dumping the chute. I did this two or three times before hitting the ground.

A Danish resistance fighter led me to a house where we waited for the Germans to arrive. As the Germans came in the front door, unbeknownst to them, the Danish resistance fighter went out the back door. About 2 p.m. I and the rest of the crew members began 11 months and 5 days as unwilling guests of Hitler's military machine.

The Germans took us prisoners and we were taken to a submarine base. These kids (myself being 19 at the time) who came and got us were all Krieg marines. The Germans, having lost a large part of their marine force, enlisted teenagers probably fifteen or sixteen and were training them for submarines.

They treated Lt Hatten's eye, which had been injured during the crash landing, then they put us back on the truck and took us to a Luftwaffe (German air force) base. We were put in the guard house there overnight.

At one point they searched us and we had to turn over everything out of our pockets. The search was performed by a woman's unit. They wore Alpine jackets with an insignia of a helmet on the lower right part with crossed cannons on it. One woman spoke English. I asked her about the insignia. She said "we're height finders. You know, the ones that shoot you down." She was real proud of that. It was a joint military-civilian jail. It had communal quarters for German prisoners so they could make kids. Hitler didn't want to lose a chance of getting one.

We were fed well at the airforce base. They brought us black bread and blood sausage. Lt. Pullen said "what's this?" I told him it was blood sausage. He said he wouldn't eat it, so I got his sausage. The next day the Luftwaffe put us on a train.

They took us down the Ruhr Valley to Frankfurt to Dulag Luft, which was the centralized interrogation point. They put us in solitary confinement for six to eight days. They fed us black bread. The Germans were well informed about the Americans. They had military news items on Captain Clay. The Germans didn't torture us in solitary. Just being there was punishment enough.

When they took us out of solitary, we went into the outer compound and joined people that we knew nothing about from other units. It was here I noticed an individual with his head wrapped in toilet paper which was covering burns he had received when his plane caught fire before the crew was able to bail out. He was picking grass and eating it (due to hunger). I learned his name was Earl Campbell and he was from Kentucky.

The Germans then put us on another prisoner train with guards on top of the train armed with machine guns in case we tried to escape. They took us to a base named Wetzler in Germany. When we got off the train, I never saw so many pregnant teenagers in my life. I didn't understand how and why.

Then we went through the gate. On the right hand side, there was a swimming pool with a bunch of German GI's in there and a bunch of women. That was a breeding camp. This was also a supply point, where they gave us a Red Cross suitcase. Our red Cross suitcase had a sweater, some soap, safety razors and a box of blades, two pair of socks, two or three packages of Chic-O- Lick chewing gum and underwear. The Krieg marines that captured us were never informed what damage we were doing to their country.

Wimmer, our tail gunner, spoke German and was able to tell the marines what was going on. They didn't believe us when we told them we had bombed Berlin. We were the biggest bunch of liars they had ever encountered. This was a rest camp for them with good food and entertainment and women. They were then put back on the train with curtains over the windows so they couldn't see out and taken back to the subs.

The next day they put us back on the train with the guards on top. We saw a lot of slave labor in our travels. We saw women picking potatoes and women stacking wheat and barley.

We went to a depot called Keifiede. It was about two miles to the prison camp. This was way up in Poland and called Stalag Luft IV.

The camp wasn't finished yet. I think we were probably the first prisoners there. My Prisoner of War number was 1680 so it was pretty new. It was here I ran into Earl Campbell again and we became the best of friends during our time of confinement.

About October the Germans brought in prisoners from Stalag VI as the Russians were getting too close to VI. Amongst the prisoners was our old crew member, James W. Riley, who had gone down on the February 11th raid at which time he had taken a 20mm shell through the stomach. Luckily for Riley the shell was a dud which did not explode. Somewhere the German's slave labor had probably duded the shell purposely. Riley told us the Germans and the French doctors had operated on him and after his wound was healed he had been sent to Stalag Luft VI.

We stayed in Poland for about six or seven months.

As the Russians got closer they started moving us out. Riley was with one bunch which left by train. In the next few days they sorted out another bunch of us and put us on another train. They boarded up the windows and there was no air at all. There were 50 of us in each continental box car. There wasn't enough room to sit down or lay down. We were on that train for nine days and nights.

In about four or five days we got to Berlin. They stopped in the train depot, call the marshalling yard, and some prisoners took off a prisoner who had died. We were brought in some water. By this time, it was getting dark. We heard air raid sirens. Every man on that train was a flier. We knew how you were briefed on targets. You had a primary target. Then you had a secondary target. The marshalling yards were targets of opportunity. If you couldn't get into your primary or secondary target then you were free to bomb anything you could see. That's when marshalling yards would get hit.

Berlin was the primary target that day. I don't know how many bombers went over, but it seemed like they went forever. Not one of them ever dropped a bomb in that marshalling yard. I figure the good Lord had a hand in that. We were asking him to do so. I sure was. You don't have anybody else to turn to. There's nobody that's going to help you. I told Him I'd count my blessings everyday if I could get out of there alive and I did. So, I pretty well count them everyday, too.

The POW train took us to Nuremberg. When we got to Nuremberg and they opened the box car doors to let us out. The first three or four men that went out fell to their knees when they hit the fresh air. Then the Germans marched us about one and a half miles to a former Italian prison camp that was loaded with fleas and lice.

It was pretty rough living there. There were no beds and we were packed so close that we all had to roll over at the same time. The Italians had taken the wooden walls of the buildings to burn over the years leaving no shelter for us, and this being a cold hard January we struggled to stay warm. We were fed black bread, carrots, cabbage and rutabaga. We were there from about January 10th until April 5th. While at Nuremberg I discovered some of our officers, Captain Clay and Lt Hatten, were in an adjoining compound and I went to visit them.

We left there, on foot on April 5. There were thousands of us. That first night they put us in a stand of woods in the rain. It rained all night. The next day was my brother's birthday. Every year on his birthday I call him and ask him if he knows where he was on April 6, 1945. He was in Dyersburg, TN. He had finished his last mission the day I went down.

We walked for nine or ten days. We would up at Moosburg. They say that there were about 180,000 prisoners in Moosburg.

Around midmorning on April 29th, we noticed that there weren't any guards in the tower yet. Then we saw three American tanks coming.

There were ground force troops behind them. They knocked some of the fenced down. Only two tank cannon shots were fired. A German sniper was in the tower of a church. He fired on the tanks. One tank said "kaboom!" and there was no tower left. Another German down town then put up some resistance. They used a tank on him too. He was in a glass store. You can imagine how cut up he was. He was dead.

We armed ourselves with weapons the Germans had dropped. We went to a doctor's house and liberated a team of horses. I had a black fat brimmed hat I had liberated from the doctor's also. I picked up a pack of cigarettes from a drawer. I lit one of them and took one puff and couldn't get my breath. They went into the fire.

Then we went to another house in a different part of town. One of the boys with us spoke fluent German, Italian and French. There was an old man and woman, two younger women and two little kids. The youngest of the two women was six or seven months pregnant. The older one's husband had just been killed on the eastern front.

We had asked the tanks for something to eat. It was the first time I had seen 10 in 1 rations. It was a box of rations for 10 men for 1 day. They were delicious. We gave them to the women and they fixed a feast for us. They wouldn't eat any. They were probably afraid of what we were going to do to them. We were there for about a week. Some of the former POWs started finding their own way back to our lines. But they had a long walk. We waited.

On the sixth or seventh day, we went back into camp and the next day we were on a C-47 that took us to Lucky Strike camp in Janville, France. There they deloused us and gave us $20 partial pay. They gave us new uniforms with no stripes, but many wrinkles. They looked terrible but at least they were clean.

At that point they put 400 of us aboard each Liberty ship. We were on the high seas for 13 days. The bulk of the time there was bad weather.

The Liberty ships had no ballast and bounced like corks. When we got back to the States the olive drabs, or OD, uniforms didn't have any insignias and had never been pressed. An Army Colonel met us and welcomed us back to the USA. He had the best looking WAC driver we had seen recently.

Immediately they put us on trains by area and we were also given partial pay. All the people in my car were going to Leavenworth, KS. We had priority. Even fast passengers trains pulled over for us. After Leavenworth I went to Wichita where my folks lived. The M.P.'s picked me up because my uniform looked so sorry. I convinced them I had been a prisoner and had just been released. They took me to my parent's house. I was glad to be finally home.

Post War

In 1975 we bought this farm east of El Dorado Springs, MO and moved there in September of that year.

I kept seeing trucks from Kentucky at the local cattle auctions and always asked if they came from anywhere around Napfor, KY as I wanted to make contacted with my best friend I had made while I was a POW.

One day one of the truck drivers asked, "Why don't' you check with a telephone operator?" Tthat night I did and located Earl Campbell. He said his crew got together every year for a reunion. He had heard for Branson, MO and asked how far away from Branson did I live. I told him about 100 miles. He asked then if I would meet with them if they had their reunion in Branson. I said "sure"." He checked with the four that were still living and they agreed and so they decided to go to Branson, MO in September of 1993.

My wife and I went and checked into the motel. However, on his way to Branson, Earls wife had a stroke in St. Louis so they went back home. We did get together with the other tree crew members for a good long visit during which time they told me about the Ex-Prisoners association which I didn't know about. My wife and I joined and have lifetime memberships.

As a result of joining this Association, I made contact with other personnel with whom I had served and joined other associations one of which was the 351st Bomb Group which was an active Guided Missile Unit at Whitemen AFB which is located just 85 miles from my home. Being furnished a copy of their membership I contacted LT Pullen and Captain Clay, LT Arnold and SGT Jilcott. LT Pullen and I phoned each other frequently. LT Pullen called and told me that Stalag Luft III was having a reunion in Kansas City in 1999. Although he would not be able to go he suggested to me that I do so and meet with Captain Clay. I agreed and he gave me the dates.

Just before going to this reunion, I received the latest copy of the Polebrook Post , which gave us contacts in England and Denmark. There was a letter and a picture of our wrecked airplane in the Post. My wife and I went to Kansas City and I met Captain Clay at his hotel and took the Polebrook Post with me to show him.

Sometime after returning to our farm, I was contacted by Captain Clay's daughter, Karen, who wanted to know if I was interested in going back to England, Denmark, and Germany. I told her I would like to go to England and Denmark, but I wasn't interested in going back to Germany. While I was in the service, I had been back to Germany twice. Later Karen called and asked if we would go to England and Denmark and I answered in the affirmative. Captain Clay's family got the ball rolling and made all the arrangements and everything worked out perfect.

On May 19, 2000, we met Captain Clay and his family, Lt. Hatten and his son Robert and Sgt. Jilcott and his daughter, Linda, in the Atlanta airport. I recognized Captain Clay and Sgt. Jilcott, but didn't really know Lt. Hatten. Then we boarded the plane and made the flight to London.

I had been told by another man from the 351st Association to look up an English man by the name of David Gower when we were in England. David Gower owned what was once the Polebrook Air Field. When we arrived in London David Gower met us with a bus and driver. They took us to Peterborough, where hotel accommodations had been made for us at the Bull Hotel. That evening Mick Austin and his wife, Karen, who we had corresponded with and talked with by phone came to the hotel, also another Englishman and his wife [Mike and Brenda Hollingdale]. Then most of us went out to a pub for fish and chips.

When we went to the American cemetery at Cambridge it was breath taking and very impressive. The chapel was beautiful. The cemetery was very well taken care of and they had flags at all the 351st graves.

We went to the old base at Polebrook. They have a nice memorial and it is well taken care of. After visiting the base, we went to a local pub for an excellent lunch. After lunch, we went to the local church for a short service. We visited the 8th Air Force Museum and enjoyed the afternoon looking at the planes and it brought back memories of the war.

After this we went back to London and flew to Denmark where we were met by a military bus and driver. The facilities were excellent and the food was outstanding as were all the people that made it possible. The Danes had a celebration for us at the crash site of "Stormy Weather" on the 57th anniversary of our original crash landing in Denmark.

I would rate it as one of the high lights of my life. I was highly impressed with the appreciation expressed and demonstrated by the

Danish people I met. In fact the whole trip was one of the highlights of my entire life.

From Nazi Germany to U.S. and the 8th Air Force.

Narrated by Bernard Fridberg 381st Bomb Group.

My family tree dates back to the early 1700's in Hannover, Germany, where I was born. My father served in the German Army for three years during WWI, and was awarded the Iron Cross.

The Nazi era officially started in 1933 and a short time later, our American relatives started making plans to bring the immediate family out of Germany. The children were to come out first. My brother and I, at 14 and 13 years old, as well as three other cousins left together on a ship to America in January of 1936.

After a short stay in Binghamton, N.Y., we moved to Washington, D.C., where we grew up and went to school under supervision of family cousins. My parents left Europe on one of the last ships in 1940 to Cuba, while still waiting for visas to enter the U.S. We were reunited in 1941, when they were allowed to move to Washington.

After Junior High School, I went to vocational school in the printing department. As soon as I could, I got a job as an apprentice printer-typesetter. After Pearl Harbor in 1941, I wanted to enlist, but I wasn't a citizen, so I had to wait to get drafted, which I did in the Spring of 1943 and became a citizen in Tampa, FL, while in basic training.

After signing up for flying duty, I was sent to Gulfport, Miss. for Aircraft Mechanic training and then to Aircraft Gunnery training in Harlingen, TX, where I received my gunnery wings.

Heavy bomber crews were assembled in Salt Lake City, Utah, where I met my crew of nine others in January of 1944.

After training as a waist gunner in our combat crew for several months, we were assigned a brand-new B-17 in Kearney, Nebraska, which we ferried overseas to Belfast, Ireland via Gander, Newfoundland on a stormy ice-cold North Atlantic night on April 21, 1944.

The Crew!

Bernard Fridberg and his Crew. It's Fridberg standing no. 4 from the left.

A number of planes were lost that night—we almost didn't make it either. The vacuum pump failed, causing problems in several systems. Our pilot, Frank O'Black, had to fly the plane by the seat of his pants without the automatic pilot, while dodging in and out of the ice storm, and depending entirely on our navigator, Ralph Sims, for positioning. Due to excellent flying and navigational skills, we made it the following morning to Belfast with only ten miles off course.

After several weeks of orientation and training, we and several other crews, were assigned to the 381st Bomb Group near Cambridge. Our first mission on May 19 to Berlin was ample introduction of what was in store. I flew as waist gunner most of the time, but once as tail gunner and once in the ball turret. Out of 25 missions, 13 were to German targets, including three to Berlin, while 12 were to the Low Countries and France, including the morning of June 6, 1944, to Cherbourg, France.

The German targets were always tough, and flak damage, at times very heavy, was always part of the mission. On one mission, the hydraulic system was shot out, and we had to attach parachutes out of the waist windows to act as brakes upon landing. On another mission, we had to hand-crank our ball turret gunner out of the turret. He had passed out due to lack of oxygen. His oxygen hose had become disconnected and he didn't answer the 15-minute check-in call. Luckily we got him out, put him on an oxygen bottle and he came to a short time later. Our bombardier had a nervous breakdown on our second Berlin mission. At that same time, a large piece of flak missed me by inches and tore a big hole in the roof of the plane. There were many close calls. The real heroes, though, were the many fellows who died in combat during all those missions.

The last mission to Peenemunde and then to Sweden, was unusual. We were flying squadron lead, but mechanical engine failure occurred on two engines one over the North Sea and the other near Denmark. Both engines had to be feathered. Swedish fighters escorted us to Malmo, where Lt. O'Black landed the plane with only two engines running on one side.

That was July 18, 1944. We were interned in Sweden until November 18, 1944. For several weeks we stayed in Falun and then on to a pensionat near Jonkoping (Mullsjo).

We were under the supervision of the Swedish Army, even though we received our expense money, etc., from the American Embassy in

Stockholm. We bought civilian clothes from an allowance. Life was easy, but permission was needed to travel outside our immediate area. On November 18, we were flown out of Stockholm airport in unmarked blacked-out civilian airplanes over German-occupied Norway to Northern Scotland and then back to England.

After staying in England several weeks, getting new uniforms, etc., I was sent back home to Washington in December. I reported to Miami Beach after three weeks, took tests and was approved as a cadet for navigator and started training in San Antonio in the spring of 1945. The war in Europe was soon over, and those of us who had flown combat, were transferred to bases near home. I ended up at Dover Air Base in Delaware with the Air Transport Command. I flew as flight engineer on C-54 transport planes to Europe, bringing back the wounded. In October 1945, I was discharged.

As a new civilian, I picked up on my apprentice-printer training, became a journeyman in 1948, started a typesetting business in 1955, in which I was active until retirement in 1998.
Looking back, the war years were indeed an important, meaningful and exciting part of my life with a great many memories. I do derive satisfaction in having had a small, direct part in Germany's defeat. Many of my relatives and childhood friends died in the Holocaust. I was lucky and thankful for the opportunities I've had. However, the real heroes of the war are those who gave their lives.

The Easter Sunday Mission 1944

Narrated by Fred H. Calfee 401st Bomb Group.

On December 7, 1941, as you know, the Japanese bombed Pearl Harbor. I joined the Air Force and was called to active duty in November 1942.

After having done various flight training in various planes, I was commissioned 2nd LT in August 1943. My next phase was to start training to fly the B-17. We were given three months of training in the B-17 certified as combat ready and assigned to the 8th Air Force in England.

We arrived on Christmas eve, 1943 at Deenethorpe being assigned to the 401st Bomb Group commanded by Colonel Bowman. I flew 13 missions, and on our 14'th we had to land in Malmo, Sweden, due to heavy battle damage. My missions included the targets of Frankfurt February 11th, 1944 and Frankfurt again February 14th. February 20th we bombed Leipzig and this was a rough one. Back to Frankfurt March 2nd . Our next big mission was to Berlin on the 4th. This mission was recalled due to bad weather. However, one bomb group did continue on to Berlin but did minor damage.

On March 6th, we flew our first big daylight raid on Berlin. Our fighter escorts left us prior to the target and for the next 45 minutes we were without fighter protection. This one I did not figure how we would make it back to England as the whole German Luftwaffe seemed to attack us. Fortunately, we did survive to "fly" again.

March 8th we bombed Errner, Germany and March 13th we hit the "bussbomb base" in Pas De Calais, in France. We thought it would be a "milk run" but we lost one of our crews. March 18th we bombed Lundsberg, Germany. This was another rough mission. March 27th we bombed a target in Tours, France. March 29th, back to Germany bombing Brunswick.

On Easter Sunday, April 9th, 1944, we were scheduled for the longest mission of the war. Our target was in East Prussia, which is on the other side of Berlin. We formed over England, flew out over the North Sea, across Denmark, where we received damage to our #2 engine, down the Baltic Sea and then to our target of Marienburg which was a ME 109 fighter aircraft factory.

Just as we dropped our bombs, our #2 engine started losing oil pressure. We activated the feathering system. This normally causes the propeller to go into a stationary position which produces the least amount of drag. The propeller would not feather, and now we have a runaway propeller in "flat pitch" which produces the maximum amount of drag. We now have in effect only the equivalent of 2 ½ engines. We are vibrating as though the airplane may fall apart.

About this time the German fighters start attacking us. We push the three remaining throttles all the way forward and decide if the old bird comes apart, this is better than being shot down. We finally regained a loose formation position and start checking our fuel consumption.

The fighters didn't try to attack. We figure we may be able to make it to within 250 miles of the English coast and ditch in the North Sea and if you are not rescued within eight hours in the month of April, you usually die from exposure to the weather.

We can see Sweden off to our right as we head west toward Denmark. At this point the decision is made to land in Malmo, Sweden. Sweden is supposedly a neutral country; however, they were actually very pro-ally.

We successfully landed on a sod airfield and immediately we are met by two Swedish truckloads of soldiers. One group is directing us to turn left while another group is attempting to enter the airplane by the rear entrance door. We blast the two good engines on the right, as we were beginning to sink into the sod, and blow the Swedes away from the tail of the aircraft. Eventually they did get aboard, and as we are taxiing, two of them made it up to the cockpit. Their first words were: "Welcome to Sweden".

We are all searched for weapons when we left the aircraft and then taken to the mess hall for some food. As we began to eat, someone said: "Hey, this is blood pudding," but I continued to eat mine as it tasted fairly good to me. Mind you, we all were dressed in our flying gear, leather jackets, fur-lined boots and helmets.

Six planes landed that day, all with heavy battle damage, plus one aircraft that had seven fatalities on board. We were all taken downtown into Malmo and put under guard in a brick building with straw mats on the cots.

The Crew in Sweden.

Photo taken at Bultofta, Malmoe April 9, 1944—shortly after the landing.
L to R: 2nd LT W. Patterson Navigator, T/SGT D. Patterson Turret Gunner, 2nd LT F. Calfee Co-Pilot, SGT F. Skelton Ball Gunner, 2nd LT G. C. Byrd Pilot, 2nd LT C.Vickrey Bombardier, S/SGT J. Exnowski Radio Operator, S/SGT M. Holzmann Tail Gunner, SGT L. Muscarella Left Waist Gunner and S/SGT W. Hussey Right Waist Gunner.

It wasn't long before a crowd of young Swedish citizens gathered in the streets outside our windows. Some of us still had a few chocolate bars from the mission and tossed them out the windows to the young girls. They saw a candy store nearby and tossed candy back to us. We spent one or two nights there. The third night they marched us to the street cars to cross the city of Malmo. Then we were put on Pullman railroad cars with the most beautiful woodwork I had seen on any train car.

We were transported to Falun which is about the center of Sweden and then taken to a civilian store to buy clothes. This turned out "hilarious" as none of us had worn civilian clothes for over two years. Everyone was having a field day. The air attaché from the American embassy arranged all this and the officer's expenses were taken out of our pay but enlisted crew members did not have to pay theirs.

We now split into two groups and the group I was in was then sent further north to a resort town of Ratvik. We were then billeted in boarding house type hotels. We could come and go as we pleased, provided we stayed within a ten mile radius of the town. We had a Swedish officer who monitored us and the Senior American Officer functioned as our C.O.

Sweden was pro-ally since Count Bernadotte married one of the Dupont girls. Believe it or not we would get three passes to Stockholm. If you will look at Sweden, you will see there was not way to escape due to its geographical location. Norway, remember, was occupied by the Germans. We spent most of our spare time chasing the Swedish girls and riding bicycles, going to Swedish dances, hiking, boating on the lake starting in July.

I was issued a ticket for illegally riding my bike and had to go to court where the judge fined me $ 2.50 and told me in excellent English that what I had done was illegal. I said "Yes, sir" and paid the fine.

Some of the Swedes wanted to put us to work on the railroad. I was known as the "West Virginia Revenuer". West Virginia, it seems, was known for its moonshine.

The worst thing about this ordeal was that my folks at home received a "missing in action" telegram instead of being told I was interned in Sweden. This was eventually straightened out by a friend of mine who was flying off our wing in the same mission and who wrote a letter to Mrs. Fred Calfee, which there wasn't any at this time, advising that I had gone into Sweden, a neutral country. My uncle, Howard Faulkner, worked in the post office in Bluefield, West Virginia, and by chance happened to see the letter.

He immediately opened the letter, read the contents, jumped in his car and drove to my parents to tell them that I was interned in Sweden. My mother wrote the War Department advising them as to my where-abouts. Remember, there were 11 million men in the service at that time. They wrote back thanking her for advising them as to where I was. This eventually was worked out between the War Department and the American Embassy in Sweden.

We were finally repatriated in November 1944. This was a real cloak and dagger operation. The Swedes traded one German for one American. We were taken to Stockholm, billeted to what looked like a health resort.

B-24s were flown into Stockholm. These B-24s hade been stripped of all their guns and the bomb bay modified with benches to carry passengers. Sweden being neutral would allow any unarmored ship to land in Stockholm. It was not unusual to see Germans, Japanese, Italians, etc. all landing in Stockholm. Twelve times (totally) at night we would go to the plane loaded up and taxi out for take-off the taxi back in and return to our quarters. We assumed this was to confuse the German espionage agents and evidently it was successful for on the 12th attempt late at night we departed Stockholm. We flew north and right above the clouds. When the pilot approached the narrow part of Norway we turned due west and out over the North Sea and on into England. I assumed we would all have to finish our missions but this was not the case. Perhaps this had to do with the Geneva Convention concerning the rules of war.

We returned to the States and I ended up being assigned to Memphis AFB. Here I checked out in the fighter type aircraft, P-51, P-47 and P-40. We ferried a few of these planes to a base in Mississippi. I thought we might be sent to the Pacific. Of course, when the atomic bomb was dropped on Japan, the Japanese surrendered shortly thereafter.

I was discharged from the Air Force in September of 1945 and returned to civilian life.

The Leipzig Mission

Narrated by Carroll Gouger 401st Bomb Group

The Crew of "Doolittle's Doughboys"

Standing L to R:
Dale W. Minard Engineer, Horace H. Shelton Co-Pilot, Carroll A. Gouger
Navigator, J. L. Foster Bombardier & Edward Gardner Pilot KIA.
Front row L to R: Fred Monnes Radio Operator KIA, Steve Bosowski Tail
Gunner, Pete Piazza Ball Gunner, Salvatore Trupia Waist Gunner KIA,
Francis Durben Waist Gunner.

This was a replacement crew who arrived at Deenethorpe just after Christmas 1943 and who went into combat about two weeks later. We were shot down on February 20, 1944 on the mission to Leipzig, the crew's 9th mission. The regular Co-Pilot, 2nd Lt. Horace H. Shelton, was on a 24 hour pass on this day and his place was taken by 2nd Lt. G. L. Carter.

The 401st were leading the Leipzig mission on February 20, 1944, and our crew was picked to fly in "Purple Heart" corner of the Lead group of the formation, when we were attacked by a strong formation of enemy fighters near Magdeburg, Germany from a 12 o'clock position.

Our plane "Doolittle's Doughboys" was immediately hit by 20 mm shells directly behind the navigators compartment and the electrical generators were knocked out. The engines lost power and the ship dropped back out of formation.

I crawled up to the cockpit to advise the pilot of the damage because the intercom had also been knocked out. The pilot and co-pilot decided to "hit the deck" and try to make it to Sweden, but, at that moment, the fighters, seeing us falling out of the main bomber formation, made a concentrated attack on us. We were hit throughout the plane by 20 mm cannon fire and #3 engine burst into flames. At that time Lt. Ed Gardner gave the order to abandon ship.

Lt. Gardner and myself paused in the heat of the battle to shake hands in a farewell gesture, then I hurried forward to inform the bombardier, Lt. Foster that we were to bail out through the forward hatch.

In the meantime Lt. Gardner had sent the engineer S/Sgt. D. W. Minard, back to the rear of the ship to inform the rest of the crew to bail out. He found Sgt. Fred Monnes, the radio operator, mortally wounded in the radio room and Sgt. Trupia, one of the waist gunners, dead from a direct hit from a 20 mm shell. The other three crew members had already left the now doomed ship.

S/Sgt. Minard later learned that Sgt. Durben and Sgt. Piazza had taken the badly wounded tail gunner, Sgt. Steve Bosowski, out of his tail position to find his right leg almost blown off. They had quickly put on his chute and threw him from the aircraft, hoping he would get the much needed medical attention on the ground. In fact he came down in the city of Magdeburg, where he was taken by civilians to a hospital where his leg was amputated. Steve Bosowski was repatriated six months later.

S/Sgt. Minard and Lt. G. Carter left the plane through the bomb bay, leaving Lt. Ed Gardner to follow them. Like so many other airplane commanders, Lt. Gardner choose to be the last to leave the ship to ensure that all his crew had left, and this very correct and brave behaviour probably cost him his life.

Three weeks later the body of Lt. Gardner was found in a field near Pilm, Germany. He had obviously left it too late to bail out or his chute had failed to operate. Lt. Gardner was awarded the "DFC" (Distinguished Flying Cross) post humously to his wife and son.

I fell out of the nose escape hatch, bounced off bomb bay doors (still open), hit my head on the tail wheel—semi conscious—my chute opened okay. Two ME 109's were flying around me but did not shoot at me. I landed in open field near the town of Gommern approximately 10 miles south of Magdeburg. I was captured by six Volksturm Home Guard members by the near by woods. While held by them, a German Army Sgt. (walking in the woods with his lady friend) saw the commotion, came running to us with pistol drawn and took me as his prisoner—up to the town jail in Gommern.

All the crew were captured, myself Lt. Foster and S/Sgt. Minard ending up in the same civilian jail in Gommern. We were later taken to the Magdeburg Air Base and then to Dulag Luft at Frankfurt for interrogation. The officers were later sent to Stalag Luft I where they again met up with Lt. Carter.

S/Sgt. Minard eventually joined Sgt. Durben and S/Sgt. Piazza in Sta-lag XVI in Latvia. These three men, in February 1945, landed at Stalag Luft I where they had marched on the road in advance of the Russian Army.

My POW experience was nothing out of the ordinary. Food was very scarce at times—I lost 40 lbs (from 185 to 145 lbs). After the interro-gation at Frankfurt I was sent by freight train in a box car to Stalag Luft I, Barth, Germany.

We were "Liberated" by the Red Army (the Russians) on May 1, 1945—and flown out by 8th Air Force B-17 bombers on or about May 17th. We flew at 1,500 feet down the Ruhr Valley and saw tremendous devastation down there.

We landed in Reims, France and then by train to Camp Lucky Strike, near Le Havre. I got out of there by "stowaway" on a B-17 from my Bomb Group—the 401st and visited the Bomb Group for two days. Then I was sent to a hospital in Cambridge, England and then to a hotel in London for two weeks.

Finally homeward bound on a Liberty Ship out of Southampton, England and got to No. Adams, Mass. On June 29th 1945.

A Ball Gunner's Story

Narrated by John Lewis Hurd 401ˢᵗ Bomb Group

I was inducted into the army on the 13ᵗʰ of January 1943 and left home for military service on January 20ᵗʰ 1943. I was inducted at Lynwood, California.I was first sent to the 402ⁿᵈ Technical School Squadron at Sheppard Field, Texas for basic training in the Army Air Forces & more tests & evaluation. Upon leaving basic training I would be receiving instruction in B-17 mechanics & aerial gunnery.

I am now being sent to the 623ʳᵈ Technical School Squadron at the Amarillo Army Air Field for training in B-17 aircraft mechanics. I completed training on September 24ᵗʰ 1943 and received my diploma in mechanics on the 25ᵗʰ of September and became a private First Class at this time.

After completing the B-17 aircraft mechanics course I was sent to Las Vegas, Nevada for ground schooling in aerial gunnery and then to Indian Springs, Nevada for actual firing of aircraft machine guns from the ground and from aircraft. Here I made my first airplane ride ever. I flew in a North American AT-6 advance trainer firing a 30 caliber machine gun from the rear seat at a target sleve being towed by another aircraft. I made one gunnery flight in a B-17E from Indian Springs firing from the top turret. On completion of this training I was made sergeant.

The later part of October 1943 I was sent to Moses Lake, Washington to join a B-17 crew and start training as the Ball Turret Gunner with that crew. In November we moved to Ephrata, Washington and became members of the 457th Bomb Group, 750th Squadron and began bombing and gunnery training with that group. This group was known as the "Fire Ball Outfit". In December 1943 the 457th Bomb Group moved to Wendover Field, Utah. This was to be our final month of Group training before moving to England and the "Eighth Air Force".

The crew.

Photo taken at Wendover Field, Utah. December 1943.
Back row L to R: Carl. F. Hansen Navigator, Alfred L. Autrey Bombardier, William R. Cole Co-Pilot & Francis L. Shaw Pilot.
Front row L to R: Howard S. Kneese Tail Gunner, Robert Gordon Waist Gunner, Richard W. Macomber Top Turret Gunner, Kenneth A. Terroux Radio Operator, John L. Hurd Ball Turret Gunner & Carl K. Seagen Waist Gunner.

This crew was transferred to the 401st Bomb Group, 614th Squadron February 1944, Deenethorpe England.

Carl F. Hansen did not transfer with crew. Elmer W. Engelhardt transferred with crew and became Navigator.

Howard Kneese became a POW in early March 1944 when on a Mission over Germany flying as tail gunner with another crew. Howard and crew bailed out when their B-17 was shot down.

On April 11 1944 Harold A. Highlen was flying as waist gunner with this crew when the B-17 "Battlin Betty" was shot down over Germany. The entire crew bailed out safely and became POWs in Germany.

Gordon, Macomber, Terroux, Hurd, Seagen and Highlen were all POWs at Stalag 17 B located in Krems, Austria.

In January 1944 my crew picked up a new B-17G at Grand Island, Nebraska and flew it to Presque Isle, Maine for our first leg on our journey to England. Over night stop here and the next day we were off for Gander Lake, Newfoundland. Fog and plenty of snow here. On our third and final leg we landed at Valley, Wales on 20th January 1944 after a flight of ten hours. We crossed the north Atlantic by deadrechoning not using radio navigation due to possibility of interference from German submarines.

On approximately the 21st of January 1944 we flew to Station 130 the home base for the 457th Bomb Group at Glatton, eighty miles north of London. In early February 1944 my crew was transferred to the 401st Bomb Group, 614th Squadron. Our navigator now was LT Englehart. Our new station now is 128 at Deenethorpe.

On February 22 1944 I flew my first bombing mission and it was with Pilot LT Samule P. Wilson and his crew as their Ball Gunner was unable to fly this mission.

The primary target was Oscherleben, Germany. Our route to the target took us over Holland, and the Zuider Zee. The only time I ever fired my two 50 caliber machine guns in anger at an enemy fighter plane was while on this mission and over Holland. He was too far behind us and going down behind some other B-17s but I fired a short burst anyway. No other time while flying combat missions did I fire the guns other than the test firing while we were heading out over the north sea toward another target.

I saw two B-17s go down on this day but I don't know from what Bomb Group they were. One was on fire and exploded and the other one banked over and went into a spin and down. Some crewmen bailed out and I believe that all were out by this time. Our ship was hit a few time by flak but nothing serious. We were running low on fuel and coming back across the North Sea so everything loose was thrown overboard. Even the waist position machine guns. We finally arrived at an emergency field along the coast of England and stayed there overnight. Flew back to our home base the next day. Quite a beginning for a new combat crewman.

On February 25 1944 I flew my second mission and this time it was with my own crew. Our target was Augsburg, Germany. Don't recall any problems this day.

Third mission was to Frankfurt, Germany. This was on March 2 1944. I made two missions with a LT Peterson and his crew and this may be one of them.

My next mission was on March 11 1944 to Münster, Germany.

On days I was scheduled to fly a mission I got up at 3 a.m. Had breakfast the first thing after leaving my living quarters which was a Nissen Hut. All crews scheduled to fly were then assembled in the briefing room to learn about the target for the day. We were also briefed on the route to and from the target and possible trouble with flak and enemy fighter aircraft. We were told about friendly fighter aircraft we might see along the way. After briefing we went to the equipment room and picked up our flight gear, parachute, life jacket, heated suits, heavy flying clothes and miscellaneous other gear. Next we were trucked out to the aircraft and wait for take off around 7 am. Sometimes the mission would be scrubbed (cancelled) due to weather and then I would go back to bed and wait another day.

My next mission was to Augsburg, Germany on March 16 1944. I flew as ball gunner with LT Peterson and his crew on this day. We completed mission but due to mechanical problems with aircraft we did not arrive at our home base until the following day.

Sixth mission was Landsberg am Lech. Don't remember this day but it was March 18 1944.

Big "B" Berlin, Germany was my seventh mission on March 22 1944. Flying between 20 and 25 thousand feet I felt the cold weather on my feet so I kept turning the temperature up on my heated suit to warm my heated boots. In doing so I burned some blisters on my knuckles and other places which were treated after returning to base. I was grounded a couple of days while they healed. On the bomb run over the target there was a lot of flak but it missed us a mile. After leaving the target we had a Lockheed P-38 fighter fly along with us on one engine for a while. It had the left engine propeller feathered.

Eight mission was to Ahlen. Don't remember this day. It was March 23 1944.

Ninth mission was to Tours, France on March 27 1944. Mission completed without difficulty.

John Lewis Hurd----after his 5th mission. Photo taken in England March 1944.

Mission number 10, April 9 1944 was on Easter Sunday. This being my longest flight lasting twelve hours.

Our target was a German Focke-Wulf 190 fighter aircraft assembly plant. Our flight path took us over the North Sea and east over Denmark and the Baltic Sea. We headed south of Danzig in the Polish corridor and struck our target at Marienburg, East Prussia with incendiary bombs.

One large building was already smoking. Our route back to the base was the same as to the target.

Flying west over the Baltic Sea and heading back to England the first thing I knew something had happened as I was looking down from my turret a B-17 was on its back underneath us. I was looking south over northern Germany and saw a German fighter streaking back over Germany. It was hard to see as it blended with the background of the earth.

About this time three P-51 Mustangs came across in front of my turret. They came up in front of our formation and by the left side of our B-17 around behind us and up our right side at which time I lost track of them. I also looked around to see if any German fighters might be coming up at us which they normally don't do.

Looking straight back behind us and far back one of our B-17s headed for Sweden. I did not see the B-17 that was underneath us crash into the Baltic Sea but it did for a total lost crew and aircraft.

After these happenings I was looking straight ahead and saw two P-51s chasing a German fighter in a circle when the fighter nosed over and flew straight into the ground. I did not see any parachute from the aircraft. I figured the third P-51 Mustang was watching up Sun as we were flying directly into the afternoon Sun.

Over the North Sea our ship "BATTLIN BETTY" #42-39847 was running low on fuel so in order to lighten her and save gas we threw the waist machine guns and other equipment overboard. We were flying low over the North Sea and ready do ditch but we managed to land at another field and safety. We gassed up and flew back to home base the next day.

Mission number 11 on April 11 1944 was my final mission as my favourite aircraft B-17G "BATTLIN BETTY" #42-39847 was shot down over Germany.

Our target for the day was Politz near the Polish border. According to the official history of the 401st Bomb Group the target bombed was Stettin, Poland.

Out flight path took us east over Holland and into Germany and as we flew near Hannover our squadron was hit by flak. One B-17 blew with eight crewmen going down with it. Two ships were damaged and tried to get back to England but were shot down by enemy fighters. A Co-Pilot was killed in one of these B-17s. I learned about these happenings from other crewmen that bailed out from the other B-17s and were captured. We all were sent to the interrogation center at Frankfurt, Germany.

Getting back to our B-17 in heavy flak I would watch under the wings for fires. The Pilot wants to know if any fires get started. I could hear the flak shells explode around the aircraft. Our #4 engine started smoking and may #3 engine was damaged. In order to watch under the wings for fires I would rotate the Ball turret so the guns were level. Then the door to get in and out of the turret from inside the aircraft is out side of the aircraft and I'm in the turret without a parachute. That will make you nervous.

Our Pilot LT Francis L. Shaw jettisoned the bombs to prevent an explosion from them. The bomb bay doors remained open. My ball turret was hit by a piece of flak above the seat. It broke a piece of the turret loose and stung me in the right Buttock. I let the Pilot know I've been hit. The Pilot asked me to come out of the turret and have Radio Operator attend my injury.

I had too many clothes on so nothing was done. That was OK. My injury was not so bad. While still in the Radio Room with the Radio Operator I tried to make myself as small as possible because flak was still flying around outside. The skin of a B-17 won't stop anything such as flak from coming inside. By this time our B-17G Vega built "BATTLIN BETTY" #42-39847 was out here in the sky all by herself and no place to go.

About this time the Pilot gave the order to bail out.

Every time I got into our aircraft to start a mission I tied my GI shoes string together. Before I finally bail out I put the shoe strings inside my left leg parachute harness and buckled up. The shoes hung there on my leg. I now hooked on my chest type parachute. We were lucky the aircraft was still on an even keel. The two waist gunners and I were ready to bail out the waist door when I heard a loud crash sound and the B-17 rocked to the left and we stumbled against the left side of the B-17.

At this time I decided we had enough and I pushed the two waist gunners in front of me and all three of us were out the door. We had been hit by a German fighter. Good thing that fighter pilot wasn't shooting where we were in the B-17. I pulled the ripcord early and looked up at the chute and saw the Bombardier's feet near my chute. I also heard machine gun fire and saw some smoke on the ground. We were hanging nearly over a river or canal. I didn't want to land in the water. We drifted away from it. Thank goodness.

I had company on my trip to the ground as the Bombardier and I were able to talk to each other. We saw our beautiful B-17 "BATTLIN BETTY" crash into the river or canal. Fire and smoke then nothing. Water was clear no indication there was a crash. At this moment in this adventure I believed the Pilot crashed with the B-17.

As I neared the ground it came up with a rush. I hit the ground and finally came to rest on my back. I struggled for several moments getting to my feet as I wanted to keep my injured right buttock out of the dirt. At this time a saw a German in the blue uniform with a luger pistol in his hand approaching. If there was such a thing as a good sign at this moment it was the blue uniform.

The Bombardier Al Autry landed near by and I walked over to him. He started to look at my injury and tear a bandage from his chute and I started to put my shoes on when the German Air Force Officer motioned for us to walk over to an open military vehicle near by and get in. The Navigator Elmer Engelhardt was already in the vehicle. I now put my GI shoes on. Soon a motorcycle with side car came along and the Bombardier got into it.

As we were being driven away three P-51 Mustangs came down very close and looked us over. It was good to see them looking after us.

Shortly after we stopped in a small town and our Pilot was brought out of a building and got into the car with us. It was good to see the Pilot again as I thought he went down with the ship.

We were then taken to a room in what looked like some kind of an administration building. We were told to empty our pockets and the items were put in a large envelope. Later I was taken to another room were the items were listed and typed on paper by a secretary. I had a Milky Way candy bar with me and the German checking the items said I had to eat it now or give it up. So I ate it. It was tasty.

I was then escorted by a guard to another building where a medical person applied medication and put a bandage on my injury. I was then taken back where the other crewmen were. Some time later two more of our crew arrived.

After dark we were given some bread and jelly to eat. Later the seven of us including the four officers and three enlisted crew members were escorted to a train station near by.

As we arrived at the station the Air Raid sirens sounded. The British were flying somewhere in the area. We pushed our way through the German civilians to a small alcove in the station and waited for the all clear.

We finally boarded a passenger train for Frankfurt and the interrogation center. The passenger cars had out side doors to each compartment. The Germans escorting us wanted us in compartments side by side so they kicked the civilians out of one compartment so we were side by side five in one and four in the other. We changed trains during the night and had a cup of coffee at this time. Sure glad I had my GI shoes on.

At the interrogation center I was first put in a room by myself and given a bowl of Rutabaga soup. Shortly after I was interrogated in another room. I gave name, rank and serial number. Then I was escorted by a guard to a third or fourth floor room. The room was about four by eight feet in size. I had to leave my shoes out side the door. Was fed some bread and jelly and maybe some tea.

The next morning before leaving the room I had to sweep it out. I didn't think I got it that dirty overnight. I finally got my shoes back and was taken to the barracks where POWs are kept while waiting to be transported to a permanent POW camp.

On April 15 1944 a group of us walked to a railroad siding and boarded some box cars for our trip to Stalag 17B Krems, Austria. I boarded a box car with other injured POWs. I spent three days to sit and sleep on a couple 2x4s. Did not sleep or have much to eat. We finally arrived at Prisoner of War camp Stalag 17 B Krems, Austria around nine o'clock the evening of April 17 1944. By this time I was tired and hungry.

The first thing the Germans did on entering the camp was take some of my clothes from me which was OK. They took a sleeveless sweater, my electric one-piece suit and my jump suit. I had plenty of clothes left.

There was one POW in the boxcar I was in that had no clothes except maybe a pair of shorts on. He got my electrically heated suit. He definitely needed some clothes. He was recuperating from having a 20 mm shell go through his upper part of his left leg. The shell did not hit the bone but the leg needed a lot of work. He was later repatriated back to the States.

John Lewis Hurd, immortalized by the local photographer at Stalag 17 B Krems, Austria.

Next the Germans took my picture and assigned a Prisoner of War (KRIEGIE) number (105070) to me.

Afterwards my hair was cut with a pair of barbers clippers. Now I took a shower and all of us POWs that just arrived were standing in a room with our hair cut off and no clothes on while our clothes were being gassed to get rid of any bugs. After a while my clothes arrived and I put them on. My clothes had an odor of gas.

Now I was taken to a barracks where other POWs were already living and stayed with two other POWs at their bunk until Germans opened another compound, which had four empty barracks. Some time later I was moved to this other compound and found my permanent "home" in barracks 31B. I took a lower bunk with head against the out side wall.

The barracks had a wash room across the center which split the barracks into A and B sections. My bed was near to the wash room wall with a window between me and the next bunk which was against the wash room wall. I had plenty of elbow room. Most of the other bunks were close together. Some times during night I would look out of the window and gaze at the milky way.

I was given a spoon and a bowl to eat with. I would cook some meals in the wash room and with others cooking it became quite smoky. We had no cook stove at this time. We received American Government food parcels from time to time which helped keep us going. We got hot water from the camp kitchen for our morning coffee. I got a ration of bread each day. I would get about five small boiled potatoes for my noon meal and or my evening meal. Some times boiled rutabagas or pea soup with bugs in it or spinach with sand in it. I recall not eating any of the soups. I was not that hungry. There was one time I helped carry a tub of pea soup to the Russian POWs and they went at it eagerly.

One of the guys next to the one I was in fixed his mattress like a hammock so he wouldn't be sleeping on boards. I decided to fix my mattress like his too. He (Wally) helped me do mine. One night the head of my mattress broke loose and my head landed on the floor. Wally and I set some newspapers on fire for light and anchored my mattress back on the bunk. Wally is the one I teamed up with to play bridge after we learned how. Our bunks were built to sleep eight POWs.

On April 8 1945 we were forced to leave camp because the Russian Army was approaching from the east and the German garrison here didn't want to be captured by the them so we gathered into groups of 500 POWs and started walking toward the west. We walked for eighteen days and covered about 250 miles. We stopped at a wooded area on the banks of the Inn river near Braunau, Austria.

There was no shelter in the forest except trees. I made a one man shelter for myself from small tree branches I could pick up from the ground and break off trees. For coffee I would go down the banks of the Inn river and hold a tin can against the rocks because water was dripping out of the rocks. We were here in the forest for ten days.

On May 2 1945 an American Captain in a jeep came into the forest where I was and talked to the American POWs who were our leaders. The Captain was from General Patton's 13th Armoured Division who were advancing into southern Germany. Some one from our side of the Inn river swam across the river and made contact with General Patton's forces.

On May 6 1945 I and other POWs walked back to the town of Braunau, Austria and went into an empty factory building. GI trucks brought food to us. On May 7 we were trucked across the Inn river and into southern Germany. On May 8 1945 I boarded a C47 aircraft and was flown to France and trucked to Camp Lucky Strike. About ten days later I boarded an old Liberty Ship at Le Havre, France for my trip to the USA. On June 2 1945 I arrived at Boston Harbor. I was sent home on a 66 days furlough.

On November 6 1945 I received my Honorable Discharge. I received the Air Medal with one Oak Leaf Cluster, The Purple Heart Medal and the Prisoner of War Medal.

The Mission to BIG "B" And The ME-262

Narrated by George A. Paull 401st Bomb Group

I entered the US Army Air Corps in early 1944 and went through the usual basic training at an unusual place. Miami Beach was the location and we enjoyed being quartered in the tourist hotels. After various types of testing and medical exams, I was classified as pilot material and would soon be sent to a flight school. While waiting my dreams were shattered when we all attended a meeting called by General Yount. He broke the news to us that we would not be going to flight schools but instead we would all become aerial gunners due to a shortage overseas. This presumably was due to the fatalities of aerial gunners in combat. This was a terrible shock to me since I entered the service to become a pilot.

Since I had considerable radio operating experience working for Pennsylvania Central Airlines, and held the highest classification of Commercial Radio Licenses, I was sent directly to gunnery school, bypassing the usual Air Corps Radio School. I received my aerial gunnery training at Kingman, Arizona and from there I was sent to Lincoln, Nebraska to be assigned to a B-17 crew for combat crew training at Sioux City, Iowa. From there, our crew went again to Lincoln to get a new B-17G to fly to England.

Our first stop was at Bangor, Maine where we were snowed in for 10 days. We thought that was a good rest stop but then on to Gander, Newfoundland where we spent 16 days waiting for a sufficient tail wind to enable us to fly non-stop to Valley Wales. We accomplished that flight over the Atlantic Ocean with no problems. Upon arrival at Valley, Wales, we left our new B-17G and boarded a train to Stone, England and then to our airbase at Deenethorpe, Northamptonshire, England, home of the 401st Bomb Group Heavy. We were first assigned to the 615th Squadron and later we were briefly assigned to the 613th Squadron. We had participated in 10 missions prior to the BIG ONE and had bombed Molbis the day before on a 9 1/2 hour mission.

The crew.

Back row L to R:
Howard Ludwig Ball Turret Gunner, Bob Espy Tail Gunner, Gene Swift
Eng. / Top Turret Gunner, George Paull Radio Operator & Right Waist
Gunner, Yancy Collins Waist Gunner & George Knight Armorer
Toggelier.
Front row L to R:
Don Volz Co-pilot, Fred Eglin Pilot, Gordon Hutchison Bombardier (was
replaced prior to leaving the U.S. by John Sites, not pictured) & Frank
Schmidt Navigator.

It was during our assignment to the 613th that we experienced our most dangerous mission, the Capital City, Berlin was our target on March 18, 1945. Of course we knew that Berlin was the most protected city in Germany and this was emphasized at our early morning briefing, well before daylight that day. We were told that there would be at least 1,000 bombers on this mission and I found out later that there were 1200.

Our squadron was at the tail end of the huge formation and our plane was in one of the "tail end Charlie" positions. We had fighter cover overhead as we progressed toward the target,

On leave in London at Picadelly Circus: Yancy Collins, Bob Espy &
George.

Piccadilly

mainly P-51's I believe as they had droppable tip tanks giving them extra range and that at first gave us some consolation.

We knew that we would have many German fighter planes to contend with but hoped that the P-51's would keep them occupied while we worried about the flak batteries that were sending large amounts of anti-aircraft fire into the sky all around us. The sky was colored with smoke from the exploding shells. Then came the real shock.

Germany had the only jet powered fighter planes that were used in World War II, the ME-262. Until March 18 1945 we had never encountered one of these fighters but had seen photographs. Prior to this time, the German jets would attack a bomber formation head-on and they were quickly seen and challenged by American fighter planes.

Now their method of attack had changed. On this day over Berlin, they attacked from the rear, flying through the bomber vapor trails and were shooting down bombers before our fighter escort got the message that the ME-262s were attacking.

It was our vapor trail that at least one of the jets sneaked in on and our tail gunner, Bob Espy was the first to sound the fighter attack alarm.

I had been wearing my flak vest and helmet and I grabbed my parachute, fastened it to one ring on my harness so it would hang and not be in the way across my chest, and immediately headed from the radio room in the center of the plane to the right waist gun position. Yancy Collins was manning the other waist gun.

An ME-262 fired his cannon shells into the formation ahead of us, made a wide sweep to the right and then turned back toward us on a standard pursuit curve maneuver. I began firing my 50 calibres as he approached our formation and surprisingly he flew into a position parallel to our plane and slowed down considerably to our speed as he fired into the formation ahead of us.

I kept firing 50 calibre bullets into the ME-262, raking the torpedo tube-like engine on his left side mounted under the left wing and then when the engine did not catch fire, I continually raked the cockpit canopy and since 1 out of about every 6 of our bullets was a tracer, I could see exactly where my bullets were striking the cockpit.

Very soon the canopy flew off and our Navigator, Frank Schmidt, who was at the nose turret of our B-17, saw the ME-262 going down. The jet had turned slightly to the left under the nose of our plane. No one of our crew was able to witness the crash but there was no doubt that the airplane was disabled and the pilot probably killed. We were at an altitude of 26000 feet and the pilot could not survive without oxygen and that system was probably disabled.

I did not get a great feeling of satisfaction by having destroyed a fine flying machine, the ME-262 and possibly killing the pilot but this was WAR, a game of adversaries, and I had to do all possible to protect our plane and those planes ahead of us.

We returned from the Berlin Mission, BIG "B", surprisingly unscathed. We were so thankful to have survived the mission that upon our return to our airbase, Bob Espy, the tail gunner, Yancy Collins, the left waist gunner, Gene Swift, the engineer, and I met with the Base Chaplain in the little Chapel for a short service giving thanks to God for our safe return.

Within a few days, we were transferred back to the 615th Squadron which supplied Lead Crews and Deputy Lead Crews for 401st bombing missions and those crews had to have special training. While training, we missed the next 16 missions that the 401st participated in and flew only training missions around England and Scotland until April 14. On that day we flew on a "milk run" mission to Royan, France where a pocket of German troops held out after most of the rest of France had been liberated. Then came missions to Regensburg, Dresden, and the last mission that our bomb group participated in, to Brandenburg on April 20, 1945.

Soon the war was over at last and our next mission was a humanitarian one. At Linz, Austria, there were Thousands of French soldiers who had been prisoners of war in Germany for 4 years.

We removed all of the armament from the B17's and put some flooring in the fuselage of the bombers aft of the radio room and flew to Linz to help return these French soldiers to France. En route to Linz, we flew over a number of German cities at low level to witness the destruction that Allied bombing had caused.

We loaded twenty French soldiers in each bomber and I will never forget that although these men were weak and sick from having been force marched prior to Germany's surrender, they were able to stand up and cheer loudly as we approached Paris.

Prior to leaving Linz, I had removed the plexiglass cover over the radio room to allow some cooling while we were on the ground, as it was a very warm day. In flight it got much colder and I began to replace the cover overhead when the slipstream caught the forward edge of the cover and while balancing it on the rear edge of the opening, my hat flew off and I thought I would be next. As I struggled, I had visions of flying out of the opening and being cut in two by the vertical stabilizer. Fortunately some of the French soldiers were sitting on the floor in the radio room and they came to my assistance and pulled me down just in time.

Back to the ME-262. It was a remarkable plane and if it had been produced in greater numbers and if Hitler had listened to General Adolf Galland's ideas of utilizing that plane, we would have lost many more bombers.

Many years after the war ended, in 1985 to be exact, I had the pleasure of meeting General Galland when he appeared as a guest speaker just outside of Washington, D.C. The occasion was a "Reach for the Skies—The European Campaign" along with a display of Aviation Art featuring scenes from World WarII. This was organized by Aviation Art Studio owner Virginia Bader.

I was able to chat with the General and he autographed my copy of his book "The First and the Last." In his book, he mentions that on that Berlin Mission on March 18, 1945, 17 bombers were so badly damaged by flak that they had to divert to Russia and that 25 American Bombers were shot down by German fighter planes. There were 37 ME-262's defending Berlin on that day.

At our meeting in 1985 I asked General Galland if there was any way for me to find out who was the unfortunate pilot that I shot down over Berlin. Galland's ME-262 group JV44 was based at Munich but he suggested that I write to the German Fighter Pilots Association.

I didn't get around to it until just recently when I sent an e-mail to the group and was advised that only 2 ME-262s were shot down that March 18, one by a P-51 and the jet pilot was severely wounded and had to have one leg amputated.

The other jet was shot down by bomber defensive fire and fell to his death 5 Km south-west of Perleberg, Germany at approximately 11:10 to 11:15.

That was no doubt the one that challenged me on that day over Berlin.

Rice & Rose

Narrated by Edward J. Rice 401st Bomb Group
(Written by Edward J. Rice September 27 1989)

The war being over for 44 years—before being questioned as to why I had not put my experiences down on paper, I find time has dimmed many happenings in my memory. I think it's natural for anyone to forget some of the hard times and remember only the good.

Had I known when I enlisted in the Army Air Force (AAF) in 1942 that the following story was to be my life for the next 3 years, I'm sure I would have had second thoughts about putting my name on the dotted line! But a war was going on and it looked as if it would be but a short time before my age bracket would be called and I would have a chance for the Air Force if I enlisted...and that's where I wanted to be—I thought.

I was inducted on my Dad's birthday—September 17, 1942. Dad went with me to Eau Claire where I was to get transportation out, and we lifted a few together. I can't remember if I left by train or bus. A succession of events carried me from Eau Claire to Milwaukee to Texas for basic training and Aviation School at Sheppard Fields, Texas.

From there I went to factory school at Lockheed Vega—an aircraft plant in Burbank, California and to Gunnery School at Las Vegas, Nevada. Things were really getting serious now.

Mounted in the rear of a cockpit of AT-6 fighter planes were 30 caliber guns. Fun? Yes, of course I mean the part where you shoot a hole through a wind sock pulled by obsolete AT-11 planes. But that other part where you cease fire and the plane tips over on one wing…drops for the ground…down…down…until it's time to pull this baby out. Everything going from head to the other end—or is my head down here too? Oh well, at least I can't fly out—I'm glued to the seat. I begin thinking to myself now—'Are you sure this "Flight Maintenance Gunner" position that you signed on for is what you want?' 'Why not the ground crew mechanic job?' Too late now, buddy!

From here we are headed for Moses Lake, Washington and will fly on the B-17 Flying Fortress. The B-17 takes us on training missions over the Pacific Ocean. Then to Walla Walla, Washington and more gunnery training. Our 10 man crew is put together here and we fly as a crew from now on—but we don't fly over seas—we go by boat on November 2, 1943 for the European Theater and land in Scotland on November 9. We spent a week in a kind of rugged replacement center before being assigned to the 401st Bomb Group.

Two crews were to a hut or barrack. We are replacing a crew that was shot down the day before. My squadron number is 613, but I'm not superstitious. There are a lot of things going through my head though. We are kept busy—one day I got the call.

My crew is not scheduled to fly, but I am. I and my right waist gunner, Hubert Holland from Georgia, will fly our first mission with another crew who somehow had 2 men on the sick list.
We bombed an airfield in France which was not a long trip really, but was long enough. I found out what FLAK was. The French coast was lined with flak batteries. No thanks. From now on I will fly all of my missions with my own crew…except the last one.

At this time heavy bombers must fly 25 combat missions before they go home for furlough. It was a good thing that nobody knew what the percentage rate for completion of 25 missions was. The 8th AF initiating the strategic daylight bombing of Germany and the price was going to be high.

The Royal Air Force (RAF) bombed at night only. Our crew was destined to finish 25 against the odds. We only had three engines running a number of times and once made it across the English Channel only to land at the first airfield we could sit down on. I flew 30 combat missions out of England between 1943 and 1944. It took me a year and a day to complete the 30th mission however, so I should say 1943 thru 1945. The other sad part of this story is that we were supposed to fly 25 missions only before we could go stateside on furlough.

Arriving back to base after our 25th mission we buzzed the tower, waved, almost blew down the warm-up tents put there for the line crew. Our pilot was highly reprimanded for this. Extra Scotch we saved from previous flights was brought out and we drank well.

The original crew.

Back row L to R:
LT R. L. Stelzer Pilot, LT W.L. Johnson Co-pilot, LT H.L. Hobbs Navigator
& LT R. Warren Bombardier.
Front row L to R:
S/SGT J. O. Pack Engineer, S/SGT E. J. Rice Ass. Eng., S/SGT T. H.
Holland Right Waist Gunner,
SGT J. P. Black Ball Turret Gunner J. P. Black, S/SGT R. G. Smith, SGT
J.H. Nicely.
(S/SGT Don Hecker replaced S/SGT Smith and flew 30 missions)

Two days later came the blow—prior to the date we finished our 25th mission, new orders had been issued from the States. The requirement now will be 30 missions to be eligible for furlough to the States.

They can't do this, we said—They did it. I found out later that this was not a full truth. What happened was that the four officers (Pilot, Co-Pilot, Navigator & Bombardier) were flown home for their furlough, but the rest of the crew would receive their vacation in England. What a vacation—in a war torn country with black outs—curfews and air raids.

Part of the reason I thought we were fighting this war was for equal rights. Oh well, I didn't know this until long afterwards, so it didn't hurt so much at that time. All ten of us were back to pull the last five missions. They turned out to be 5 Berlin area missions in a row.

The first 25 missions had brought me the D.F.C. (Distinguished Flying Cross) and the Air Medal with 3 oak leaf clusters—Also a presidential citation for the Oscherleben Mission in which the 401st bore the brunt of the attack.

Our B-17 was named "The Saint and Ten Sinners". It had taken good care of us. Now on my 30th and last mission, I was to fly on "Old Massa". My Co-pilot, top turret gunner and myself are the only members of my original crew on this one. However, I did know the pilot, navigator and tail gunner of "Old Massa".

The mission was proceeding as usual. Never can tell what might happen when approaching the enemy coast. They have flak batteries that are moved up and down the English channel by boats so you can't always know where they are. We are routed around any known batteries, at least on the way to the target. However, when on a long mission, we may have to come home the way the crow flies or run out of gas and that, you know, can become very interesting.

We are flying up front on this one. Good of the Colonel, not to put us in "Purple Heart Corner" on our last mission. The different groups and squadrons take turns flying the low box of the formation. The tail end formation in the low box we call "Purple Heart Corner". A little flak as we cross the coast, but not hitting right where we are. Our fighter escort was right on time and they must have scared the Luftwaffe away today. They don't like our P-47s.

The flak is coming now—we are on the bomb run. Bomb bay doors are open, there will be no evasive action now until the bombs are gone—straight ahead, like the crow flies again, right through the middle of a big black cloud of flak—that damn flak—it's always here. I hate flak—I hate flak—you hear me?

Bombs away! This old bird does a little jig when getting rid of the bomb load. We are on our way out now. Damn that flak. Won't it ever stop—oh oh—we got some—we got some in the wrong place again—sure enough—we got it on No. 4 engine—home on 3 engines again. I hope we are going home on 3.

We move out of the flak and start to breathe easier. Flying a little low and offside now as we have trouble keeping up. This could be bad. Being out of the formation makes us vulnerable for fighter attacks as the fire power the formations affords us is lost. It seems our escort is doing a good job. The Jerry's aren't coming back today. Once out of the flak zone, they usually move in again. About 100 miles from Holland it happens, so close to home yet so far.

A loud, hard, explosion toward the front of our plane woke me from my attempts at catching a few winks. I had never felt or heard one exactly like this before and I know this is it. But I did the right thing for a change, I asked God for help just as the second blast went off right beside me.

The plane was flying level as a die, but the whole tail was gone. Just a great big hole looking out at the sky. No parachute. The blast blew everything toward the front of the plane. The plane chutes were next to the radio compartment wall. The plane can't fly this way.

Everything is going thru my head fast. The next thing I'm doing is kneeling by the ball turret and snapping my chest chute on. I'm bringing the other chute back with me. I don't know why. The right waist gunner, Cole, is lying crumpled on the floor of the fuselage. No Blood, is he dead or unconscious?

Turning him enough to snap on his chute I felt the plane lurch. Something inside is telling me, get out! Couldn't see the static line to hook the chute to. Must have blown off with the tail. I got to get out of here!

I ran straight out into space thru the open fuselage. The chute opened and snapped me up and around. The plane was diving straight down or so it appeared. It nosed into the ground and exploded. Fire and smoke shot skyward.

It would have been a nice quiet sunny day without the war going on. The smoke climbed straight up, higher and higher.

There are soldiers and civilians coming across the grain field in which I must land. The plane must have went into a dive while I was sleeping as it seemed to be about 12 to 14,000 feet when I jumped.

We were hit at about 22,000 to 24,000 feet. God alone, it seems, is the only one who could have leveled off "Old Massa" long enough for me to get out.

There is another chute in the air below me and behind me. Somebody else got out. I look for more but see none. The Germans will be practically on top of me when I land. I'm feeling very low now. This is really it, trying to remember how I was supposed to land. I hit on my feet right and then over kind of head first, getting shook up a little, but I'm OK.

The soldiers are shouting at me with rifles at ready. I think they are saying, hands up, as they keep coming toward me. I'm on my knees, unsnapping the chute and for some reason was paying little attention to them. I wasn't scared I don't think or maybe I was scared stiff—just completely given up maybe.

I was grabbed by the arms. A civilian looking guy was in front of me and reached for my hand to pull my mitten off. I don't know how they stayed on all this time. The whole back of the left mitt was shot off and when removed it looked like the back of my hand also.

The soldiers motioned their guns in the direction for me to go and I was marched across the field to a small building that seemed to serve as a first-aid field station where the wound was temporarily bandaged. Through a window in the building I saw more guards marching another prisoner by—it was my Navigator LT Bennett. I made a start for the door to shout at him but was held back. He never saw me unless he happened to see my chute in the air.

A limousine arrived with a chauffer and some high ranking German official. I was put in the back seat with him and the car took off for I knew not where. It turned out to be a prison hospital near Osnabrück. Here my wounds were taken care of a little better. It seems I had a small piece of shrapnel in my right thumb also.

An English flyer was in the room I was assigned to. He had broken a leg. The Russians were in the room next to us but we couldn't see them. We could reach out of the barred window and around to shake a hand or as happened later, pass a cigarette butt.

A week passed and then one day the door opened and a surprise package was wheeled in. It was my tail gunner, not in A-1 shape, but there he was with a surprise look on his face that I am sure resembled mine—what a day!

Tony rode the tail down that was blown off "Old Massa" and lived to tell about it.

Anthony F. Rose from 1322 S. Campbell Avenue, Chicago IL. His story was that he came to after the explosion. He was floating down in the tail section and concussion from the explosion had folded the ammo boxes across the tail section behind him. As he put it, "I couldn't get out even if I could get out". Then he passed out again. I don't blame him, I would have too. The next thing he knew, he hit a building of some kind and bounced off. Then people were cutting him out.

Tony had a full package of Lucky Strike cigarettes with him. He couldn't smoke, it made him sick. I'll never know how he managed to hang on to them. I and the Englishman shared them along with the Russians. I passed a butt thru the bars one day and a Russian put a ring on my finger. I still have the ring!!

Another morning we awoke with air raid sirens again, but this time they didn't stop. They stayed on all day. We knew something different was happening and guessed it. The invasion was on.

Another day and we were leaving the hospital. Armed guards led us to an automobile which took us to a train which took us to another rail station and there taken to solitary confinement for interrogation. A week or two of this is supposed to loosen your tongue. Of course, if you don't know anything then there is nothing to loosen.

The cell was solid on 3 sides with metal bars and door on the other. A high ceiling with a small window toward the top of the outside wall. A wood plank bed with one blanket. Call the guard if you have to go potty. A tin cup of warm black stuff that didn't taste at all like coffee and a slice of heavy dark bread with some kind of thin syrup came 2 or 3 times a day until they were done pumping you. Usually they call you in one day, then skip 2-4 days and call you again.

The last day they call me in, the English speaking German who went to school in N.Y., so he said, told me the answers to all the questions he had been asking plus knowing the names of ranking officers from my group, whom I didn't even know.

From Dulag Luft (the interrogation center near Frankfurt) located S & East of Berlin, we went by rail spending a very unrestful night in box cars in the Berlin RR yards. Too many people to a box car and not a bit comfortable. The RAF didn't bomb the yards this night nor did USAF before we left in the morning. My last 5 missions being the Berlin area, you can guess what I was thinking of most of the night.

The guards hustled us out this morning to do our morning job along side the railroad tracks, then back into the cars and railed to a station in N. E. Germany "Grottyschow", I believe was the name.

Most of my imprisonment was spent at Stalag Luft IV, but the daily routines were pretty much the same at each place. Roll calls could come any time of the day and could range from 2 to 5 times a day. The only 2 roll calls one could bank on for time was the sunrise and sunset.

Inspections came whenever they felt like it. While everyone is outside the barracks for roll call, the Germans go thru and check everything and if they felt like it a full inspection on this day, then you'd find your bunk and the whole room in disarray when you returned.

Our mattresses were big burlap sacks filled with straw. Getting the straw replaced when it was worn down to nothing required many reminders by our compound leaders before the wagons would bring us new straw. The mattresses were stuffed as full as possible as there was only six slats in the bunk to hold them up and keep it from sagging.

The winter months were uncomfortably cold. Fuel was rationed very close. A small pot stove in each room of the barracks heated the 16—20 man room. The people more than the fuel is what heated the room. The fuel being a compressed brick of sawdust and something black like oil. Don't know for sure what it was, but it did burn once you got it lit.

The rooms were very stuffy in the winter and the men welcomed a walk around the compound after roll call. You could walk around the inside of the compound, but stay well clear of the warning wire which was placed about 20 feet inside the 10 foot high barbed wire. There were 2-10 feet high barbed wire fences with rolled barbed wire between them and stretched around the whole camp. Guard towers were on each corner with machine guns and spotlights. Guards with dogs walked patrol at night.

Aside from walking the compound, there was not much to do in the winter. Comfortably that is. The rooms being crowded with one table and a couple of benches, most of the time we sat on our bunk and half of us had top bunks. I for one took the top.

I had a friend, Gerald Quakenbushch, from Wisconsin, he had the bottom bunk. He was still recovering from a broken leg. We played cards. However, with home made cards. The deck was so thick because of the thickness of the cardboard that it had to be shuffled one third of a deck at a time.

We wrote letters but most of them never got further than the Germans who censored them. A lot of poetry was written, however, which was passed around for all to read. I'm sure we would have had mail every day or so, but it came so seldom that mail call became a joke.

Whenever our barracks got hold of a pair of traveling scissors, we could have a "hair-cutting bee". Either exchange haircuts or someone would cut yours for something from your Red Cross Parcel. Mustaches were a fad for quite a while.

One barracks size building was both latrine and washroom for the compound. In the winter it was an oversized outhouse and no one stayed in there any longer than they had to. Needless to say, there were a lot of beards and mustaches walking the compound.

The spring would change much of this and also enlighten a lot of spirits. Some were fashioning soft balls out of whatever could be rolled or twisted into a ball. Our compound leaders were usually someone who could talk some German and they would try to con some of these articles we needed from the enemy. The bat might have to be a slat from some ones bunk. But the game was a welcome diversion and sometimes even became serious.

Food would have taken up a lot more of our time if available, but unless our Red Cross Parcels got thru, it was better if we kept our minds off that subject. The Germans gave us what they called Ersatz—black like coffee, but it sure wasn't. It came for breakfast with dark bread with a sweetened syrup on it. The next meal was soup. There may be some potatoes in it but it was more apt to be kohlrabi or cabbage and then one bowl with a slice of dark bread.

While at Stalag Luft IV I chanced to come face to face with a red head I had known throughout my high school years. Red Knoble from Altoona, Wisconsin, whom I had met on the basketball floor each year up until graduation. That was a great day and from then on we had some nice get-togethers.

Then there was another day when the camp was being partially evacuated, some would stay as they not capable of marching. My tail gunner, Tony Rose, would stay. I told him I'd see him in Chicago when the war was over—and I did!

I stayed at Luft IV until February 1945 when the Russian offensive was driving in from the East. As this would be the second march for me, I was smart enough to fall in on an inside column. If you are on an outside column and things are not moving just right, you are more vulnerable to a rifle butt or bayonet. This march will be different, we will march west instead of east as the Russians are coming in from the east.

We end the march at Stalag Luft I. It's an officers POW camp at Barth, Germany. I became sick shortly after arriving at Barth. I had a very high fever so I was taken to a special barracks that served as their hospital. I'm sure that hospital is the wrong word, but for want of a better word, I must use it.

They treated me for Diphtheria. If not for receiving shots in the rear-end it was a better bed and it was warmer here. They found a little more food for me and first thing I knew, I was getting well. I tried playing the sick game as long as I could, but they were wise to that game and kicked me out.
On May 1, 1945 we awoke to find the Germans had evacuated the camp, No Guards, Nobody, we were on our own, Free—almost! Contacts had been made with the Russians and we were told to stay put and don't leave the camp until further orders.

I would not say that these orders were followed to the letter because a whole POW camp with no enemy guards, and within a very short time, no fences either, would be very hard to control, much less, stay put.

This camp, being on an inlet from the Baltic Sea, was a fisherman's paradise also. Boats were on the bay and with a little ingenuity, the nets were pulled and the camp was soon cooking fish and also eels. On the peninsular they were butchering cattle and we were soon to be eating beef. The Red Cross Parcels were found and distributed to all. We had a feast!!!

The nearby villages were checked out for something to drink and the wine flowed. The Russians came up later with the Vodka. Our Red Cross Parcels afforded us cigarettes, which we exchanged with the Russians for their brand. We got beat on that deal but we were comrades in arms and were drinking to many years of friendship to come. Take the whole package and thanks for dropping in.

After we wake up from this one, things will be different. We are still prisoners, so to speak, but our captors are not enemies.

Landing strips were being cleared and by May 8, 1945 I would complete my 30th mission and go home.

We were flown out of Luft I to France where we were to stay until transportation came for us. We slept in tents. Planes were landing every day but not for us. Checking with a couple of pilots I found they were coming across the channel from England and if my C.O. would supply clearance papers, he could take us back with him.

The C.O. checked to see if the 401st Bomb Group was still in England. They were, so he gave me papers to go. Getting there I find that the flying crews had flown home the day before and only part of the base personnel were there. I must still wait for the next available transportation home. Finally made it aboard the Queen Mary.

That Statue of Liberty was beautiful to see !!!

"A Kriegies' Consolation"
by POW Edward J. Rice

A sleepless night, a worried mind,
And why?, I cannot say.
Man surely wasn't ever designed,
to live in such a way.

Oh why don't God tear out the leaf,
in the book of human life;
Which associates the world with grief
and locks it there in mortal strife.

Despite these thoughts and other too,
Which come and go, as thoughts will do,
Despite the troubles everywhere,
I've found a consolation here.

For in my simple, flustered mind,
One dream contents my lasting stay;

Thoughts of loved ones left behind,
Dreams of our meeting again some day.

Rose & Rice 1992.

"Old Massa"
Monday May 8 1944

The actual story of Anthony F. Rose, Tail gunner 401st Bomb Group on the "Flying Fortress" "Old Massa" as told by himself:

When returning from a Berlin raid, on the eight of May 1944, our Fortress, "Old Massa", suffered two direct flak hits. One of which severed the tail section off just forward of the tail wheel.

The left ammo box was bent inward from the explosion, and I found myself trapped in my rear gun position. I was wounded, and lost consciousness. When I came to, I felt the tail roll over once, then unconsciousness again.

We fell, myself and the tail, 24,000 feet, and finally landed on a small guard hut, where the Germans found me.

What I believe saved my life is the fact that I was unconscious and perfectly relaxed, coupled with the fact that the small guard hut broke my fall.

Nellson Liddle meets with Rose in 1948

By Nelson Liddle 401st Bomb Group

After the war I reenlisted in the Air Force in 1947.

I was assigned to Langley Air Force Base in Virginia. In a casual conversation soon after I discovered that Anthony Rose, who also had reenlisted, had also served in the 401st, during the air war over Europe. So naturally we started exchanging stories. We both had been shot down in May 1944.

He then told me of his amazing story of falling to the ground in the severed tail section of their B-17 bomber. Soon after I was sent to Frankfurt, Germany to serve on the Berlin Airlift. I lost all contact with Rose, but could never forget his story.

Many years later I obtained the 401st casualty report and found Anthony Rose's crew in it. I discovered the names of three survivors of that crash. Two others besides Rose. One was Edward Rice.

I then checked in my 401st BG Association Membership Directory and found Edward Rice's address and phone number. I gave him a call and found he was a crew member on the bomber with Rose. Also found he had an amazing story to tell which he sent me thru the mail.

Called him again to get his permission to send the Rice and Rose story to Erik Dyreborg to be published in his book.

Nelson Liddle
Blacksburg
Virginia
May 10 2002.

The War Years—
The Way It Happened To Me!

Narrated by Harry T. Watson 401st Bomb Group

On my birthday, September 4, 1942, when I became 20 years old, I went to Dallas from my home in Fort Worth, Texas, to join up. The U.S. direct involvement in the war had occurred on December 7, 1941, when the Japanese attacked the Hawaiian Islands and the U.S. immediately declared war on Japan; a few days later Germany and Italy declared war on the U.S. At that time young men were eligible for the draft at age 20, and to join the services prior to that age required the approval of their parents. My mother would not agree to me joining any earlier than was required so I had waited for those nine months until my 20th birthday.

My intention was to join the air service of either the Army, Navy or Marines. I had decided I would try the Army Air Corp first or try the others if I was first unsuccessful. I really did not want the Navy as I had little or no interest in the water and the possibility of being on a ship for long periods. The Navy trained the Marine personnel so it too was a lower choice.

A number of young men were applying that same day. We were first given a series of aptitude tests and then a physical examination as a first qualification step. All men were required to be at least high school graduates, which I was, having graduated in May 1940. My aptitude test scores were apparently satisfactory as well as the physical exam. During the prior nine months I had been working out at the Y.M.C.A.

almost every day and was in very good physical condition, weighing about 160 to 165 pounds, and was 5 ft. 9 in. tall. These were good physical specs for the Air Corp. The extremely short, tall or those too heavy were automatically eliminated.

Those of us who were accepted were sent home and were told we would be notified when we were to report for active duty. We knew there was to be a delay because the training facilities were being developed and were presently not adequate to accept all the potential flyers that were needed.

Also, new airplanes had to be manufactured and production was not yet up to the needed level. Shortly after I joined, accepted applicants were sent to various colleges for academic training while they waited. Since my group was not included in this program, we knew we would be called to active training more quickly. It was kind of a mixed bag as the immediate call up and college training would have been beneficial but the prospect of a delay in flying training was the trade off.

I returned home to my job to await the call up. My physical training was intensified but other than that there was not much I could do other than wait. The war had intensified, in mid 1942 General Doolittle led a group of B-25 bombers launched from a carrier over Japan. Much flying was going on in the pacific area and the first of the heavy bombers from England were trying to make a difference flying over Germany, France and the Low Countries.

Finally, by orders dated February 24, 1943, I was directed to report to Dallas, on March 20, 1943, for appointment as Aviation Cadet and assignment to duty. Two days later on March 22, we boarded the train for the trip to Santa Ana, California, the Aviation Cadet Pre-Flight Training Center. Interestingly, my cousin Wallace Ballard, from Seagoville, Texas, was on the same orders and we proceeded together for our assignments. (Wallace, my father's sister's child, was sent to Navigation school, graduated and was assigned to a B-17 group in

Italy. He was shot down, became a prisoner until the end of the war and stayed in the Air Force for twenty years and retired as a Lt. Colonel. He later worked in Houston as the administrator of a law firm and died when he was in his fifties.)

At Santa Ana we were given an extensive series of tests, both mental and physical, to test for coordination, dexterity, eye worthiness and ability to withstand high altitude flying, among others. While this was going on we were taught how to march, stand guard duty, clean latrines and how to pull K.P. duty (kitchen police). These are many of the things that a future officer needed to know. We were also lectured on how to behave as an officer and gentlemen. We learned how to properly make up a bed, with blocked corners, and the blanket pulled tight enough so that a quarter would bounce if dropped on it. We learned how to keep our living space (what there was of it) neat and clean and with our clothes on hangers all buttoned at the top and all facing the same way. All brass buckles and insignia and shoes were to be kept perfectly shined at all times.

Military life at this time fit me fine. I even loved the food. Never in my young life had I had all the fruit juice I wanted. We would find ½ gallon cartons of orange, grape, apple or pineapple juice available on the mess table so that we could drink to our hearts content. (Some day I will tell you of the great depression and of those who did not have enough food to eat or drink—not me though). I liked the marching, the "spit and polish" and the physical training that was a part of each day's activity.

All was not work as we did get some week end leave and were able to go to Los Angeles, Long Beach and the near by coastal towns. I was lucky in that an older friend from Houston had a friend from school days who lived in Santa Ana and was married to a doctor. They entertained me and were able to take me to various places by car since they had gasoline coupons, gasoline being rationed. They introduced me to others my age and although the time was limited, we did have some nice times while at Santa Ana.

The day finally came for assignments and I was accepted in the Bombardier training program. This was not wholly to my liking, as I had preferred being a pilot. The tests we had taken were to show aptitude so I was satisfied to accept the assignment and move on. This was certainly better than having been washed out and been sent to gunners school as some had been. There was another factor, that of supply and demand, perhaps there was a greater need for Bombardiers at that time.

In May, 1943, my group of Bombardier cadets were sent to Roswell, New Mexico for detailed training. Here we were to learn how to use the famous Norden bombsight that allowed us to drop bombs with great accuracy from great heights, 30,000 feet or so. Upon graduation we were to become 2nd Lieutenants in the U. S. Army Air Corp (now the Air Force, a separate branch of the armed services) and would receive our silver wings.

We attended classes each day as well as flying. We were given such courses as aerodynamics, airplane engine and airplane frame mechanics, navigation, meteorology and aircraft recognition. We were expected to study in the evenings if we were to be proficient in our studies. I was fortunate in having a very smart roommate, so he and I worked hard and upon graduation he was first and I was second in academic standing for our class. Our wings when presented were inscribed to denote our class academic standing.We continued with some military training and physical training. Like on one of our overnight bivouacs we were bombed with sacks of flour. One of these so called bombs landed right in the middle of the mess table which caused quite a mess, not to mention the bad tasting food. All personnel had disbursed so no one was hurt. We had to know how to swim and do endurance running. As I mentioned earlier, I was in good physical condition and was our top long distance runner. My technique was to stay near the leaders of the pack during the run and then to out run them in the sprint at the end.

Flying consisted of practice in twin engine planes outfitted with practice bombs (filled with sand) and the Norden bombsight. We practiced dropping bombs from various heights. Scores were maintained for each cadet and I have that record to this day. My score didn't look particularly impressive but was obviously good enough for graduation.

After about four months we were ready for graduation. We were given money to buy our new officer uniforms and on October 3, 1943, we were commissioned 2nd Lieutenants and awarded our silver Bombardier wings at a very nice ceremony at the base auditorium. My mother, Sister Kathryn and a high school friend, Weldon Wilson, drove out to attend the big event.

My first assignment after a 10-day leave at home was to Salt Lake City Air Force base. Salt Lake City was an assembly base where crews were put together for the next phase of training. We didn't have much to do except wait for our crew assignments. Fortunately for me my older brother, Floyd, lived in Salt Lake City. He was about seventeen years older than I and had been working away from home as long as I could remember. It was great being with him and his wife, Alberta (they had no children). As I have said, I had a good bit of time off so was able to stay with them some. They entertained me and introduced me to friends.

In late November, 1943, we were assigned to a B-17 Bomber crew and were directed to go to Avon Park, Florida, for crew training. We left Salt Lake City by train to make the long trip across the country to Florida. We were on the train on Thanksgiving Day. Nice people along the way came to the train when we stopped and passed out turkey sandwiches to us. The trip took about three or four days and nights.

Avon Park was the first time the entire crew was together. We were assigned a B-17 Bomber for practice flying . The airfield was about ten miles from the town of Avon Park, way out in the Florida swamps. It was said that the swamps were so thick and inaccessible that when planes crashed in the swamp, recovery crews could only recover the flyers and instruments from the planes but could not salvage the plane itself because of the difficulty in getting in and out of the swamp. Also, there were alligators out there. We decided we didn't want anything to do with that crashing thing. We practiced formation flying, navigation and bombing in preparation for overseas duty.

We got a few leaves while there and were able to go to Palm Beach or Miami. This involved a four or five-hour bus ride or train rides down through the Everglade National Forest. Also, we were able to visit some of the local towns including Winter Haven, Lake Wales, Sebring and Orlando. Florida was a different world than what it is today with Disney Land and all the development that has come with it. The towns were all relatively small and very laid back.

Like California, there were fruit orchards everywhere. You only had to step out the door to find an orange tree where you could pick your own fruit. I spent Christmas day 1943 at the airbase. We had a nice lunch at the officers club, a very nice facility located on the shore of a large lake. Some of us officers went swimming in the lake with some young ladies who had come in from some of the near by towns to comfort the lonely airmen. The weather and the water were warm. The lakes for the most part are quite shallow with nice sand bottoms. Thank goodness, no alligators were sighted.

We completed our training in late February. We left our planes and were transferred to Langley Field, Virginia. We made the trip by train again. During the trip up north we encountered what we would call a "blue norther", a real shock after having been in Florida for the winter. Upon arrival at Langley, we were assigned to barracks that were not heated. I don't remember the temperature but I will always remember how very cold we were. We had a few blankets but they were inadequate and we resorted to putting additional mattresses over us to try to keep warm.

We were attached to a Search & Attack Group at Langley. Primarily we were to practice with some new radar equipment that was being put into service. The assignment was short and a month later, on March 23, three of our gunners and I were sent to Fort Hamilton, near New York City, for shipment overseas. It was not said but we knew England was our destination. The other crewmembers, the Pilot, Co-pilot, Navigator, radio operator, engineer and assistant engineer, were assigned a plane, which they flew over to England. Several priority non-flyer officers also flew with them including a General.

The Crew 1943.

Back row L to R: LT Harry T. Watson Bombardier, LT Albert L. Hanson Pilot, LT Fred A. Craytor Co-pilot & LT Carl Salamone Navigator., Front row L to R: S/SGT Donald L. Koons Bal Turret Gunner, S/SGT Bernard K. Green Nose Turret Gunner, S/SGT Lester D. Lyall Waist Gunner, T/SGT Donald F. Sears Radio Operator, T/SGT Homer G. Murray Eng. / Top Turret Gunner & S/SGT Dale C. Martz Tail Gunner

While at Langley we got leaves and visited Richmond and Norfolk, Virginia, one of the main Navy towns. I was amazed at the number of white navy caps we saw as we walked down the streets. Also while in Norfolk, I went to the first and only real vaudeville show I ever saw. It was great fun, filled with a great variety of acts, mostly slapstick.

We were at Fort Hamilton just a short time to get ready for the ship ride to England. We did receive on short notice a leave to visit New York City. We were dismissed in the afternoon and had to return the next morning. Someone told us how to get the subway into New York City and there I was, a little ol' country boy from Fort Worth, Texas, in the middle of that big city. We walked around the Times Square area, impressed by the sights and lights. I finally went to a movie and a personal appearance by Jimmy Durante. He did his act of playing the piano and singing. As he proceeded parts of the piano start falling off and by the end the whole thing fell apart. It was a wonderful experience.

Back at Fort Hamilton the next day we packed all our clothes and gear in one foot locker, one duffel bag and a B-4 Bag, a large suitcase with large pockets on both sides. It was amazing how much clothing could be put in that bag. The B-4 bag was to be kept with us and the other items were stored as if on an airplane with your carry on and your checked items. Our ship assignment was the Queen Elizabeth. During peacetime she carried about three or four thousand passengers and crew. For our trip, there were sixteen thousand service people and crew. I was assigned to a cabin on C deck, a very nice first class cabin that pre-war was for two passengers. We had sixteen bunks in the cabin but only fifteen officers. The empty bunk as well as the bathroom, which wasn't operative, was used to store our bags. We were crowded to say the least.

When going up the gang plank, the walk way for boarding, the B-4 bag being carried by the officer in front of me popped open like a can of breakfast biscuits. Clothes spilled out and the several of us near by scurried to help him grab them before they fell overboard into the water. Someone had some leather cord, which we used to hold his bag together as we continued to board.

On April 1, 1944, we pulled out of the harbor bound for England. The Queen Elizabeth was a fast ship, could do about 30 knots, so sailed without escort since she could outrun submarines and other surface war ships. The trip was to take about three days but actually took four as we were told she had to sail well away from the normal course to avoid a storm. I do not remember seeing any bad weather. The trip was mostly uneventful. We had access to most all of the ship except an area that was segregated for a large group of female nurses who were going to England for assignment also. We only had two meals served each day, but that was plenty since we weren't very active. I had purchased a box of almond Hershey bars before embarkation to supplement the GI issued food. We had to wait in line for a long time before admittance to the rather large dining room. The food was served cafeteria style.

We docked at Glasgow, Scotland, disembarked and were immediately loaded on trains for transfer to a holding camp near Manchester in the North of England. The train ride took several hours and we arrived at the camp before dark. My only impression of Scotland was seeing red headed and red faced little kids waving to us from the towns as we passed through.

The camp was very plain and we were crowded in rooms with double bunks, as many as could be placed in the rooms. Again, we had little to do, so we just read books and played football for exercise. We received our first leave in England. A group of us went to Nottingham, which was not too far from the camp. There we visited the famous Nottingham Castle. This was my first experience of seeing an Old World medieval castle, complete with high stone walls, great wood doors, turrets and a surrounding mote. We did not get to visit the inside as you can do today. Visiting castles was not a very necessary wartime activity.

After a couple of weeks we were transferred to an air base near London for some ground training. Some of the bombardiers (including me) were informed that we were to attend dead reckoning (DR) navigation training school. DR navigation is the determination of the airplane position from the record of the courses flown, the distance made, and the known or estimated drift without the aid of celestial observations. We were also taught to use various radio aids that had been developed to assist us in the navigation process. We were informed that our stateside-trained navigators were being sent to radar training and we, the bombardiers were to become the crew navigators. One of our two waist gunners was repositioned to the nose at the bombardier's position (without a bombsight) to man the forward nose gun position. He was taught to observe the lead plane in the formation and to drop our bombs using a toggle switch when the lead plane dropped theirs.

In mid May, 1944, upon completion of the navigation course, I was transferred to the 401st Bomb Group (Heavy) at Deenethorpe, England, where I rejoined the rest of my stateside crew. The air base had previously been an English bomber base, which was transferred to the Americans in 1943. It had been built around the little town of Deenethorpe and some of the town structures were still being used for base functions. The location was about 80 miles northwest of London in the area called the Midlands. The nearest town of any size was Keatering, located about 10 miles away and was on the main railway line to London.

We were assigned quarters in Nissen Huts, the European Theater of Operations version of a barrack. A Nissen hut resembles nothing so much as a corrugated steel tunnel with fissures in the floor, cracks in the ceiling and well-ventilated walls. We had real beds, not army steel cots, for the 16 officers assigned to each hut. Fortunately, our crew was able to talk the supply sergeant into giving us the last sets of white sheets that he had. A crew had failed to return from a mission just a day or two before which made them available. My brother Howard who was in the infantry for several years had little symphony for me when I told him how lucky I had been regarding the bedding.

Lavatories for face washing and shaving and toilets were outside in a separate building to serve the men from several surrounding huts. Bathing facilities, large bathtubs, were located near the officer's mess, dining hall, and club about a mile away. Groups of living quarters were disbursed around the base so that raiding enemy airplanes could not bomb any big concentration of facilities.

My first visit to the bathing facilities was an experience. The tub invariably was disgustingly dirty with a big dark dirt ring around the inside. A good scrubbing of the tub was necessary before there could be a scrubbing of your self. Of course, as my mother had taught me, leave things as you found them when you depart. So I did!

The next feature to strike us in our new home was the ETO bicycle, a necessity for getting around the area when most facilities, such as eating, bathing, recreation, church, fitness, etc., were a mile or more away from your living quarters. I promptly went to town and purchased one, a thing of steel and wire designated for destruction and styled for discomfort. Instead of a brake operated by a slight pressure on the pedal, these brakes were operated by hand and operated in such fashion as to make a vault over the handlebars a simple thing, even for a second lieutenant.

The group was organized into four battle squadrons and a headquarters group which included all the supporting functions such as leaders, planners, training, maintenance, armament, intelligence, weather, personnel, finance and security. A full complement of B-17 bombers, Boeing "Flying Fortresses", was about 40. It took about 400 crewmen, pilots, navigators, bombardiers and gunners, to man these planes plus perhaps 2,000 others to lead and support the effort.

The crew with me as the navigator started flying practice missions in the area of the base north of London. We also attended ground briefings to train us for combat flying, gunnery, navigation and radio techniques, and the like.

In the early morning of June 6, about 3 AM, all combat crews including those of us in training, were assembled in the briefing room. When the room had quieted down, Colonel Harold W. Bowman, our commanding officer, spoke to us and said, "Gentlemen, remember the date, June 6th, 1944. Remember it, because your grandchildren will probably have to memorize it. This is D-Day!"

The announcement was not wholly unexpected. The day before an announcement was made over the base loud speaker system, "To all military personnel on the field—you will immediately carry gas masks and helmets, you will carry a weapon with you at all times. This is all." There were more fliers in the briefing room that night than ever before and there was a scramble for seats to hear the news. Everyone was excited and most of us felt that the time had come at last. None of them really knew until the Colonel's opening remarks. Then there was a moment of bedlam, everyone yelled, laughed and slapped each other on the back. The Colonel told us that this was the day we had all worked for and trained for. It was a short speech without frills and, after wishing us luck, he sat down to listen to the briefing for the D-Day mission.

Planes from our Group flew two missions that day, a part of a fleet of some 2,362 8th Air Force aircraft flying over the beachhead before the assault. After the briefing was over and we moved out into the still dark night, C-47's could be heard overhead, some with paratroops and others towing gliders filled with special troops to be landed behind German lines. They stretched in clusters across the sky, flashing colored lights and shooting off flares as they positioned themselves into their respective formations. At our base, the noise of our Fortresses engines began to be heard as our planes began to line up and then took off one by one for the first mission of the day. Unfortunately my crew was not one of those to fly on June 6. Beach defences were the target for 36 of our planes that early morning and later in the day 6 more joined with others to bomb positions in the Caen area in support of the landing.

Our crew was called to fly our first mission on June 7. We were assigned an old model B-17 that had apparently been around since the formation of the group. We were excited since this was our first combat experience so the old plane didn't bother us. We made a routine take off and started climbing to gain our assigned altitude. Not too long into the climb one of our engines became over taxed and burned out. It had to be shut off and the propellers feathered (turned vertical to the wind to prevent drag). We immediately turned back to land since we could not keep up with the other planes with just the remaining three engines. In the process of returning to the base a second engine also burned out. With a full load of bombs you can fly reasonably well with three engines but hardly at all with just two. We looked for the closest airfield and headed in. We barely cleared a fence coming in and landed on the dirt just short of the regular runway.

We had landed at a base near ours. We were directed to a parking place and as we got out of the plane we heard the noise of an explosion, the results of two planes colliding with one another up in the clouds.

Since we lost altitude so quickly my ears stopped up and I had to go to the hospital there at the base to have the ears examined. While I was waiting for an examining doctor one of the crewmen from the two planes that had collided was brought in. He had been blown out of the plane and apparently was the only survivor of the accident.

What a way to start our tour of duty!

We were returned to our base and a couple of days later we were assigned a new silver B-17G, the latest model. "Little Pedro" was the name given to our plane. The picture of a small Mexican boy trying to pull a burro by his rope halter was painted on the plane's nose. We felt this depicted our feelings of not being "gung ho" for war but being willing to accomplish our responsibility, although reluctantly.

On June 14 we were called for what became our first completed mission. Happy to be in our new plane, this time when we climbed to the assigned altitude and arrived at the location where we thought the rest of our group was to assemble, we couldn't see them. Formations were assembled and flying toward Paris, France, the target for the day. We noticed a formation that had a plane missing from a wing position so we just moved into the spot and flew the mission with that strange group. We never knew if the missing plane tried to catch up with his proper group. We were shot at by anti-aircraft guns, but not heavily. We saw a few bursts off our right wing, which tracked us as we turned away from the target after having dropped our bombs.

It was a complicated and exacting task to properly assemble great numbers of bombers, from several hundred to as many as one thousand. There were about 60 American heavy bomber bases located mostly north and north east of London. Preplanning for each mission determined how many planes were needed from each group (base). The location over England or the sea, altitude and time for each group was determined so that the entire bomber stream for each designated target, often there were several, would be assembled and be on the way to the continent so as to reach the target areas at designated times. Timing was essential because fighters, rescue and observer types of aircraft were to meet the bombers to protect them from enemy fighters, etc. Observation planes and distinctively marked planes would take off early and be in various areas to help direct the assembling bombers. The bombers at each base started the take off procedure promptly and each succeeding plane started rolling as the one ahead lifted off the runway. Each pilot was given a designated rate of climb to maintain and a compass direction to fly, so that each plane reached the assembly area one after the other. As the planes moved into position the formation was moving toward the continent as planned. The weather was often bad which further complicated the assembly and increased the danger of collision.

A few days after our initial mission, on June 19, we were called for our second mission. This time we went to Bordeaux, France, deep in southern France near the Atlantic Ocean. We successfully joined our group as planned and flew to the target. The group approached the target at a lower altitude than usual, less than 20,000 feet, to achieve better bombing accuracy. We received some moderate but very accurate flak (anti-aircraft shots) and the group lost 3 of the 41 aircraft sent on the mission. Our plane received several hits but none of our crew was hit. This was our real "baptism of fire" so to speak.

The next five missions were to France, bombing bridges and railway switching yards in support of the invasion forces. As to enemy action, they were rather uneventful, with light flak and no enemy fighters.
One of the missions was to Toulouse, France, near the Spanish border and the Atlantic Ocean. The weather was bad for the return so it was decided to fly out over the ocean all the way around France. As we approached England we ran into a mighty thunderhead and had to climb to an altitude of about 33,000 feet to get over it. The temperature was about 40 degrees below zero in the plane. We wore heated suits over our uniform but it got cold never the less. Due to the distance and the altitude required to get over the front, we were getting low on fuel as we approached the coast of England. We decided to drop down and look for an airfield in case we needed to land. We dropped down into clouds and as we broke out below we saw barrage balloons just in front of us. We quickly pulled up and decided we must press on to our base.

We made it but with precious little gas left in our tanks. We were in the air for 9 ½ hours.

Mission No. 8 was to Leipzig, Germany, our first to the "big league." Heavy flack was encountered over the target. Just as we dropped the bombs, flack hit one of our engines forcing us to shut it off. The whole formation quickly dropped down about 5,000 feet to pick up speed leaving the target. With our increased drag and slower speed on only three engines, we were quickly left behind. Enemy fighters traditionally jumped a straggler so we expected action at any time. Good fortune smiled on us and after a short time a group of our P-38 fighters came into view and stayed with us in the general area until we reached the English Channel. We were considerably late in reaching our base and had been reported as missing by the other crews at debriefing.

There was certainly a "fear" factor in flying combat missions. Being attacked by German fighters was our greatest concern. They were much faster than we were and were much more deadly with their guns than we were in return. When under attack the formation flew very close together for added defensive reasons, being able to direct more of our guns at the incoming fighters. By the summer of 1944 when I was flying, fighter opposition had greatly diminished but was still a genuine concern. Some fighters attacked somewhere along the formation on nearly all missions. It was a matter of luck as to where your plane was positioned in the formation and just where the fighters made their attacks. "Tail-end-Charlie", the plane or planes in the lower back position were considered the most vulnerable. Often the German fighters would pull up along side the formation out of range of our guns and then they would break off and drop down to hit the lower planes. To this day I remember looking out and seeing this single fighter who had pulled up along side us, we were at the highest outside position in the formation, and I clearly saw the pilot turn to look at me as if it was a personal thing. Actually the top turret, the waist gunner and my forward nose gun were all pointed at him. We alerted the ball turret gunner who waited for him to break off to attack our planes in the lower positions, which he did.

Flack was our ever mission nemesis. All German cities with industry had many numbers of guns, hundreds. They were quite accurate up to altitudes of 30,000 feet, the altitude at which we often bombed. They knew that for the 5 to 10 minutes that we were on our final bomb run, the planes had to fly straight and level so that the bombardiers could line up their bombsights. The flack gunners would throw up a large box of flack that we had to fly through. Before and after the actual bomb run we could alter altitude, move side to side or up and down so we were less vulnerable. You could see the explosions, the large black smoke it caused, sometimes be close enough to hear the explosion, smell the burnt explosive and hear or feel the pieces of shrapnel hitting the plane. In spite of all this, the sky is awfully big and space can absorb a great deal of flying pieces of metal, so most of us continued to make our way through the area where the explosions were occurring. You approach the bomb run with much trepidation, fear if you like, and then as the shells start bursting around the plane you try to make yourself as small as possible and have faith that you will make it through. Normally you are also busy with your duties but over the target there isn't any-thing for the navigator or gunners to do because the fighters would not follow us into the flack so you just had to "sweat it out." I was hit once by a rather large piece of metal, jagged, about the size of my little finger, but it had already come through the side of the plane, knocked the corner off an ammunition box and creased a large oxygen bottle before hitting my leg. The force was enough to move my leg, but the force was spent and it then logged in my heated suit pants leg. I reached down to feel what I thought would he blood running down my leg. What a relief to find no running blood and that piece of metal there in the fabric of my pants. Strangely I don't remember the fear factor being any greater in the late stages of my tour as we approached that magic number of 35 missions. Believe me though, there was great relief when we flew that last mission knowing we would no longer be shot at and would soon be homeward bound.

Our next six missions, numbers 9 through 14, were to targets deep within Germany. Four of them were to Munich in a period of 5 days. We experienced very heavy flack on all these missions and occasionally fighter attacks. In July, we were getting good fighter support from our P-51's, P-47's and P-38's which considerably cut down on losses. Another notable mission was to Peenemunde, Germany, up on the Baltic Ocean, the location of their rocket experimental and manufacturing works. This was one of the first 1,000 plane missions to a single target. Our group was approximately in the middle of the bomber stream and I could see planes to both horizons as I looked forward and backward. The time in the air was 8 ½ hours, 3 of that on oxygen.

On July 24 and 25 we flew with the group to bomb St. Lo, France, low level missions in support of the Allied forces trying to break out from the Normandy beach area. We carried fragmentation anti-personnel bombs to be dropped very near our own lines. We were to be very careful to not drop short into our own troops. The first day the target was obscured by smoke so we did not drop our bombs. The mission on the second day was successful.

We now had credit for 16 missions and were considered an experienced crew. We were awarded our second Air Medal and the other two officers and I were promoted to the rank of 1st Lieutenant and our Sergeants were all promoted to the next rank as well. Our crew had qualified for better positions with in the bomber formation. We had put in our time as "Tail-end-Charlie," the lower and more dangerous positions.

During August and September we flew 17 more missions to various targets in Germany. We were primarily bombing oil refineries, chemical plants and manufacturing plants at or near cities like Berlin, Frankfurt, Cologne, Ludwigshaven, Hamm, Mannheim and another to Peenemunde. We experienced the usual flack, a few fighter attacks, had our first sightings of the greatly feared jet fighters and were very thankful to God that we would soon be finished and could go home. After finishing 25 missions all our crew members were awarded the Distinguished Flying Cross for "extraordinary achievement" while participating in combat missions over Germany and German occupied countries.

In April 1944, Germany had adequate supplies of oil. Over the next year the 8th Air Force dropped 70 thousand tons of bombs on refineries and the 15th Air Force flying out of Italy, dropped 60 thousand tons. A year later in April, 1945, their production of oil was 5% of the previous year. Of all the bombs that struck the Reich during the war, 72% fell after July 1, 1944. In the following nine months the bombing campaign wrecked the enlarged German economy until it could not support military operations or supply the basic needs of the population. We were a part of the successful effort to starve their war machine of that much needed oil and other resources.

On October 3 we went to Nurnburg, Germany, the later site of the famous war crimes trials. It was a long and tiring trip, our number 34, the next to the last. On October 6, we were dismayed to have Berlin announced as the target, a much dreaded destination since the Germans defended their capital to the greatest extent. Five or six hours later the bombers approached the city, which we found, was covered in clouds. The group commander announced that we would not bomb there but instead would bomb a fighter airfield in the vacinity that was in the clear. It was lightly defended and happily we were soon on our way back to England, my final mission!

The Crew in late August 1944 after 30 missions.

Back row L to R: Koons, Green, Murray, Sears (note the 30
bombs----jacket) Lyall & Martz
Front row L to R: Watson, Craytor & Hanson

After our final debriefing session we all had a drink from the spirits bottle we had been saving for this great occasion. It was the practice to offer each crewmember a shot of whiskey at each debriefing session. None of us cared for the liquor at that time, we were tired and hungry, so we accumulated it in a bottle for a celebration at the end of mission number 35.

All of the crew except the pilot and front nose gunner (the one who actually dropped the bombs) were removed from combat crew status and started making plans to return to the U.S.A. These two were required to fly one additional mission. Earlier on one of our missions deep in Germany as we were approaching the target we found that our bomb bay doors would not open due to mechanical failure and it was too late to manually crank them open. We all agreed that there was no sense in our continuing to fly with the formation into the flak field since we couldn't drop our bombs. Since we were on the outside of the formation we were able to just slide out to our right to get out of the flak, but knew that if fighters should attack we could easily slide back into formation to fulfill our responsibility in protecting the formation. When we got back to our base, the pilot was called in and was reprimanded for what they considered as an act of weakening the formation. The two crewmembers were not given credit for that mission and thus were one short when the rest of us finished. Those of us who received credit for the mission felt badly because it was a crew decision, but we didn't feel bad enough to protest and run the risk of not getting credit for the mission.

I had been told that the Air Corp/ was accepting requests from non-pilot officer to attend pilot school as their new state side reassignment. I immediately made such a request and the indication was that my request would be considered when I returned to the U.S.A. I don't remember just what I did for the next couple of weeks but I started getting the paper work in order, sold my bicycle and got my personal effects ready for the trip home. Soon I received orders to proceed to a port of embarkation and was assigned a place on an Army troop ship. The ship was only about one-forth loaded since we were returning to the U.S.A. right in the middle of the war. Most of the passengers were aircrew members such as myself who had completed their required number of missions and a number of American prisoners (bad guys) in the hold below, closely guarded by military policemen. We joined a large convoy of various other ships and started the long, slow trip to New York. It took about two weeks to make the crossing since we were restricted to the speed of the slowest ship. Several destroyers guarded the convoy.

We had one scare during the trip. We woke up one morning and found that our ship had stopped and the rest of the convoy was already out of sight. We were told that they had some steering problem and couldn't keep up with the group. We felt rather uneasy out there in the middle of the Atlantic Ocean knowing of the terrible losses other convoys had experienced from attacks by submarines. Fortunately nothing happened and the crew was able to correct their problem and by the next morning we had caught up with the convoy and were back in our position.

The ship was very comfortable with each officer having his own cabin as compared with the trip over to England on the Queen Elizabeth where we had 15 officers in one cabin. We were served breakfast, lunch and dinner in the dinning room and were waited on by white-coated stewards. The food was very good and plentiful. We had a nice library on board and spent our days reading, playing bridge, sleeping or just sitting on deck watching the waves go by.

We steamed into the New York harbor area one beautiful, clear morning and it was a wonderful experience when we passed by the Statue of Liberty. We disembarked and were taken to Camp Kilmer, New Jersey, for disbursement to our respective homes. Camp Kilmer will always remain in my memory for that wonderful milk shake I had there after being gone from the United States for so long. A couple of days later I boarded a train along with 3 other officers and 12 enlisted men for the trip to Fort Sam Houston, San Antonio, where we received our orders for a 3-week leave. It was another long train trip but this time quite comfortable as compared with the one from Salt Lake City to Florida. We stopped in W. St. Louis and all were permitted a few hours in town. When we got on the train for the continuation of the trip, several of the enlisted men didn't make it back on the train, but who cared. I'm sure they somehow found their way to San Antonio on their own.

Being home in Fort Worth with my mother and sister was great. (My brother, Howard, was still overseas in Italy at that time. He was an army Staff Sergeant in the quartermaster Corp of the 36th Division. He served about 36 months overseas, having joined his Division in early 1941, almost a year before the Pearl Harbor attack by the Japanese on December 11, of that year. He would have had a great story to tell regarding his experiences overseas. I wish he had recorded it before he died. A reading of the history of the 36th Division during WW II would tell the big story for he was with them all the way.)

It was great fun being a returning war hero during the midst of the war. Several of my old friends who were stationed stateside were able to get home on leave during the time I was there. I have some pictures of our celebrations.

The three weeks past quickly and I was assigned back to the Santa Ana Army Air base where I started. I spent a couple of weeks there awaiting reassignment. The married officers were sent to Miami, Florida, for their reassignment. We singles felt put upon. However, I did get to visit with old friends whom I had met when I had been there a year and a half before. I did spend Christmas, 1944, in Santa Ana but I don't remember anything special about it, must have been rather quiet.

In late 1944, I was transferred to Midland Army Air base, back in Texas, to await acceptance in the pilot training program. After about a month I moved on to San Antonio where we underwent further testing to determine fitness for pilot training. Finally, in March, 1945, I was sent to Garner Field, Uvalde, Texas, about 90 miles west of San Antonio, to attend Primary pilot training. The base had been a pre war private flying training school, a neat country club style layout of administrative, service and dormitory buildings. The airfield was mostly grass on which we did our take off and landings. There were a few hangers along a concrete tarmac and one small concrete landing strip for larger planes.

We learned to fly in planes called PT-13 trainers. The PT-13 was a rather small biplane, two wings, with two open cockpits, the front for the student and the back for the instructor. They weren't very fast, maybe 120 miles per hour, but were great fun to fly. They were very maneuverable, could glide a great distance with the power cut off and were relatively easy to land. In addition to take off and landings, we were instructed how to do basic maneuvers, recovery from spins and how to make dead-stick landings (without power). After about 9 hours of flying with the instructor, one morning he said, "you are ready to solo, take off and fly around the field on your own." After two months and about 65 hours of flying time in the PT-13 we were ready for graduation from primary training and a move on to Basic training.

In late May 1945, I was transferred to Mission Army Air Base, at Mission, in Deep South Texas. Here we were to attend Basic flying training and fly in the famous AT-6. AT as in advanced trainer. Earlier trainees flew a plane designated as BT for basic trainer, but it was determined that pilot trainees now could move directly into the AT-6, and perform at a faster pace. The AT-6 was a much more powerful plane than the PT-13, it had a single low wing, was all metal framed and had a closed cockpit for two, for the trainee and instructor. We learned how to handle the additional power and speed, learned about radio procedures, navigation and instrument flying, i.e. blind flying, where we depended on our cockpit instruments rather than visual observations. Instrument flying under those big South Texas cumulus clouds where the air currents would sometimes drop you a 1,000 feet was really a challenge. We did some cross-country flying up around Corpus Christi and would sometimes get jumped by advanced Navy flyers in much more powerful planes. It was good training for us less experienced pilots.

During June and July we logged 82 hours and were graduated from Basic school to move on to advanced flying school where we were to fly in twin engine planes, B-25s. In early August I was transferred to Pampa Army Field, in the Texas panhandle about 40 miles north east of Amarillo. From August 11 until the 24th I flew 12 hours as a trainee-copilot in this much bigger and more powerful bomber plane. It was a thrill but not nearly the thrill that occurred on August 25 when the Japanese surrendered and WW II came to an end.

Our training immediately stopped and plans were made to close down the training center. We were offered the opportunity to continue our training at another base but if we continued and graduated we had to agree to remain in the Air Force for at least one year. I was very anxious to complete the course so I agreed to stay in. A week later we were again given the opportunity to discontinue the course and be promptly released from the Army. I considered the fact that I had not been to college, didn't really think that Army life was for me and that I would be a new pilot in the service with many, many experienced pilots staying in the peace time Air Force.

Prospects didn't look too good, so I decided I would resign and go home to start a college career.

After a week or two the base was closed and we were transferred to San Angelo Army Air Base to await discharge. Once again we waited around for a week or two and on October 18, 1945, orders came through transferring me to the separation center at Randolph Field near San Antonio. Four days later I was discharged and I headed for home.

I learned that a new semester was to start at the University of Texas in Austin within a week, so I immediately bought some new civilian clothes and headed for Austin. My days as an Army officer were over and I was now to start my new life as Mr. Freshman, University of Texas Longhorn. It had been a thrilling and fun ride but I was not at all sorry to become a new kind of student.

One Airman's Story

Narrated by Jack Young 401st Bomb Group

Jack Young 1944

To England

About July 10 1944, after our transition training was completed of learning to work with each other in the crew, we headed for Camp Kilmer, New Jersey for the same old processing we had whereever we went. Then off to Brooklyn Navy Yard to catch an ex-Italian luxury liner for anything but a luxury cruise.

With over 5,000 troops on board, bunks (canvas stretched over pipe frames) five tiers high, two meals a day, and just plain crowded, I knew it was going to be a GREAT cruise. We left in the middle of the night, so I never saw the Statue of Liberty. That kind of ticked me off!!

On awakening the next morning, and being able to get on deck, I looked around to see us at sea with nothing but ships around us as far as I could see. I counted around forty ships in our convoy, and I knew that wasn't all of them.

To keep from starving, I volunteered for night K.P. Then I got three meals a day.
One thing that impressed me, and I've never forgotten, is how rough the North Atlantic can be in a storm. For at least four days the weather was so bad that we were riding fifty to sixty foot waves at the same time.

Eleven days after leaving New York, we dropped anchor in Liverpool Harbor, debarked, and proceeded to a staging area to wait assignment at a B-17 base. While here I turned twenty years old on July 31. No cards, no presents, no cake.
Then August 5th rolled around and we got orders to report to the 401st Bomb Group. This was near the village of Deenethorpe—70 miles north of London. After a little bit of interrogation, briefing, and practice flying in our newly assigned plane, we were ready to conquer "Der Führer". Our plane was an old B-17E—combat weary, lots of patches from flak damage and the same old O.D. (olive drab) paint that was painted on in Seattle. All of the arriving new B-17Gs had shiny aluminium finish. They discovered unpainted aircraft were harder to see. The name of this plane was "Pakawallup II", and it had been in service since early 1943.

The Crew & their ship "Net Results"

Back row L to R: John Udy Pilot, Billy Hockaday Co-pilot, Dale Youel Navigator, Bob Jencks Waist Gunner & Jack Young Engineer / Topturret Gunner.
Front row L to R: Al Warn Tail Gunner, Harry Knowles Radio Operator, Earl Oviatt Togglier & Russel Alber Ball Turret Gunner.

Off Into The Wild Blue Yonder

The big day finally arrived. On August 16, 1944 at 2:30 am, we were awakened for our first mission. At 4:30 we had our mission briefing. When they uncovered the mission map, we discovered our target was Leipzig. I believe the target was a ball bearing factory.

We started our engines around 6:30 am, waited our turn to taxi into position, and then took off into the wild blue yonder. It was a beautiful day for flying. At ten thousand feet we put on our oxygen masks, and then I got up into my position—the top turret. Here I spent most of four hours checking the heavens for enemy fighters. We climbed to 27,000 feet and flew our mission to the target at that altitude.

("Hey, what are those black puffs of smoke out there? Oh. That's anti-aircraft flak. That's interesting. Holy cow—it's getting closer, and there's lot more of it. My God! It's so dense, so close to us they're trying to shoot us down!! Oh, shit!!")

"Bombs Away!!" Our plane jumped upward as all 6,000 pounds of bombs were dropped at one time and we were free of our load. It was up to me to check the bomb bay to be sure no bombs hung up. Everything was OK!

Our formation then turned back to England. We were shot up, but no planes were lost—one co-pilot killed though.

Nine hours after take-off, we landed at our base. The brakes had been shot out, so John (Pilot) had to ground loop the plane at the end of the runway ("Thanks John"). As soon as we could after landing, we checked our battle damage. Besides losing our brakes, we counted over 250 holes in our plane.

The next few missions were rough also, but not as bad as our first. In a sense, it was better to have our first mission be the worst, because all the rest seemed so much milder. We could come back with only 200 holes from anti-aircraft-fire—and flat tires. Once we had to crank down our landing gear.

After five missions we got a "stand down". We got a four day furlough for "Flak Leave". Three of us, Harry, Earl, and myself who always chummed around together decided to see London. FANTASTIC! Westminster Abbey, St. Paul's Cathedral, Buckingham Palace, Tower of London. We were able to get to London twice more, to Edinburgh, and to Nottingham.

Concerning these cities, I thought Edinburgh was the most beautiful and friendly city. It was not damaged by German bombardment, was not overcrowded as was London, and was so tranquil. There was one site I would like to have visited. That was the Palace of Mary, Queen of Scots. Impossible!! It was home for over 5,000 German POW.

It was during the "stand-down" starting September 28, that we had our chance to visit Edinburgh. After arriving, the three of us—Harry, Earl and I, purchased a very good bottle of 7-year old Scotch. The next thing on the agenda was to get a room in a small hotel. We asked the proprietor to bring us three glasses—"And bring one for yourself". Well—that bottle went down in a hurry, and the proprietor's nose got redder and redder. But as he was imbibing, he told us much about the history of the region and pointed out the bridge across the Firth of Forth, which is one of harbors of Britain.

We probably had too much Scotch ourselves, because I don't remember too much more, except that the weather was beautiful. Anyway, we had a very relaxing vacation.

After coming back to our base from Edinburgh, we noticed our plane was not in its hard stand area. "Hey, where's our plane? What happened?"—"The day after you left on flak leave, it was shot down over Cologne. The crew got out OK". The end of an era.

By the way, our last mission before our leave was to Cologne on September 26, 1944. It wasn't that rough a mission. It was a beautiful, sunny day, snow on the ground, and I could see the shadows of the Cologne Cathedral on the ground. Even at an altitude of 22,000 feet, I could visualize the extreme beauty of the Gothic architecture used on this structure.

Shortly after we were assigned a brand new, shiny B-17G. We named it "Net Results".

Most missions after this seemed more like "Milk-Runs"—very little flak damage. Oh, sure we had missions like Meresburg, Frankfurt, and Peenemunde, where the flak seemed thick enough to land on, but we had minimal flak damage. We had to have a guardian angel. At some of these targets, it was estimated that over 10,000 anti-aircraft weapons were firing at each group that flew over the area (48 B-17s in each group).

"Net Results" was a great plane—got us "There and Back". But it had one little quirk. On every mission, right after crossing into enemy territory, the gyro compass would QUIT. It would just go "round and round". When we crossed back over friendly territory, it would stabilize to give us correct readings again. We thought the cause could be cold temperatures, altitude, vacuum lines, vacuum pump and / or the compass itself. They eventually changed everything and we even flew for two hours over England at 38,000 feet and—65 degrees, and could not get it to malfunction. The next mission over enemy territory—the same thing happened, The problem was never solved. The conclusion: The compass was "chicken".

On October 6, 1944, we were slated for a very long mission to the Politz / Stettin area in Poland. The round trip distance of at least 1,500 miles at an average air speed of 160 MPH made for almost 10 hours of flying time. A very long time when we're watching for both flak and fighters—much of the time right into the sun. One consolation though, was the beautiful scenery. To the south we could see the Alps; to the North we saw the mountains of Norway—a distance of about 1,700 miles between them.

When we got to the target area, I believe it was oil and fuel, we could see nothing on the ground. Smoke screens covered the entire target area. We saw no flak or fighters.
When you can't bomb the primary target, you then go to a secondary "target of opportunity". So we bombed an airfield. Later we found out

it was a Luftwaffe training base, and the only damage was to trainers that could not fly. Oh well, you can't win them all. With that long flight behind us, we got a good night's sleep.

Bright and early the next morning on October 7, after a delicious breakfast of scrambled eggs, hot cakes, sausage, orange juice and coffee (they fed us every breakfast as if that one was the last meal we would have), we went to the mission briefing. When they uncovered the map of the target area, we breathed great sighs of relief ("Oh, boy! Milk-run!! Long but easy!"). The Target was Politz again! No flak—no fighters.

One thing we didn't think of (which was good) was that the Germans would gamble on us coming back the next day. They would be ready for us—with everything they had. That was a pretty accurate assumption. As we went in toward the target, the sky got black (Oh, God, the flak is so thick we could land on it, and it's getting thicker ahead").

Then—"Poof-Poof-Poof-Poof". Twenty millimetre shells were exploding in our right wing. "Bandits—4 o'clock high!!". I got one burst of 50 caliber A.P.I. (Armor Piercing Incendiary) into a FW 190's underside, and he was gone—no more fighters.

As we neared the target, the flak got worse and worse. The heaviest we'd ever seen. It seemed everything was against us ("Oh, God, help us with this mission. Help us get through it safely, Lord. We're the good guys.")—"Bombs-Away". I checked the bomb bay—all bombs released OK. But BOOM! A burst flak barely missed exploding directly in the center of the open bomb bay. I slammed that armor plated door closed in a hurry and checked myself for wounds. I was OK—but scared. No place to dig fox holes at 27,000 feet.

On our way north to the Baltic Sea, I could see two or three planes going down—parachutes opening thank God. We passed one crippled B-17 whose crew was jettisoning everything that could—machine guns, ammunition, whatever they could lighten the load to get to Sweden.

After this Politz-Stettin "affair", our entire group had a stand-down for several days of R&R. It gave us a chance to relax, breathe, play games and talk. During this time, we had some enlightening conversation with members of another crew. "The first crew that slept in your bunks were shot down on their first mission. The second crew went down on their second mission and the third crew went down on their third mission. You are the fourth crew to make these bunks "home" and you've made it through your fourth, fifth, six missions and many more. You've broken the trend and will make it through your tour OK". That conversation helped make my day. And, oh yes, about the same time I got my final promotion to Tech. Sergeant. They finally realized I was an asset to the organization and worth more money.

Not all periods of relaxation were spent around the barracks or on leaves to London, or other large cities. Instead, many afternoons and evenings were spent at the smaller city of Kettering. This was fourteen miles from our base at Deenethorpe, and an easy ride by the one and only bus that made the run every two hours or so.

The people of this community were very easy to talk to, and very proud of their heritage. The houses were like row houses—made of stone with a common wall between them. Most of them had no plumbing, and many had no electricity (three rooms and a path). The dates of construction? The cornerstones dated about 945 A.D. These dates are unbelievable but factual.

One Sunday early in September 1944, the sun was shining, it was 86 degrees, and we (Harry, Earl and I) found ourselves walking around a very peaceful park with hundreds of other people enjoying the last warmth of summer. Suddenly we found ourselves near a Tea House—why not? So we went in and had tea and scones. It was neat! We thoroughly enjoyed our first English experience with High Tea.

You know? For a while this brought us back to the real world.
There were other ancient landmarks that we had toured and forgotten
but specific places that we frequented on occasion.

They had established dates from 1500's to the 1700's, and they had
names like "Black and White", "White Horse", "Pink Elephant", etc.
The buildings were old, but the refreshments were newer. Bitters and
milds, pints, cellar temperature. The old saying was that we had to
drink it before it got cold. I remember one time at the "White Horse"
where I had imbibed a few pints. I really had to go. I walked my way
through a door, down a hall, around a corner to a privy, where I found
relief. Oh, how great. As I was doing my thing, I could hear women's
voices outside. I pulled the chain, buttoned up, opened the door, and
heard feminine squeals. "Oh! You're in the wrong one!". I never did see
the men's john. Oh well, you can't win them all.

Meanwhile the war continued, and we continued flying. Not all our
missions were hazardous. Some could be classified as "Milk-runs". One
beautiful sunny day as we were travelling south at about 25,000 feet,
basking in the sunlight at balmy 56 degrees below zero and relaxing
since there was no anti-aircraft or enemy fighter activity. Suddenly,
directly in front of us—WHOOSH!! "Hey! What was that? Where did
it come from?". From nowhere (it seemed), a V-2 rocket was fired and
through our formation on its way to England. All we had seen was a
contrail, with no beginning or end—at least as far as we could see.

Occasionally little things happened to individuals that have no effect
on a mission. I was that individual once. On some forgotten mission,
flying toward our target on a beautiful day, John asked me to get something for him behind his seat. I got out of my turret, stepped down,
picked up what I had to and handed it to him. I then proceeded to
climb back up into my turret. As I was just straightening up to be able
to look out—"BANG!"—I heard a very loud explosive sound. I suddenly had a pulverized Plexiglas throughout all of my flight gear—from

head to toe. Even inside my long johns next to my skin—even in my heated flying slippers and boots. Something had gone through the windows of my turret. When I finally got up enough courage to stand up and inspect the damage, I discovered something had come in through the back glass, behind where my head would have been, and exited at the front left panel. If I had been in position, whatever it was would have gone right through my skull. This cat would have had one less life. There was no enemy activity around, so I thought it was the accidental firing of a machine gun from one of the planes in our flight. The hole made by the missile was so large that I could get my entire arm out and wave at the other planes. They all waved back.

When we saw some fighters—ME 109s and FW 190s, they could be deadly. On three of four different missions, we were hit by 20mm shells and were able to fire back and do damage to them. Unconfirmed, but we think we got a "kill"—possibly downing a FW 190.

Then came December 24 1944—the Battle of the Bulge. Very cloudy and foggy on the continent. We were flying at 27,000 feet near Koblenz to bomb German troops and transportation. Our troops fired some anti-aircraft in front of us to show where we could start our bomb runs. And guess what—the Germans fired at us to show where they did NOT want us.

The first burst of enemy flak got our number one engine. I tapped John on the shoulder and pointed out the stream of black oil that was pouring out of the engine. "We need our power for the bomb run. Shutting down number one will overload number two. Remember, that one is a new engine change, and overloading it can burn it out prematurely. Then we are REALLY in deep trouble. We'll feather number one when we have to."

When that time came, we found there was no oil reserve for feathering the prop and the engine started running away.

We had to break formation and turn back. Normally, our engine cruising speed was around 1,200 R.P.M. But this one was running away at 10,000 R.P.M. Since there was no oil, it was "freezing-up". The engine would seize, stop, and buck down around 45 degrees, twisting the wing. It would then relax, speed up, then repeat this performance four times more before shearing the propeller shaft so the prop could windmill freely.

We had to travel as slowly as we could to prevent the prop from running away, and still be able to maintain a proper altitude to get across the English Channel. Over the channel, we dropped our bomb load—a safe area. No "innocents" could be hurt here. It ended up that we got back to "Mother England" OK. Despite being very foggy, we were able to find a Canadian training base to land at.

Then is when we learned the extent of our damage. We could rattle the number one prop in any direction. Little holes were punched all over the left wing near the aileron (these are used to stabilize the plane in flight). The counter balance for this had broken loose and punched a hundred holes, but fortunately had not jammed into the aileron. This would have caused us to loose control and crash. We also found the main spar to the left wing had snapped. We could have lost the wing and we would have crashed anyway! (God bless the B-17).

Then our Christmas holiday began. After getting our billets, we were able to get dinner and TEA (England, you know). Then off to the Sergeants Club. They wouldn't let us buy a drink. WOW!! Then off to the dance. I was OK, but Harry was spending a lot of time leaning over a Quonset Hut. I understand others had the same problem. Merry Christmas—1944. One of the most popular songs with the G.I.s at this season was "I'll be home for Christmas".

Our tough missions were finally over. We had some very bad missions, many rough missions and a few milk runs. I flew my last mission on a milk-run to Paderborn on January 17 1945. It was great that this was an easy mission, and there were no fighters or flak. At this point our minds were starting to think of other things ("Oh, God. I hope this mission doesn't go bad. I'm ready to go home"). The only things I remember about this final mission is that it was short—probably five to six hours long, and it was sunny with scattered clouds below us.

Whenever we completed a mission and the plane had taxied into its hardstand area, we would have to clean our machine guns, turn in our parachutes and Mae West (floatation device), and then go to debriefing. Here we would get a straight shot of Scotch, cake and coffee through the Red Cross gals and tell all we could think of about our mission.

After our last mission on January 17, we turned in the rest of our combat gear—flight helmet, electric flying suit, insulated coveralls and jacket and winter fur lined boots. And the to debriefing....

This last debriefing was slightly different than the others. When we sat down we didn't get one shot of whiskey—we got the whole bottle! (And I was only a minor—not even twenty-one yet). We started celebrating that ended up at the N.C.O. club. Obviously we slept in the next morning. We had completed our thirty-five mission tour.

The Escape From Bornholm 1944

Narrated by the crew—401ˢᵗ Bomb Group, their helpers on Bornholm and the Author.

Prologue

by Erik Dyreborg

This story, "The Escape from Bornholm 1944", is dedicated to the ten Airmen who crash landed with their B-17 on the fields at Sose, Wednesday May 24, 1944 and last but not least dedicated to the people on Bornholm who helped them evade and escape.

As mentioned in "About The Author—A Dane's Story", "The Escape from Bornholm 1944" was published in Danish in May 2001, but has not been published in English, I therefore decided to include the story in this book.

The story is about people who all participated in the war in one way or another. It is about the American airmen who were "thrown" into WW II with very little training. It is about the people on Bornholm who found them, took care of them, helped them evade capture and escape to Sweden and thus saved the airmen from an uncertain destiny as POWs in Nazi Germany.

When I started my research I found that the people on Bornholm, who risked their lives by helping the airmen, were only mentioned on a couple of pages in a few books and in a few columns in some newspapers.

These operations, carried out by the local people, were not only voluntary but also extremely dangerous—beyond any imagination! And sad as it may be—they were soon forgotten!

This is the detailed and true story, narrated by the Airmen themselves and their helpers on Bornholm.

The holocaust, the terror and the horror, which took place in WW II should never be forgotten and I wish that future generations will be reminded again and again—and will remember, because it is said:

"Those who fail to remember history are doomed to repeat it!"

The Plane And The Crew.

B-17G "Flying Fortress" No.: 42-31619, name: "BTO in the ETO"

8th Air Force, Deenethorp, England. 401st Bomb Group 615th Squadron

Target: Berlin, Germany May 24, 1944

CRASH LANDING ON BORNHOLM MAY 24, 1944 02.12. hrs pm

LOCATION: "SOSEGAARD" Sose, Bornholm

Reason for crash landing: Plane damaged by anti aircraft shelling over Berlin.

COMBAT CREW:

Pilot	2nd LT	John S. Whiteman
Co-pilot	2nd LT	Horace H. Shelton
Navigator	2nd LT	Seymour Ringl

Bombardier	2nd LT	James A. Stevenson
Radio operator	S/SGT	William G. Nunn
Top turret gunner	S/SGT	Richard H. O'Bannon
Ball turret gunner	SGT	Heath Nelson Liddle
Right waist gunner	SGT	Marwin L. Carraway
Left waist gunner	SGT	Orlando J. Yemma
Tail gunner	SGT	Jack R. Culliton

Co-pilot Shelton was assigned to fly the first two missions with this new crew, as an experienced one.

The crew

Back row L to R:
Richard O'Bannon, William G. Nunn, Jack R. Culliton, Heath Nelson Liddle, Marwin L. Carraway & Orlando Yemma.
Front row L to R:
John S. Whiteman, Swisher, Seymour Ringle & James A. Stevenson.

To England And The E.T.O.

By Nelson Liddle, John S. Whiteman & Seymour Ringle

Liddle: Crews were formed and trained for combat on B-17 bombers for 3 months in Alexandria, Louisiana. Our crew picked up a brand new B-17 in Nebraska and flew it to Bangor, Maine and then from Bangor to Gander New Foundland and from Gander, Newfoundland to Nutts Corner, Ireland on April 22, 1944 and finally to our destination Deenethorp in The United Kingdom.

We were assigned to the 8th Air Force, 401st Bomb Group, 615th Squadron, stationed in Deenethorp.

Whiteman: In connection with our departure from Gander, I had a problem with the tower. We were third from last to take off and as our engines had been running for about one hour, I had to demand that the fuel truck top my tanks. We took 160 gal.

We took off from Gander Newfoundland at about 11p.m. Instruments all the way. We had a 2000 pound overload which was bolted into the bomb bay. As I climbed to assigned altitude, 11,000 ft I tried to salvo the load but it wouldn't salvo. The load damn near cost us our lives.

We were past the point of no return, 1000 miles from any land with 30 feet waves below, cruising at 150 indicated and had just put on some carburated heat because we were in a raging storm.

It had everything ice, sleet, St. Elmos fire and the props slinging ice up against the plane as we had prop de-icers on. I had just downed a half cup of coffee when Swisher "Swish" the C.P. hollered. Look at the #2 & #4 manifold pressure, they were slowly falling. I shouted to Swish to hit the #2 & #4 hand primer which injects fuel directly into the engine, which he did, and in the process took the flesh on his first two fingers of his right hand right down to the bone.

That's how much of an emergency he thought we had and he was right. I had closed the turbo gates on the #2 & #4 and high rpm's when the engines backfired and blew the ice out of the carbs. with a spectacular belch of fuel in front of the engines and back over the wing.

We put on full carburator heat & closed everything back to normal at which point I threw up the coffee on the flight deck, that stayed in my throat.

Ringle: On this flight I had access to only one method of obtaining fixes and that was celestial sightings with a sextant. I would get a fix every hour and Whiteman would give me wake up calls every few minutes to make sure that I was not sleeping on the job.

Whiteman: The engines were new and burned just below the 50 gallons per hr, which was the limit or the engines would be changed.

The icing caused a fuel emergency and we had to make an instrument landing at Nutts Corner, Ireland.

When we landed in Ireland we had 189 gal. left. The overload and the storm burnt up the gas.

I was never taught to backfire the ice. "Someone" put the words in my mouth.

The Boeing representative in Ireland said when we described what happened: "You could have blown the carburators off". What was the difference with 30feet waves below we were dead no matter what.

When we took off at Gander I just had 25 hours of flying in a B-17, the co-pilot less and the rest of the crew even less.

62 planes took off from Gander that evening, only 44 made it.

Erik Dyreborg: We know that 4 planes crash landed in Greenland. The remaining 14 missing planes? You can only guess! The bad weather? Germany was not the *only* enemy!

Ringle: As to the 14 missing planes that took of from Gander, I'm sure that a number of them fell victim to the German operation known as "meaconing".

There was a powerful radio station in Prestwick which was used on the final portion of the flight for homing. The navigator would tune it in on his radio compass, identify the station which would be sending its letters in Morse code and then rotate the loop antenna until it was lined up 90 degrees to the bearing of the station. At this point he would get an oral null (absolute silence) and his compass would give him the correct bearing.

The Germans built a more powerful radio station on the coast of France and superimposed its transmission over that of Prestwick on the same frequency and call sign and, if the navigator used that bearing in his calculations, he would ultimately find himself "position uncertain" and, at this stage of the flight, very low on fuel.

However, if he rotated his loop antenna through 360 degrees, he would pick up four oral nulls instead of two and, ascertaining that he was getting two separate and distinct stations, he would use his DR (dead reckoning) position to home in on the correct one.

Whiteman: We continued our trip to our destination, Deenethorp in England.

At Deenethorp we were, like all new crews, assigned an experienced co-pilot—2nd LT Horace H. Shelton and our original co-pilot, Swisher, was transferred to other duties.

I never saw Swisher after he was replaced by Shelton. I heard that he flew as a co-pilot for the rest of the war and then went to 4 engine to become a first pilot on B17s.

As far as we know, he died of a heart attack about 1997.

Liddle and I tried everything possible to find him for our reunions, just like we did with Stevenson, but I guess we just ran out of luck.

The First Combat Mission
May 23, 1944

Narrated by Seymour Ringle

"Drop your ~ocks and grab your socks"—was the wake up call echoing through the Nissen Huts and announcing the start of our first combat mission.

We dragged our weary, half-asleep bodies through all the preflight rituals and were finally airborne, one small piece in a jigsaw airplane formation.

All we had to do was maintain our position and blindly follow the lead ship to our target in France, where the lead would unload his bombs using the Norden bomb sight and the rest of the airplanes would follow.

My job in this situation was not to give the pilot headings but to maintain a log and plot our flight path on my chart so as to be prepared to react as lead navigator in the event of any trouble.

The lead ship finally turned to a northerly heading, which was the heading of our bomb run, and his bomb bay doors opened—20 miles west of our I.P. (initial point)! We flew this heading for about 20 minutes with bomb bay doors open and experiencing light flak with bombs exposed.

The lead then executed a wide turn to the left and continued turning through 360 degrees with the entire formation in trail and ended up on the same northerly heading.

Our Bombardier James Stevenson—"Shorty"—was seated in the nose looking down with his hands on the toggle switches and I was crouched behind him, looking over his shoulder when I perceived the bombs falling from the planes ahead of us. I looked over into Shorty's face and—he was fast asleep. I nudged him and he proceeded to toggle out our bomb load. I guess they are still trying to determine where on God's earth those bombs landed.

The Second And Final Combat Mission
May 24, 1944

Narrated by John S. Whiteman, Seymour Ringle, Nelson Liddle & Horace H. Shelton

Whiteman: I will never forget the 2nd mission May 24 1944 Berlin!

Ringle: It was some ungodly early hour in the morning when we were all aroused for another "all out effort" and we dressed and ate and departed for the various briefings.

The pilots and navigators were addressed by the C.O. who dramatically raised the shade covering the blackboard and disclosed the route and target of the mission:—Big "B" (Berlin) and the noise in the room rose significantly.

The individual officers gave their particular briefings concerning weather, start up, times, radio frequency, form ups etc.

The intelligence officer informed us that the envelope of fire of the 88 mm guns was only five miles at an altitude of 22.000 feet so that our bombs would be falling directly on them, thus decreasing their effectiveness (HA!) He was probably the travel agent who booked the passengers for the Titanic!

Whiteman: The mission started normally. The 615th Squadron formed up over Deenethorp. We then tied in with two other squadrons over Bury St. Edmunds (three squadrons to a group and three groups to a wing).

The wing formed up over The Wash. Then the wing took off for the Dutch coast. It paralleled the coast and cut inland at the North end of Holland and took East South East, heading for: THE BIG "B" .

Radio silence!

We got very little flak when going in.

Ringle: The flight itself was a beautiful thing to witness. It was like a ballet with all these gorgeous aircrafts in formation at different levels with contrails streaming back from each airplane like the long trains on the wedding dresses of 2.000 new brides against the background of a clear cerulean sky. 500 ships were heading for Berlin.

Whiteman: I got my first look at The big "B" (Berlin) from about 100 miles out. It looked like a big mass of black flies—FLAK !

I said to myself "Holy....", how can a plane survive in that mess? WE DIDN'T !
The initial point of the bomb run started at 24 thousand feet. The flak was very heavy.

We had just dropped our bombs, when out of the corner of my left eye, I caught the explosion of a shell off our wing tip. The core was cherry red and I could hear the pop. Next second we got a runaway propeller on the #2 engine.

The temporary co-pilot Horace H. Shelton (all new crews were assigned an experienced one on the first two missions) gave a bail out order. However, I told the crew to stay put.

Shelton: We had a direct hit on #2 engine, blowing off the reduction gear housing. The left wheel dropped and flaps came partly down, couldn't get them up. One of our concerns was, since the hit had brought down our landing gear, whether our fuel would last. To overcome that, I activated the landing gear and it came up but the flaps were still partly down.

We thought we were on fire so we had the ball gunner come out and get his chute on.

Liddle: Soon after the bombs were dropped a flak burst hit number 2 engine knocking the entire nose of the engine off and started a fire in that engine. The prop could not be feathered and it started wind milling causing a terrible vibration. Someone gave the order to prepare to bail out. We left our assigned positions and were at the exits ready to go out. However, the engine fire went out so the order to bail out was not given.

Ringle: The co-pilot saw flames issuing from one of the engines and cried into the intercom: "Prepare to bail out!"
The bombardier Alex Stevenson only heard: "Bail out". His position was in the nose and my position, as navigator, was directly behind him. He dashed passed me—his intercom wires, connection to his heated suit, oxygen and mask connection, all pulled out and he pulled the release on the escape hatch.

He had one foot out when I grabbed him. I had heard some cruel stories about angry Berliners and what they did to captured airmen. I held him while I watched the altimeter at my station and pulled him back in.

Erik Dyreborg: The reader should keep in mind, that the situation onboard the plane, at that time, must have been extremely hectic and confusing with heavy flak, hits, explosions, fire, loss of gas etc. Some crew members thus perceived the order as: "Prepare to bail out" and some as: "Bail out!"

Shelton: We met more flak and it was damn accurate. Radio silence was the emphasis but I thought this warrants a call. I called the group leader requesting him to contact air-sea rescue to watch for us. The answer was: "Maintain radio silence!"

Ringle: We finally stabilized at 12,000 feet and took a northerly heading to the Baltic Sea. At this time some ME-109's took the opportunity to attack us but were engaged by some beautiful P-51's who drove them off.

Whiteman: I told the co-pilot to feather #2. It couldn't be done. The ship was shaking like hell. The governor on #2 didn't work and we got a runaway prop. When I tried to feather, the oil came out under pressure, all over my side of the ship. I was "blind" on my side.

Erik Dyreborg: The feathering of the prop on a B-17 could only be done hydraulically and not manually. Due to lack of oil to feather, the prop will just keep rotating and causes the plane to shake violently as it gets drier and hotter.

Whiteman: I started to fly the plane down, when we got hit again. I didn't realize it at the time, but something happened to the #4 engine. It was putting out 19 inches of merc, so I ignored it. I had other problems.

Liddle: We received damage to #4 engine causing the engine to loose power although it was still operational. We had a flak hole in the left wing and also in the inboard gas tank causing a loss of much fuel. We lost part of the oxygen system forcing us to fly at reduced altitude.

Whiteman: During this period, I never even felt it, a shell went through the #2 gas tank. Thank god it didn't go off. If it had blown, none of the crew would have survived. We lost 175 gallons of gas over Berlin.

This loss is what brought us down. The ball gunner confirmed the hole in the back of #2 nacell. I saw the hole on top, after the oil had cleared.

nacelle

Liddle: Another bomber had a similar hit in the gas tank over Germany but made it back to England. The mechanics took out the tank and found an unexploded shell in the tank. They disassembled the shell and found there was no explosive charge in it. However, there was a note written in Czechoslovakian, saying: "This is all we can do for you!" The shell was made by slave labour and many of the shells were intentionally made as duds.

Whiteman: We could not maintain our position in the bomber formation, so we were forced to drop out and go alone. We couldn't maintain altitude or air speed and started down.

Ringle: Due to flak from some islands, we would take some slight evasive action. The airplane threatened to stall out. We were now flying on only two engines and barely capable of maintaining our altitude.

Whiteman: I tried to get rid of the windmilling prop which was shaking the ship like crazy. I dived the airplane to build up air speed and then pull up sharply. It accomplished nothing, except loss of altitude. I did it twice and then gave up.

I still could not maintain altitude so everything movable was thrown overboard, guns and all.

I could not even hold about 12 thousand feet.

Then a P-51 Mustang fighter showed up on our right and we tried all channels on our radios and could not connect with the fighter. We realized then that we had no radios.

A big cloud bank showed up and we dove into it. Now we are on instruments. The ship stalled at 122 mph and indicated airspeed was

138 mph. Again we ran into flak and did some evasive action. Then shortly afterward we broke out over the North Sea.

This is when we realized that the loss of gas would make us ditch 75 miles or more off the British coast. At this time of year, we had about 20 minutes of life in The North Sea and also I had no idea what this battle damaged ship would do in a ditching and as the odds of being picked up were slim, I told the crew we were headed for Sweden.

We turned back into the soup and the navigator gave a heading on dead reckoning that took us right over the tail of Sweden.

We were running out of fuel and I was starting to go down when a hole in the soup opened up.

We were at 8000 feet and we went down through that in a very tight bank and broke out at 900 feet looking right at a German warship on the south east of Bornholm. The Germans were running like hell for their guns. I hollered to the co-pilot, to get on the left rudder and we whipped that ship, still diving. The Germans started their flak, however nothing hit our ship.

Erik Dyreborg: The German warship "SCHLESWIG-HOLSTEIN", anchored at Nexø roads had lost one anchor including 250 metres of anchor chain and divers were looking for the anchor and chain and investigating the possibilities of getting it back on board the vessel. For this reason the vessel had been at Nexø roads for more than a week.

According to reports concerning the German air space, allied aircrafts were all over Germany and German occupied territory, bombing heavily night and day.

At least once a day they had air raid warnings onboard the vessel and this Wednesday May 24, 1944 was no exception.

This is the report from "SCHLESWIG-HOLSTEIN"

"Just before 2.00 hrs p.m. a bomber with 4 engines (Fortress II) broke through the cloud ceiling at an altitude of approx. 700 metres. The bomber flies direct on to the port side of the vessel and in a short while we started anti aircraft shelling with an 8,8 cm and a 3,7 cm. The bomber turns off and climbs back into the clouds and disappears. We did not observe any hits on the bomber, however, later the same day, we received the news about, that this bomber had crashed near Rønne".

It is obvious that the Germans are talking about the B-17G that crash landed at Sose.

Whiteman: We were still diving, over and around a point of land. We were running on engines #1 and #3—on fumes only—and we went along the South Coast of Bornholm up to Rønne, parallel to a small cliff, when I decided to land on land.

Erik Dyreborg: Another "contact" with the bomber was made from The Air Report Centre at Rønne airport.

Journal no.: 13878 Date: 24th May 1944 Time: 02.10 hrs p.m.
One American "Flying Fortress" has been spotted from the airport of Rønne and reported flying at an altitude of approx. 100 metres—course southeast.

This message, however, was "delayed" for some time and passed on to the Germans later on, thus making the Germans' work more difficult and enabling the US airmen to gain valuable time for their escape.

Whiteman: I swung out over the water and headed back for the cliff. I fire walled the engines just before the cliff and eased up over and damn if we were not headed straight for a German machine gun nest on the edge of the airport. We were so low, I swear that I could count the teeth of the two gunners in the nest.

We continued inland for 4 or 5 km and turned down in. Now it was fish or cut bait.
WE REALLY WERE ON FUMES.

A large field was spotted and we made a pursuit curve approach, as I expected #1 or #3 to quit momentarily and just then the damn #2 prop comes off seconds after we hit the fields of "Sosegaard". A good landing was made, wheels up.

The landing was perfect and none of the crew was injured. The crew kids me, that it was the best landing I ever made. In truth it was! So many things could have gone wrong on that belly landing, I hate to think about it.

One thing did go wrong though: On the approach, when I pulled the throttles off, the right wing took a sharp dip. I had forgotten to take out the trim! I corrected with power to the #3 engine and eased the wing back down. I think that, if there had been no power in the #3 and that the wing had grabbed the ground first, we would have cart wheeled down the landing area.

Anyway everything turned out well. We all got out of the ship, PDQ, when it finally stopped.

One of the crew tried to set fire on #2 engine by opening a parachute and stuffing it around the engine. Our phosphorous bombs had been thrown overboard, when we unloaded everything.

A flare pistol fired a star shell at the engine. The shell hit the top of the nacell and caromed straight up 150 feet. Saying to the Germans: "Here we are boys".

With that, we all took off for the farmhouse, where we met the farm-hand Hans Christian West, who told us that the Krauts definitely were on the way. I think "Pee Wee" the Bombardier wanted to stay in the farm's hay loft, but was talked out of it. Then Hans Christian West told us to go North East to the big forest, Almindingen, so we did.

Our evasion & escape had begun!

"BTO in the ETO" on the fields of Sose May 24, 1944. German soldiers at the tail.

Hans Christian West and the Airmen

Narrated by Hans Christian West

After I had been in the army, during the summer of 1943, detained by the Germans 29th August and discharged in October, I was employed as a weeder by farmer Poul Jensen Sosemosegård. There are 3 farms around the town of Sose and they are all named "Sosegaard" and Jensen's farm is the one in the middle. The others are located to the north and to the south.

On the 24th of May 1944 I was busy weeding using a horse hitched in front of a weeder. The farmer and his wife were not at the farm that day. Suddenly I heard engine noise and I saw a plane coming from southeast, flying just above the water. There is approx. 1 kilometer from the farm to the beach. I could hear that the plane had problems, but I didn't give it much thought.

After a while the other farm hand—16 year old Poul Andersen—who was whitewashing the southern wing of the farm, came running towards me and said that there was a group of soldiers headed for the farm. He took over the horse and I ran back to the farm. I didn't know much English, but I understood that they had made an emergency landing on one of the fields below the southern Sosegaard by the water.

There is one thing which I cannot to this day understand. They thought that Bornholm was a part of Sweden and therefore neutral ground. They got very upset as I told them that Bornholm was Danish territory and occupied by the Germans.

After that, one of them was determined to hide in the hayloft. When I told them that the Germans used to stick their bayonets into the hay when they were looking for refugees, and that they could be here any minute, they immediately prepared themselves to move on. However, the one who was on his way up to the hayloft didn't want to come down again so his friends had to pull him down.

I still don't get it. If they thought that they had landed on Swedish territory, they didn't have to hide but just wait for the authorities to contact them and pick them up.

I explained to them, to the best of my ability, that there were resistance people on the island, but that I unfortunately didn't have any contact with them. I told them that I had heard about people in the Northern part of Bornholm, who helped refugees to Sweden and that they should go to Almindingen, which we could see from where we were standing, as quickly as possible and hide until they were able to get in touch with someone who would help them.

Our conversation probably didn't last for more than 10—15 minutes. I parted with them and wished them the best of luck. At that time there were 10 airmen. I then went back to work in the field, while I kept them in my sight until they disappeared in the terrain.

About half an hour later I saw a group of German soldiers, walking down the private road, which passes by the Northern Sosegaard and Hallegaardsvej, but fortunately they didn't contact me. Just like the Americans they had followed the creek and walked across the courtyard and knocked on the kitchen door. There was only a young girl at home, and she told me afterwards that she had been scared, because one of the soldiers had behaved in a very threatening manner, but then one of the older German soldiers in the group had padded her on the head and said that she should run back to her mother. She didn't understand much of what had been said, but just pointed in direction of Hallegaardsvej, which is 90 degrees to the east compared to the route that I had given the Americans. Fortunately she didn't mention to the Germans that I had talked to the Americans. Good girl!

I went for several days wondering what had happened to them, and I guess I was a little bit sorry for not being able to give them more help.

Fortunately I heard, a few days later, that they had all evaded to Sweden, safe and sound.

Knud Marcher—"The Thief" !

Narrated by Niels Christian Bohn Pihl

Knud Marcher, who lived near Kjølleregårds Station where his parents had a small house, was studying to be a dairyman on the Østerlars-Dybdal Dairy, however Wednesday 24th May 1944 was his day off.

He saw the bomber flying at a very low altitude, making a lot of smoke so he was sure that it would land very soon. He took his bike and went southeast.

He found the bomber abandoned on the fields of "Sosegaard" south of the country road Rønne—Pedersker—Nexø and Knud Marcher was definitly the very first person arriving at the bomber, after the airmen had left.

As he did not observe any people at all, he went into the bomber, picked up a pair of flying boots, a flashlight and a signal pistol. Then he left the bomber, realizing that the Germans would soon be there.

He went back on the country road and drove west. Then he met a German patrol car, however the Germans did not pay any attention to him.

A truck loaded with clay approached from behind. The truck driver drove alongside Knud Marcher and shouted at him that he should give him the boots he was carrying on the back of his bike. Knud Marcher refused and told the truck driver that he intended to keep the boots, as he himself had stolen the boots from the bomber. The truck driver then shouted, that he would report him to the Germans, but Knud Marcher shouted back: You don't know who I am and where I live.

Knud Marcher continued on his bike until he reached his home, guarding his stolen merchandise and according to Knud Marcher he still has it, somewhere.

The Evasion & Escape of: The Navigator 2nd LT Seymour Ringle & The Bombardier 2nd LT James A. Stevenson

Narrated by Seymour Ringle

We attempted to destroy the airplane by wrapping a parachute around the #2 engine, which was saturated with gas and oil and setting it on fire but to no avail. We were told at our debriefing later, that parachutes were made of nylon and non-inflammable.

When a German plane came overhead and started circling we ran for the woods and decided to split up in pairs.

Stevenson and I paired up and we headed north.

I don't know what the weather is generally on Bornholm but, for our brief stay, the climate was miserable, rainy and cold and we were both sick almost from the time that we touched down.

We discussed our situation and decided that our best bet would be to attempt to contact the vaunted underground that we had heard so much about and we knocked on quite a few farmhouse doors saying: "Americanske Aviators".

We were greeted amiably by all and given food and drink but no one would harbour us.

We were walking along a road one day and a man in running clothes jogged by us saying: "Good morning" and kept running to the inter-section where he stopped next to a hay cart and started urinating. We approached him and he told us that the Germans were in the midst of an intensive search for our crew and he reached under his sweat shirt and gave us a bag full of food and directing us to hide out in the woods until dark and then proceed to the town of Gudhjem and steal a boat and sail to Sweden.

When it got dark, we headed for Gudhjem. We didn't reach Gudhjem but hid for a whole day in bathing cabin no. 23 on the Beach of Mel-sted.

The next night we walked along the coast path to Gudhjem in heavy rain.

By the time we got to Gudhjem (meaning God's Home), we were completely discouraged and disheartened since neither of us had even elementary knowledge when it came to operating a boat and we could see German soldiers on patrol at the docks.

The only encouragement was the fact that every citizen we had approached had treated us with kindness and consideration. So we decided to approach the first light we encountered in town and knock on the door and play it by ear. We headed for a light up the street but came across an intersection which showed a light that was closer. We turned to the light and knocked on the door of that house. A woman opened the door and I said "Americanske Aviators". She pulled us in and that morning another man came to that house and we followed him to another house where we went up to an attic bedroom and they fed us.

Erik Dyreborg: Both airmen were now in the safe house of Mr. Kaas Hansen, Gudhjem. Mr. Kaas Hansen's daughter Vibeke, now Vibeke Bech, talked with the airmen a few times and Shorty gave her an Air Force insignia, which she is still wearing.

Ringle: Mr. Kaas Hansen told us that their son who had previously occupied "our" bedroom was now living in Minnesota.

When we described the location of the first light we had headed for, we were informed that it was same municipal building that the Gestapo had taken over.

We were given civilian clothes and I.D. papers using the photos from our escape kits and were then escorted right past the German guards on the wharf and on to a boat.
Shorty was dressed in a sailor suit and looked young enough to be my son.

The boat dropped us off near Malmö, Sweden and we were met by the American Consul and then we were put on a train to Stockholm.

We were classified as refugees and flown to Scotland on a B-24 without military markings and crews in civilian clothes.

Shorty and I were then taken to Widewing H.Q. in London where we were interrogated by the British Admiralty. It seems that a raid was being planned by the commandos on an installation on the northeast end of Bornholm, which they suspected would be launching V-2's and wanted confirmation from us.

We were finally flown back to the U.S. in a C-54 which was scheduled to land at Mitchell Field in Queens N.Y. but over flew it instead and dropped Shorty and myself off in Washington D.C. where we were interrogated for a couple of days with our stories, getting shorter each time we told them and we were then released to go home on leave.

Well, when we did not return from our raid on Berlin, M.I.A. telegrams had been sent to our homes. When we were officially located D-day intervened and nobody at home was notified of the good news.

I will terminate this account by leaving you to imagine the scene as I walked in on an unsuspecting family and friends at home.

I am a member of the Air Forces Escape and Evasion Society—AFEES. The AFEES put out a publication wherein are recounted many exploits of evadees and escapees most of which are of such an incredibly harrowing nature that our misadventure was a comparative walk in the park.

Ringle: That morning on May 24th Shorty had shaved for the first time and had forgotten his dog tags in the latrine. When he proclaimed his fear of being shot as a spy when caught, I showed him the "H" on my dog tags which automatically entitled me to become a member of the "final solution" club.

James "Shorty" Stevenson, December 1943.

Shorty, however still had his small winged propeller with him as some sort of proof of being an airman and it was Shorty who gave the insignia to Vibeke when we were in Gudhjem in her father's house.

I feel that the entire mission (as is just about all of life) was a series of random happenings—luck?

The only portion I was personally proud of was what I consider the professional job of navigation I performed. I was on DR (dead reckoning) for over three hours under the most difficult of flying conditions and, if we had descended at the time of my ETA, we would have hit it right on the nose.

We were certainly fortunate to have finally landed and ended up in the protective hands of the valiant Danes / Bornholmers who saved our necks. Myself, my wife and all join in grateful gratitude.

The two Airmen in Gudhjem

Narrated by Vibeke Bech, daughter of Mr. Kaas Hansen.

When the two airmen arrived in Gudhjem, it must have been during the night of the 25th May 1944, they knocked on the door at our neighbour Christian Holm and they spent the night there as well. They were put in an attic, which could only be accessed by a ladder and a small hatch. It probably wasn't very comfortable but a good hide out it sure was. The next day they were taken to my parents' house.

The airmen had to be extremely quiet during the daytime as you could hear every sound and especially when someone was visiting Kaas Hansen.

In such a small town, where everybody knows each other, it is not easy to hide when something unusual is going on. I know that the baker in town was wondering why all of a sudden we bought so much bread.

My mother did the cooking for the airmen and once she served a well known Danish desert called "Rødgrød med fløde"—almost impossible to pronounce for a foreigner but this desert is actually some sort of red fruit juice thickened with flour and on top of it you put sugar and milk or crème.

The airmen had NEVER seen anything like it and simply refused to eat it. How can you eat fruit-something with milk on it? No way!

The postmaster in town, H. Sørensen, fortunately, could get hold on fake ration cards. He could also make fake identification cards for the pilots, and he did this in agreement with Policeman Dinesen. As I remember it, one of the pilots was named Peter Pedersen—or something like that—a common Danish name.

We were quite impressed that the airmen, in their situation at that time, were thinking of our safety.

They said: "If the Germans find us, we will "just" end up as POWs, but your, unknown destiny will probably be far worse".

On the other hand, the airmen also were very pessimistic regarding their own survival of the war.

The two airmen were given civilian clothes but it was not possible to get civilian shoes for them.

I myself saw when the two airmen and Policeman Dinesen walked toward the steamer "CARL", passing 16 German soldiers on the dock. Since the Germans knew Dinesen well and trusted him blindly, they probably thought everything was okay and the airmen got onboard the steamer, as other tourists, without any problems.

The Germans didn't even observe that the two airmen still had their flying boots on.

During the trip to Sweden, the airmen were placed in the Captain's cabin and got a good meal. At Falsterbo, Sweden, the airmen got on board the Coast Guard pilot's boat from the "CARL"and their evasion and escape had come to an end.

After Ringle and Stevenson had arrived in Sweden, my father got a message from them, through Captain Einar Mikkelsen (The Polar Scientist), who had met them in Stockholm. They told him that they had lived in a house with the house end towards the water. Einar Mikkelsen then thought that they had lived in his house, because his house also had the end wall towards the water.

The airmen never mentioned any names.

After the war my parents got an inquiry from the American Embassy who offered them a financial compensation for the costs that they might have had with the pilots living with them. It was a fine gesture from the Americans, but my father turned it down. I guess everyone who was involved in these events was given that offer.

About Father Hjort Lange, I know that he visited "our" pilots several times. He and my father often talked on the phone about fugitives who should be transported to Sweden. They used their own secret language, e.g. when they were talking about the fugitives they mentioned them as a number of jars of honey.

Also Policeman Dinesen from the Danish Coast Guard and 1st Officer O. Hansen from "CARL" visited the airmen, instructing the airmen about their coming escape on board the "CARL".

The evasion and escape of the two airmen was well planned and it became a success.

Had the Germans launched house searches, the whole thing could have ended very dramatically. There is no doubt, the Germans knew about the airmen. However, maybe the Germans in Gudhjem didn't want too much trouble. Bornholm was a far better place for a German soldier than the Eastern Front.

The Evasion & Escape of:
The Radio Operator SGT William Nunn &
The Left Waist Gunner SGT Orlando Yemma

Narrated by Orlando Yemma

After the crash landing at Sose and after having talked to a farmhand at Sosegaard, we all went together towards the forest Almindingen.

Now Bill and I went into the forest and it was starting to drizzle and we saw two hunters with their Half-short Pants-etc. We walked right up to a small town and observed people walking in the streets, then we went back into the forest and the first night we slept in an abandoned hut, it was chilly so we put a broken door across for heat.

The next day, 25th May 1944 we were walking on a road when we saw a neat little cottage in the middle of a green field, but as we walked we noticed a Bornholmer sawing some wood. We looked at him and he looked at us. He was wearing a red & black jacket like we have here (Checker-board). We did not talk with the sawing Bornholmer but we remembered the neat little cottage in the field, and we decided to rest there.

We just started to lie down and the door shutter opened. A German Soldier stood there and pointed a small gun at us and told us to come out. We did.

The German Soldier came on a bike as we were walking toward their base, on the Street, Bill whispered: "Lando, I am going to say Fräulein (The German word for Miss) and then I'll point to the hill and then I'll jump the Kraut".

Bill said Fräulein, pointed to the hill, jumped the Kraut and took his gun. We ran all we could up the hill and hid behind a tree. From there, we could see about 20-25 German Soldiers in their Green-grey uniforms with bayonets, looking in the direction, where we were.

Bill threw the gun away and we continued our escape.

Then as we were walking we saw a clothesline with two jackets and pants. We took it all and went back in the woods, changed and left our clothing in the forest.

I had my High School ring in the airman jacket, I remembered that later, so somebody on Bornholm has a "Haverhill High School Ring" in his possession—may be.

We dug a little hole to cover our uniforms and that night, we slept in the open.

The next morning 26th May 1944 we were walking on a road about 50 yards from the ocean. The two airmen were now at Stammershalle just south of Tejn on the North Coast.

A small group of German soldiers were guarding the area near a little hut.
I looked them right in their eyes and Bill said :" Don't look" and I said: " Too late, I already did". For some odd reason and to our luck, the Germans did not pay any attention to us.

We just walked on, saw a stone mason making stones for probably Danish people.

We approached him and he looked around and took us into his little hut, walked away and came back with sandwiches and a drink. We swallowed them—we were so hungry. He told us, that he had a sister who was a school teacher in California.

(The two airmen had met Oscar Fält, living near Allinge. They slept in his hut that night, which was near Norskehus.)

Next day 27th May 1944 the stone mason brought food and coffee. He also brought his two young daughters down. The girls wanted to know if we knew about Hollywood ?

This was our third day on Bornholm and he said it was a full moon and we had to wait until the next night.

On the next day 28th May 1944, the fourth day, the same thing happened, the stone mason brought food and drink.

Around midnight the stone mason brought his friend who had a little row boat. He pointed to a lighthouse and he said: "Row for the lighthouse, that is Sweden". We shook hands, hugged and started to row.

The Baltic Sea with small waves. I rowed the rear and Bill rowed the front, or the other way around. But after an hour we observed a German Coast Guard, a pretty big one.

We had a fishing pole like we were fishing, but they never saw us. Bill lost his oar but we got it back. We rowed for about 6 hours, then we heard a Rooster crowing, we could see land, rowed all we could towards the beach and pulled up the rowboat. It was now 29th May 1944.

A paperboy saw us, just like on the street Sunday morning and a few minutes later a Swedish Detective came down on a bike and introduced himself. Also a woman that lived on the corner came out and took us inside her house. We had arrived in the Swedish town of Simrishamn.
There were a few people that saw us in her house. We had coffee and cake. Her husband was a Swedish sailor and was stationed in New York. She spoke English very well as did others.

I remember that Bill and I still had big blisters on the backside of our hands.

After coffee and cake, we went to the police station and they put us up for one night. They treated us well.

The next day 30th May 1944, we were visited by a general and his aide who was about 6 foot 9 inches tall. The general was short.

He wanted to know why the Swedish Coast Guard did not observe us coming into their territorial waters. The tall major or higher rank was the interpreter.
Again we had coffee and cake.

Then the police had called our Ambassador and we were told that we would be put on a train to go to Stockholm. We spent 2 days at Simrishamn.

The detective that was taking care of us in Simrishamn, Sweden, his son was a movie star and on the cover of magazines, told Bill and I that we could expect a Swedish Colonel, his wife and mother in law. They would try to tap our compartment on the train. They would come in and question us on facts about our base.

Just as soon as we got on the train and into our compartment, there was a tap and it was the Colonel.

When we got to Stockholm, other detectives would meet us. We told them that we had been questioned and the detectives took them away. Later, we were told, that they were German spies.

Then we met the U.S. Ambassador and he shook our hands. We went to the office and talked for a few minutes and then he gave us $ 300.00 in Swedish money and we went to a men's store, where we bought a suit, silk underwear and shoes and a 35 mil camera.

We were put up at The Continental Hotel, nice rooms. We met a Swede who would show us Stockholm etc. Bill and I were down at a park near the Harbour and were taking pictures of it when two tall policeman came over and asked if we were taking pictures and we said yes.

They had no guns, but they confiscated our film and gave us the camera back. Apart from that, we had a good time. We went to a movie, nightclub and sauna a few times. Got stamps for food to eat—we lived well.

Every time we came to an intersection, there must have been a hundred bikes, men and women, the women would pull up their skirts as they knew we were Americans.

On June 5th 1944, after 5 days in Stockholm, we were taken to Stockholm airport , where we saw German pilots and British pilots. We got on a stripped down B-24 with a group of Norwegians on board too. They were going to England to fight for the Norway troops helping the allies.

Back to London I was first off the plane and our ambassador says:" He is an American" and Bill was behind me—what a feeling that was to hear.

Then to our base, met the Commanding officer, then on to London, where we went on a B-17 over to Santa Maria, Portugal to New York where we were for two days for debriefing.

Bill and I shook hands and bid each other goodbye and that was the last time I saw Bill Nunn.

I went home after 10 days, then on to Atlanta City for a month—delicious. Then I was assigned to Galveston Air Base which was nice.

That was when I saw Lt. Whiteman walking by, as I was on the train. I hollered at him, he waved back and the train pulled out.

Erik Dyreborg: Bill Nunn visited Bornholm in 1982.

The Evasion & Escape of:
The Top Turret Gunner S/SGT Richard H. O'Bannon &
The Tail Gunner SGT Jack R. Culliton
Narrated by Erik Dyreborg

It has not been possible to get a more detailed information from the airmen themselves as they are both deceased.

The information with regard to their evasion and escape has therefore been written off from the E & E report dated June 17, 1944.

When we split up into pairs in the woods we were the last to leave. After some distance we crawled under a pile of bushes to get out of the rain and slept a bit. A man came along on a bicycle, apparently looking for us. He pointed out a house to us and we approached it cautiously.

We were eagerly welcomed there and fed, but we were not allowed to sleep in the barn. Our hosts told us to go north to the coast between Nekso and Svaneke, where they said there were fewer Germans, and find a fisherman to take us to Sweden.
We climbed into a haystack for the night, but before we could go to sleep we could hear Germans around, poking here and there and sticking pitchforks into haystacks. We stayed where we were until about 22:30 and then started walking north again.

We tried to avoid farmhouses for fear that dogs might bark at us. We thought that everybody was watching us, and when a car stopped not far from us on a road, we thought that we had been spotted. When it began to get light, we found a haystack and dug into it from the top.

The next morning the sun woke us up. We saw a farmer in his yard and went to the house to ask for food. We were fed and given food to carry. We continued north, hiding when there was any danger of being seen.

We approached a farmer and his daughter, but the farmer seemed to think that we were a menace to his daughter.

We stopped by a stone pit to eat some of the food we carried. Later we carried on, waving at many of the farmers whom we passed. Most of them waved back.

In the woods we came upon a man who took us to a barn and showed us a large map of the island and fed us royally. He told us that some other members of our crew were in the neighborhood. Only one of us had escape pictures and we left one with the man. Both of us left our names and home addresses.

Later we stopped and built a little shelter from the rain, but it leaked and we were eaten up by ants. Later in the day, we approached a man to let us stay in his barn. He was afraid of the Germans but he fed us and directed us to a shed which afforded shelter from the heavy rain. Early the next morning we were told where to go to try to find a boat.

Walking in the woods, we met a man on a bicycle. When he learned what we wanted to do, he took us to a lake, showed us a rowboat, and made us understand that we would have to steal a boat to get to Sweden. Then he took us to a barn, hid us in the hay, and took our socks to dry. Later we were fed.

About noon we approached another farmhouse near the coast. A young fellow was very glad to see us, but was trembling while he talked to us. He told us that two of our crew had been caught by the Germans. (The young fellow was referring to Bill Nunn and Orlando Yemma). He gave us food and directed us to the coast to get a boat.

After a fruitless day of dodging patrols and hiding among the rocks, a girl took us to a farmhouse and fed us. Later at night we went with her and found a boat which we took and pushed out into the water, making all too much noise, we thought.

We saw a number of surfaced submarines which we passed safely. We headed north steering by the North Star and the Dipper. We saw submarines for hours.

At daylight we checked our course by our escape compasses. We had been told that Sweden was only 7 miles (The distance from Bornholm to Sweden is 25 miles at the nearest point) and we knew that we had rowed at least that far; still we could see no land, except a group of islands on our left. We rowed all day and the next night. The second morning we could still see nothing but the little islands.

In the early morning we ran into a fog bank, which we welcomed, because we had seen a submarine's periscope directed at us. We began hearing boat whistles, which we took to be fog horns. About 11:00 we could see the sun and things cleared a bit. Still there was no land.

At last when we were about to give up, we saw a boat. We waved at it and it came toward us. Fortunately it turned out to be Swedish. We were brought on board, fed and taken to Sweden.

Both airmen were back in The United Kingdom on June 5, 1944.

The Evasion & Escape of:
The Co-Pilot 2nd LT Horace H. Shelton &
The Righ Waist Gunner SGT Marvin L. Carraway

Shelton's story is narrated by Dary Shelton after an interview in 1994.

After having talked with the farmhand Hans Christian West at "Soseg-aard", who told us that the Germans would soon be coming, we all started walking heading North.

When we left the open field a German plane flew over at about 200 feet, looking for us but we were well hidden.

We took off our heavy clothes and boots; some put on GI shoes, and then we split into pairs. Carraway and I paired up.

After about 30 minutes we met a boy who spoke English. He said a German airfield was nearby and about the same time we saw a plane landing just west of us. We continued north, keeping most of the time in the woods.

Finally, the woods ended and we walked down the roads trying for some hills with heavy timber. Finally, we came to a beautiful area of woods, lakes, hills and scattered fields.

We came to a farm house. Near it was a large fenced-in area for stock, stacks of hay and a large barn. The people gave us some sandwiches and we found warm places in the hay to sleep.

We were well bedded down and the man of the house came out gesticulating, very excited. You can get along pretty good with sign language if you have to.

He took us out to the big gate and pointed to fresh tire tracks. The Germans were looking for us so naturally he was scared. We left but the next day was a repeat of the same tableau.

We were constantly on the run with two sandwiches that lasted five days. We slept in a barn and the people never knew we were there. They came in to do some work while we continued to sleep.

May 25th 1944. Sometimes we became somewhat complacent, not seeing anybody around. We walked right down the middle of the road. One night I observed some lights coming into shore. They looked like they were right on top of the water. Then I saw another light. When daylight came, we could see it was submarines surfacing and coming toward the mother ship.

Later Navy intelligence told us that they thought it was a training school for submarine people.

Erik Dyreborg: It was not a school, it was an area for testing the noise of the submarines propellers.

Shelton: With a camera I could have made some good pictures.

By this time of course, everybody on the island knew about the B-17 and the crew.

We located another farm at 0100 on the 25th where we hid in the barn. We were damp and cold and our feet were wet from walking through fields. Finally, we went to an adjacent farmhouse and stayed in a shed.

At 0800 we caught the attention of a woman and she came to the shed to talk. Although she couldn't speak English she brought us a map to show us where we were. At 0900 her husband came and talked to us. She fixed us a hot water bottle to warm our feet and gave us blankets. Then they moved us to a barn with straw and with our blankets and wool-lined lap robe we were pretty warm. They brought us a large basket of sandwiches and showed us where to go on the map to possibly obtain a boat to Sweden.

After sleeping all day we were given more sandwiches and milk; and then oiled our shoes to keep the water out and we then resumed our search for escape.
Thereafter a storm arose with high winds and heavy rain so we had to go back to the same barn.

Finally, at 2300 of the 26th May we started out again walking toward the coast according to the map. Coming out near the bay we counted about a dozen submarines around the mother ship. Just before daylight we found a shed to hide in. A farmer came out of the house and we motioned to him.

He brought us sandwiches and told us to go. We noticed that the submarines were gone but the mother ship was still anchored in the bay.

We stayed in the woods until we were near the north coast. After washing our feet and socks in a pool of water, we rested until late in the afternoon. A lady at the farmhouse gave us sandwiches, cake and buttermilk.

At 2200 we went to the town of Vang and we were told that the Germans were looking for us. We left that town in the dust as fast as we could walk.

Down near the coast we found a light in a house. We knocked but when the people saw us they were extremely distraught, turning out the light and latching the door.

Out from the coast we found a small lake with a boat. We followed a trail to an inlet of the bay. We discovered many fishermen's boats tied up at the docks. Finally, we gave up and went to a haystack to spend the night.

We stayed out of sight until dark planning to saw a lock off the boat with a hacksaw that we had stolen. Finally, a fisherman came by and showed us a better hiding place and he said that someone who could speak English would be back that night.

At 2300 a man appeared who spoke fluently English and told us to follow him. We stayed in his house and after a while they brought in Whiteman and Liddle.

They brought us food and took us to see a Mr. Petersen, arriving at his home on the 29th. We went to bed for the first time in six days. We remained there until midnight of the 1st and all we did was eat and sleep.

While there, we saw a few German planes pass over and once we saw a submarine. We were unable to identify an explosion that shook the house. We were unable to go down to the landing because German soldiers were guarding the area.

Petersen was already suspected by the Germans after a previous trip to Sweden with two other American flyers. Consequently, he decided to embark with his whole family thinking he might be under surveillance.

He took his boat out into the Baltic and returned to a prearranged spot. We had two Danish police with us and boarded at 0100 on the 2nd June along with his family, two policemen and some others.

On arriving in Sweden we were taken to the Swedish police office to fill out forms and then to the American consul, a Mr. Briggs at 1900. There we met some American boys who were working on planes. They took us to the train for Stockholm where we arrived 3rd June.

After staying some days in Stockholm, we were finally flown back to the U.K. were we arrived 11th June 1944.

Shelton's Account—Stockholm, Sweden.

Erik Dyreborg: The account (handwritten by Horace H. Shelton during his stay in Stockholm) was mailed to me by Shelton's brother Gene Shelton. This newly discovered document is far more detailed, especially with regard to the stay in Stockholm, Sweden.

Shelton: We arrived in Stockholm at 08:15 on June 3rd and after spending all day filling out a few forms, getting paid, buying civilian clothes, etc. we settled down for a good haircut, shave, shampoo, massage, tonic and then a nice meal.

Went to a club and danced a few times and drank some beer. Boy what women they have over here and the towns, country and people are the cleanest I've ever seen. To bed at 01:00.

Note: From May 24th until June 3rd is written from memory of our experiences so they may not be too accurate.

June 4th up at 09:00 for breakfast. Rested some more then had dinner. Made some pictures of our crew. Four of us are supposed to leave for England today—O'Bannon, Culliton, Nunn and Yemma.

Watches, compass, etc. can be bought very cheap here so most of the boys try to take a lot home but it's hard to get them by the Customs so it may be a bad investment.

The boys left the hotel at 20:00.

Had supper then moved from Room 108 to 117 so we could have a bath. Carraway and I walked around town. Gee! What beautiful parks and restaurants. We went to the Boulevard Club again had 3 beers a piece and a sandwich. Home at 12:30.

Talked to an engineer of a crew that came over on the same boat I—Barrick and Munn are over here too. Guess I won't get to see them though. To bed at 01:00 as we have a real busy day tomorrow.

June 5th. Up at 08:00. Had breakfast then took passport photos to the office. Back to the Hotel and then started out to buy knives, watches silk and stockings, suitcases and pipes. Paid 20 kroner for knives, 18 for suitcase, 10 for suspenders, 20 for lighters, 33 for silk hose, 295 for watch, 15 for lipstick. 4 kroner = 1 US Dollar.

Were supposed to leave for England tonight but they called it off. Went to a show and saw "Above Suspicion" with Fred Mc Murray. Had coffee and cakes and to bed at 24:00.

June 6th. Up at 09:30. Had coffee and rolls in bed. Took a bath and went walking. Stopped at a Café and American Bar for a drink. Went back to the Hotel and had a large dinner.

Bought some post cards and a picture book of Stockholm. Went to bed at 14:30 and slept until 17:30. Had ice cream or "Glass" in Swedish.

Whiteman, a SGT. and I went to see "Butlers Sister" Deanna Durbin, Franchot Jones and Pat O'Brien. Had two beers at Boulevard Club and to bed at 01:00.

Invasion started this morning but we don't know what the hell is going on because we can't read these papers, etc.

June 7th. Up at 10:00. Breakfast in room. Had dinner 13:30. Went to legation at 14:00. Went to American Club and played pool. Back to hotel and shaved.

Had supper at Parrott Café. Started to a show but no reservations so waited until 21:15 for last show. After we went to the show we realized it was a French Picture and translated into Swedish so we couldn't understand a word of it. Left and went home. Had two dishes of ice cream and coffee before going to bed.

June 8th. Up at 10:00. Breakfast in room then a hot bath. Dinner at 13:00. Went to legation. Back to Hotel for a shave. Had supper at the Parrott Café. Date with the girl there so we went to another café and had a sandwich and a drink. We just talked about the difference between our countries, etc. Took her home at 00:30 and then to Hotel for bed.

June 9th. Up at 12:30. Had dinner. Then went to store to get watch regulated. Went to legation and we are on the alert. Drew 36 dollars. From the 3rd through the 8th drew 173 Dollars. Had supper and then a shave. Packed my suitcase but it's called off for today so we are here for at least 24 hrs. more.

Bought a shirt. 2 pair of socks, etc. today. Meet LT Sills tonight. We went on a tour of night clubs. Danced quite a lot tonight and had a pretty nice time talking with some of the girls. To bed at 00:30.

June 10th. Up at 09:30. Had fresh eggs for breakfast for the first time in about a month. Got a haircut and a shampoo. Had dinner at 14:30 then went to the store to get the watch set. Bought a cigarette case with a map of Sweden and Norway on it for 5 kroner. Back to the Hotel for ice cream then had cakes and milk. We are alerted for tonight.

At 20:30 we took a taxi to the Airport and flew to England.

Horace H. Shelton. Photo taken in England winter 1944. Shelton died September 25, 2001 in Texas.

An Airman's Diary.

Shelton's day-by-day Record from WW II

The diary covers incidents from November 1st 1943 till July 13th 1944.

1943

November 1st	Left Kearney, Nebraska for Camp Kilmer, New Jersey by train. Went through Chicago, Cleveland and arrived in New York. In that area for 10 days.
November 14th	Left by train to board the "Queen Mary" for England.
November 21st	Debarked. Went through Sheffield, Berby and arrived at Tillshead.
November 22nd	Then on through London to Hempstead where we stayed for 21 days, visiting surrounding towns.
December 11th	A German Junkers 88 came over the barracks real low, one engine smoking, so guess he didn't get far.
December 13th	Attending classes to the 26th. Some combat pictures and talks by men who have been on many missions.
December 21st	German planes bombed London.
December 26th	We are going to be assigned to 401st Bomb Group.
December 27th	Trucks picked us up and we went through North Hampton to base where we were assigned to the 615th Squadron.
December 28th	Had pictures made of us in civilian clothes to use for escaping from France. I won 440 dollars in blackjack.
December 29th	Sick call for cold.
December 30th	Too cold to go to school.
December 31st	A new crew of officers moved in, Bill Trimble's crew, his bombardier used to sing with Charlie Spivack and Jack Teagarden Orchestra.

1 9 4 4

January 1st	Group on mission to Bordeaux today. Weather was zero when they turned. Lost one plane due to weather, the crew bailed out, one lost over target, one landed in channel, co-pilot killed.

January 1st — Group on mission to Bordeaux today. Weather was zero when they turned. Lost one plane due to weather, the crew bailed out, one lost over target, one landed in channel, co-pilot killed.

January 2nd — Drew throat mikes and goggles today.

January 4th — Scheduled to fly. We were flying a new B-17 to test at 25.000 feet, went to 30.000, very cold, and we were lost when we came down, landed on RAF base. They were having a big party. We stayed all night.

January 7th — My pilot went on mission as co-pilot to Ludwigshaven. Our tail gunner shot down a ME-109.

January 9th — Flew today, squadron formation practice, flew into clouds and lost the formation.

January 12th — Bad news about our group mission to Berlin area, lost lots of ships, shot to hell.

January 13th — Had class, some of crews on yesterday's raid talked about how awful it was. One of the planes we flew in the day before this raid was lost.

January 14th — Operations are getting ready for a mission. Pete, Foster and I went to Kettering on bicycles, a 20 mile trip. Later we went outside in time to see the last two men bail out of ship just back from mission with the control cables shot away, pilot landing by using AFCE.

January 15th — Up at 03:00 to go on a mission to Gotha, near Berlin, mission scrubbed because of weather. We were to destroy twin-engine fighters that are made there.

January 16th — Assigned to new B-17 today. Because of weather we couldn't fly the next few days.

January 24th — 1st mission. We were scheduled to bomb factories in Frankfurt but heavy clouds broke up formation and we returned.

January 25th	Went to London, by train about 30 minutes, stayed Dutchess Club, 26th room at the Royal Hotel, dinner at the Consolidated Officers Mess.
January 29th	2nd mission. Took off for Frankfurt, bombed at 11:27, saw flak and fighters leaving target, saw a B-17 explode, 3 crews missing. We only had one flak hole in our ship. We have had several air raids lately…just stepped outside and saw sky light up with bombs the rascals brought over.
January 30th	3rd mission. To Brunswick, trip okay except bomb doors wouldn't close after we had trouble getting bombs dropped. FW-190 shot a ship down flying next to us. Guess we were lucky. I'm so tired I'll go to bed about 21:00. We may go on another mission tomorrow.
January 31st	Mission to Frankfurt scrubbed about hour before takeoff. Letter to Gene, bed at 21:00.
February 1st	Second attempt for Frankfurt, but scrubbed.
February 3rd	4th mission. To Wilhelmshaven (submarine base), took off at 08:30, home 15:30, cloudy and we had to let down from 20.000 feet to 1.500 feet, through clouds in formation, flak pretty heavy and accurate. Bill Trimble passed out at altitude and also brought a piece of flak home.
February 4th	5th mission. Raid on Frankfurt. We couldn't find group we were to go with but found another group. Flak pretty bad and saw about 15 FW-190's, one man had to have foot removed because of flak.
February 5th	6th mission. To Chateaux Roux, visual bombing at 15.000 feet. En route we were attacked a ME-109 and FW-190. The plane we were flying wing on had one man killed (Christonsen crew) and one man injured, he may die. Also the ship on our left shot pretty bad with 20 mm cannon. The attacking planes were Goerings best pilots (yellow nose) according to the Major. Eight men were killed in our group.

February 6th

7th mission. To Caen, France, but couldn't because of clouds on primary target, returned to coast and bombed an airfield and hangers, beautiful! I went back to bomb bay and watched as bombs hit hangers.
We saw 12 ME-109's today en route home. Very near. Over London. Our leaders nearly led us into the balloon barrage; we broke formation to get away from the cables. Later I went into London at Grosvenor House, tired, bath and to bed. I've flown four straight missions. We had little sleep for four days and because of fatigue, my pilot, Ed Garner and one of the gunners were put in hospital.

February 7th

Stayed in London for three days, caught train back to base on February 9th went to class about electronic superchargers on B-17.

February 11th

8th mission. To Frankfurt, formation poor and flak accurate over target. ME-109 came up behind us as we left target and shot at some planes. We heard that a German flew a B-17 in our formation today and a P-47 shot him down.

February 15th

I went into Kettering to take laundry. I had a letter from William Frank with 96th Bomb Group. He was killed.

February 19th

Snow on ground this morning. I and another co-pilot went to London. He caught the last train back but I stayed there. He was to be at base for mission.

February 20th

I caught train back to base to find that my crew was missing in action over Leipzig, were flying "coffin corner". I learned months later that fighters came up behind and hit them repeatedly with 20 mm cannon. Radio operator and left waist gunner killed. Pilots body found near wreck of plane. All five enlisted men in rear of plane wounded or killed. The tail gunner had a leg nearly blown off. Was amputated by Germans. Six in all that were still alive though wounded were prisoners for 15 months.

February 21st

Their belongings are gone from our barracks, which makes it kinda bare.

February 22nd	I am scheduled to fly with a new crew to German base tomorrow, but fuse burned out on motor for our hydraulic brakes and we went off of taxi strip into mud, had to be pulled out. That made us late to find our group so we came back. The planes were all shot to hell on this mission.
February 24th	9th mission. Off to Schweinfurt, a ball bearing plant, had one attack by six ME-109's, flak pretty accurate. By the time we dropped our bombs the factory was already burning.
February 25th	10th mission. To Augsburg, lots of fighters and many planes went down, had ten holes in our plane. Gougers friend came to visit today not knowing that he is in prison.
February 28th	We had a practice mission today. Moved part of my clothes to Barracks # 18.
March 2nd	11th mission. To Frankfurt, attacked by eight fighters before target and by two close to channel going home. Sheehan in high squadron shot down, saw four chutes from his plane.
March 3rd	Up at 03:00 mission to Berlin, weather bad, went up to 28.000 feet,—60 turned back.
March 4th	Berlin again and again bad weather, no luck, one plane couldn't get wheels down. I thought he would never quit skidding.
March 5th	I got 8-day leave. Post flew me to 96th Bomb Group, buzzed a fighter base a few times and landed to get our bearings, arriving at 18:00. Ingram is operations officer. Peterson is there. William Frank's ship exploded over France, I was told. FW-190's killed him and Mosier.
March 6th	Ingram took me to Boyington in a B-17, met his roommate, Capt. Robb, whose wife is Billie Burke, Movie Actress.
March 7th to 9th	London, met several officers that I knew from time to time, lots of nice people.
March 10th	Back to base and found out that Kobl went down on first Berlin raid on the 6th.

March 11th	Flew with Trimble on a gunnery mission over North Sea, two holes in plane we couldn't account for. Later went to officer's club dance; it turned out to be a brawl. I got letter back that I wrote to Wm. Frank.
March 14th	Flew to two bases for items, got oxygen bottles.
March 15th	Shot five landings, heard that Germans came over last night on way to bomb London.
March 16th	12th mission. To Lechfield, about 20 miles south of Augburg, about four fighter attacks by two planes, not much gas so we landed at "white Cliffs of Dover" at RAF dirt strip, a short place to land. You go down a steep hill if over shooting landing strip. I saw a hole where a German plane hit in a high dive, engine way down in ground. Dogs had eaten pieces of German crew. A Lancaster Bomber overshot landing and went off the hill; also saw a burned B-24. We stopped within 200 feet of the steep hill. A wild Texan flying with the RAF in a spitfire gave us a show by buzzing us and doing rolls about 30 feet above ground. We stayed all night in a house built in 16th Century.
March 17th	After breakfast we returned to our field.
March 20th	Briefed for Frankfurt, flying lead element behind Colonel Rogner, turned back because of clouds. Back at base received box of Hersheys from Mamma.
March 22nd	Picture in paper of our tail gunner as P.O.W., mission tomorrow.
March 23rd	13th mission. We hit a target near to Mauster. Our gunner reported that several ships blew up. I heard one order the crew to bail out.
March 25th	Passes were cancelled today; every man in squadron expected to fly tomorrow.
March 26th	Captain Rumsey lost today.
March 27th	14th mission. Two tours, missed target. We saw a FW-190 fly through middle of our formation. The next few days we flew on camera bombing course.

April 1st	London, but everything closed. We had first birthday party for 401St Bomb Group. Banquet and floor show. General Williams was there.
April 2nd	I went to London and then on to Berkhemsted, invited to home of Mr. & Mrs. Parsons; I spent three nights there. Christine Parsons, nice girl, was an actress. I went to some of her plays in London.
April 6th	Lecture by a sergeant who spent a year in a German prison camp, escaped and recaptured several times, but finally got out.
April 9th	Some men went on mission to Mariensburg, near Poland, a 12 hour mission, one plane shot down, LT Byrd probably went to Sweden.
April 10th	One plane lost today.
April 11th	15th mission. To Saru, not far from Berlin, went over Hannover and had the worse flak I've ever seen. I saw two B-17's catch fire and explode. I saw some others go down and men bailing. We couldn't hit our primary target; went to Stettin and over the Baltic and over Denmark, and back to base short on fuel, flew 1500 miles and used 2780 gallons of gas, four planes missing.
April 13th	16th mission. To Schweinfuhrt, always a tough trip. 15 German planes came up from rear, three B-17's went down. About 30 ME-109's hit us head-on, went through our formation, and back around and hit us again. I was looking right down the barrel of one plane and he came head-on, went by my right wing so close I could see the pilot clearly. Lozinski left us and started home, crash landing on English coast. Vokaty and Stimson, two pilots with their crew and planes from our squadron were lost. I saw another plane explode when we were returning toward England, in all I saw about seven planes go down, all exploded, and I saw only one chute. Nine of our men were injured, two pretty bad. However, this is still safer than going up and down that bulldozer road on your property.

April 14th	I found out we lost nine crews of nine planes shot down in last four missions. I went to town to get Fosters and Gougers laundry. LT Child co-pilot on Loziski's crew went to hospital to have piece of 20 mm cannon removed from leg.
April 15th	We flew and dropped plastic bombs.
April 19th	Two air raids last night; we heard the planes overhead.
April 20th	We lost two planes and crews today. I met a boy from Sanderson. His uncle managed the Kerr Hotel and restaurant for years.
April 22nd	17th mission. To Hamm, no fighters, little flak, I saw one B-17 go down, saw about eight chutes floating down.
April 25th	I asked Capt. Stairns if I could get on his squadron. He is going on patrol duty in North Sea to pick up men returning from missions.
April 26th	18th mission. Up at 01:15 for mission to Brunswick, only two hours sleep; home at 12:30. I found out that the Hamm mission on the 22nd were followed by German fighters who shot down several planes in traffic pattern. No ships lost today.
April 28th	A truck took Lozinski, Rush, Hughes and enlisted men to 303 hospital to see LT Child and another man. Child had flak in his ankle; gangrene had set in.
April 29th	Group went to Berlin today. Capt. Gould and two other crews in our group didn't come back. This was a mammoth raid, 2000 planes, 79 bombers and 16 fighters reported lost.
April 30th	19th mission. Went to Lyons, France, with five-1000#bombs.
May 1st	We went to France to bomb but it was too cloudy; we brought bombs home.
May 4th	20th mission. Berlin, weather caused recall near Germany, bombed airfield on Belgium coast.
May 5th	I thought I had 48 hour leave but they restricted me because I missed classes.

May 6th	Major White declared that they won't promote me until I check out and also go to classes. I have flown most of my missions except they raised the requirement to 30 from 25, and I never checked out as first pilot on B-17.
May 7th	21st mission. Up at 01:15 for Berlin. Our formations have not been good. I have been assigned to tail gunners position to watch the formations and report those who are not complying. Over Berlin two superchargers went out, looked bad for a while, flak and minus 42 degrees, landed in Bassingbourn where PFF ships are stationed, home in command car.
May 8th	22nd mission. Up at 01:30, after three hours sleep, for Berlin. Capt. Lewis leading low squadron lost engine, stayed with him for a while, but he is going to try to make it home. A B-17 blew half in two and fell just in front of us. A piece of flak hit my right window even with my neck. I saved it for keepsake. Capt. Lewis crash landed with two engines after throwing out all guns, ammo radio equipment, etc., to lighten load, had 400 flak holes in plane, one man injured.
May 9th	23rd mission. Luxembourg, bombed railroad yard.
May 11th	Took trip to Mauston to look at a crashed B-17 to see when it will be ready to bring home. All kind of planes landed here: Sitoes, P-47 after crossing channel enroute home. I flew as pilot.
May 12th	24th mission. To Mersenburg, west of Leipzig. Bad food caused several ships to abort, sick men on board…tail gunner killed on one crew, his 30th mission and was to be his last mission. 42 bombers and 10 fighters lost today.
May 13th	25th mission. We are bombing synthetic oil plants the last two days. Politz was our destination today but due to bad weather we hit Stettin. We saw about 60-70 enemy fighters in one bunch, and they shot down three B-17's one of ours was missing. Out heater out minus 40 degrees centigrade.
May 15th	My birthday, I'm 26.
May 19th	Hagen shot down on today's mission to Kiel.

May 22nd	Callisthenics, I met LT Berry at Club. I knew him in Kearney, Nebraska.
May 23rd	26th mission. I flew with John Whiteman crew to check them out on missions; we flew to Bainsville, France. John Whiteman and the other eight on their first mission.
May 24th	27th mission. I flew again with John Whiteman crew. This was to be his second and last trip toward check out. I previously checked out another crew and they were shot down on third mission. We are hit with a direct hit from flak gun on #2 engine over Berlin seconds after dropping bombs. Belly landed at Sose on Bornholm. None of the crew injured. Escaped with gunner Carraway. Evaded to Sweden helped by Danish resistance, were flown back to England from Stockholm. We all survived.
June 16th	I got order to return to my group, 401st, arrived in afternoon.
June 17th	I saw several of the men I knew before my May 24th mission; also found out several crews lost while I was gone.
June 19th	I had to clear base, left for Kettering and on to London: Reindeert Club. I met some people who wanted me to call their folks in Hollywood, met some war correspondents too.
June 21st	LT Whiteman and I are going to lecture new crews. I looked at a P-47 with equipment for rocket firing.
June 23rd	I went up to see about flying in order to get my flying pay. We flew in afternoon in a B-17F with Capt. Brown. After this I flew some nearly every day.
June 28th	We talked to two classes in morning, then two LT's came in to lecture. They both walked out of France, took them three months...I went to London to Astor Club with Whiteman. The Buzz bombs are falling on London.
July 1st	I met Reed who graduated with me at Stockman Field; still dodging buzz bombs.
July 3rd	I went to get orders and a little money; have to pack and weigh in by 15:00, shipped foot locker, left by train for Prestwick, Scotland.

July 4th	I arrived in Prestwick at 06:00, left at 11:30, landed in Iceland 16:00, left there for Harmon Field, Newfoundland about 23:30, left for New York and landed at LaGuardia about 11:30 July 5th. I went through customs and then to Ambassador Hotel; due at office at 08:00 at LaGuardia, then Mitchell Field for A-Z interrogation. Back to New York, cleaned up and went to see Foster's brother; Foster was on my crew was shot down and is now a P.O.W.
July 6th	To July 11th I was on train to California with one 24 hour delay in Chicago.
July 13th	I went to Stockton, California.

I stayed in a hotel on the beach for 30 days. Afterward I took two months training instrument landings; Columbus Air Force base and Lockbourne Air Force base. I volunteered for Pacific duty, took more training at Biloxi, Mississippi and Boca Raton, Florida on B-17's, finally separated from service August 5th, 1945.

I resumed working for the railroad as a Brakeman, later bought a bulldozer and went into business building spreader dams for the government in partnership with ranchers. Did security work at Los Alamos and after that I went back to the dirt work at Sanderson.

The next event was a chance to enlist in the war with North Korea. It was not much of a war, but it was the only one around. I flew 75 missions being involved in psychological warfare. After that I started flying helicopters and worked as an instructor for 16 years.

When I look back on the exciting and interesting periods of my life, historic and tragic, I always remember the missions in WW II. I can still see the planes going down; the losses were high. When they putting up some 2.000 planes over Europe, everyone knew that the tide had turned, but man, the losses. One day, for example, 64 heavies were shot down on Berlin mission. Think of that 64 times a crew of ten—640 men, most died though a few bailed out.

Early in the war we could send out 12 ships and only one came back. The rest of them were shot to hell!

The Evasion & Escape of:
The Pilot 2nd LT John S. Whiteman &
The Ball Turret Gunner SGT Nelson Liddle

Narrated by John S. Whiteman & Nelson Liddle

<u>Whiteman:</u> We all started to run, jog and walk and after a while, we came to a small hill with some trees on it. All fell to the ground when a Heinkel 111 went over. After that we paired up and took off in all directions. I paired up with Nelson Liddle the Ball Gunner.

When Nels and I were about to pass the main country road, a truck came along and gave us a lift, so we got nearer to the big forest faster.

Nels and I continued further inland on the same dirt road, where the truck took us, and had not gone 1500 yards, when we heard the German half trucks on the main road. The Germans were throwing a cordon around the plane out about 5 miles. Nels and I jumped into the edge of the forest, which was on both sides of the road.

We watched as the half trucks came slowly up the road. At this point when the krauts were opposite to our position, I turned to Nels and said: "Do you smell a steak cooking?" He must have thought I had flipped my wig, but I could really smell a steak. The krauts went another 200 yards up the road, turned around and went back to the main road.

After a bit of a rest, Nels and I continued up the road and came upon a mounded flat concrete area, maybe 500ft x 1000ft. Big slaps of cement with grass growing between them. Opposite to our side, there were three open steel towers about 100 ft tall with only one arm extended over the concrete. No wires, no cables etc. , we couldn't figure what it was. It was a rocket launch area, which we learned later in England.

We kept on walking and got to the highest point on Bornholm, "Ryt-terknægten". It had a lookout tower. We didn't climb it. Kept moving on. It was raining and we came across a barn, ducked in and found the co-pilot Shelton and the Right Waist Gunner Carraway.

I decided it would be best for Nels and me to keep moving. By morn-ing on Thursday 25th May 1944 we were so beat, so we pulled into a barn to spend the day.

Liddle: Soon after daylight, a lady from the farmhouse came into the building and found us. She became very excited and afraid. She did not understand English but we kept saying "Americans" and she finally understood who we were.

We tried to find out the direction we should take to get us to Sweden but she did not understand us until Lt. Whiteman said "King Gustav", he was the king of Sweden, and she then understood what we were try-ing to find out and pointed us toward Sweden. We walked for some time, I can't remember how long, stopping at farm houses and asking for food.

Whiteman: After the barn, I get kind of fuzzy and I think we spent Fri-day 26th May 1944 in a haystack. I remember leaving the stack at dark, however, we hid immediately, when we saw a car coming up the hill, probably German.

Nels and I continued up the hill and knocked on a farm house door, it had no lights, and tried to ask directions as to where we were.

The farmer handed me a slice of black bread spread with lard, he said go away and he kept saying—tyskerne, tyskerne—meaning the Germans. The bread I split with Nels. It tasted damn good after nothing for two days except a chocolate bar from the escape kit.

Liddle: We had escape kits which contained some tablets that tasted terrible but were supposed to be nutritious. The kit also contained tablets that we added to the water we took from streams to make it safe to drink.

Whiteman: The third day Saturday 27th May 1944, I will never forget. We came upon this pig farm. We were in the barn trying to talk to the farmer, when a German patrol came up his front path. The stench was pretty bad, just standing in the barn but the farmer hurriedly covered Nels and me with USED PIG STRAW. The stench was now god awful.

The farmer had to bring the German patrol leader, and I guess the stench was too much even for him, because he turned around and left without searching. Nels and I contained ourselves (barely) until we heard the motorcycles go away.

The German patrol scared the farmer to death and he asked us to leave immediately.

We left stinking like pigs and later at a small stream, we tried to clean ourselves a bit, but we still stunk.

We kept moving through the night and on the morning Sunday 28th May 1944, we broke out of the woods onto a main road.

Church bells seemed to be ringing all over. People on the road were moving in one direction.

I think the pig stench influenced our thinking because I said to Nels: "I don't know about you but I have had enough of this crap." Nels agreed so we stepped out onto the road.

I still had my 45 pistol on but we both must have looked like a couple of beat up bums.

We fell in behind a horse and wagon with three men sitting on the tailgate. We walked behind them for a while, until I thumbed my nose at them. In a little while I got a signal from one of them. He just pointed to the left down a dirt road headed toward the coast.

Liddle: When we reached the Northern coast of Bornholm, we saw 13 German submarines and a tender off the coast. We searched for a rowboat that would get us to Sweden but were unsuccessful.

Whiteman: After about a mile or so, we came upon a small house overlooking the cliffs and sea. The owner was an elderly man but he invited us into the house and gave us two fried eggs and a slice of jellyroll and a bottle of beer. After consuming the beer, I had to run outside and loose it all—only solid food for four days—since hitting the Island.

The old man asked us to hang around and soon three or four other men showed up. We all shook hands etc. and one of them asked what we wanted. We told him, a rowboat and a heading for Sweden.

The same man, asking us what we wanted, now told us that he was an ex Chicago Policeman and that he would come back again after three hours.

After they had gone, I said to Nels: "How come an American Policeman is running around free in an occupied territory?"—Something smelled besides us!

So we moved off about 1.000 yards and watched. Sure enough, the "cop" came back with the Gestapo. We didn't know it at that time, but we found out in Sweden, that there was a price on our heads, dead or alive and death to anyone helping us.

We moved on and came upon a small trail winding down the cliff, which was pretty high. We got to the bottom and continued along the trail which was right at the sea level.

We didn't know it, but this was to be our lucky night!

Came on a couple of houses and a marina, we looked for a rowboat we could steal, but no luck. We continued on the trail and soon heard people coming down the trail.

Nels and I jumped behind a light hedgerow. When the bikes were abreast of us one of the riders said: "We know you are there and when we return be prepared to jump on the bikes." The riders were Ernst Petersen and Ebbe Hasselholt.

When they returned, we jumped on. I rode the handlebar, I don't know how Nels rode.
I guess my weight on the front of the bike really was too much, because Ernst Petersen's bike broke down, just where the Germans were barracked.
I got off and walked to Ernst Petersen's house, which was up the road a couple of blocks. Ernst had to almost carry the bike—mind you this is in the middle of the night.

When we got to the house, Helga, Ernst Petersen's wife, met us at the cellar door and put up her hand, meaning stop and held her nose, meaning you smell and are not coming in here. Helga was a real gem. She spoke limited English but enough for us to understand and we had to take off our clothes down to our skivvies. She took everything to wash them.

We went up to the attic room, where we were to stay and there was Shelton the Co-pilot and Carraway the gunner. They had been picked up earlier.

We got laughed at by Carraway and Shelton, seeing us in our under-shorts.

As I said "Helga was a gem" she brought Nels' and my washed and pressed uniforms up to us late next morning. It made Nels and me feel like human beings again.

She also was a damn good cook. I had to partake of it sparingly as my stomach had been kicking up ever since Berlin.

I had a lot of stress.

After about three days with four guys in cramped quarters, things began to get testy. I guess we all had a lot of stress.

That afternoon Ernst P. came to me and said that two men claimed they were part of my crew and would I go with him after dark and I.D. them.

After dark, E.P. and I went down the coast road, past the marina, and up the cliff ways.

We came upon two men sitting on the ground and two men with pistols at their heads. They flashed a light on the faces of the sitting men, I just shook my head NO.
Ernst and I turned and went back to his house. I assume that the two men sitting on the ground were Gestapo men and that they were eliminated but I never heard shots. They were probably taken elsewhere.

On the ride back on E.P.'s bike, Ernst said to me: "They are getting too close. We leave tomorrow."

The next day Ernst took his family out about noon. He showed us how to hide under the eaves of the room and said that he would be back by seven o'clock and if he wasn't, it would mean that he had been caught and we were on our own .

In the afternoon someone came in and said there was a house to house search going on by the Germans looking for us. We ducked into the tight space under the eaves and sweated it out.

We were not in hiding too long when we heard an air raid signal. It called off the search and we crawled out soaking wet. It was really hot in there.

True to his word, Ernst returned about seven with help.

One of them was Ebbe Hasselholt.

We had Danish police uniforms on (capes). I rode Ebbe Hasselholt's bike, we were headed for the marina.

Ebbe and I had hardly gotten clear of town when I had to throw up. This slowed us up and when my pants got caught in the sprocket & chain, this slowed us up even more. When we arrived at the marina, the SWAN was pulling away from the dock. Ebbe Hasselholt hollered in Danish to wait for us and Ebbe and I ran like mad and jumped on the Swan as it was moving out.

It was foggy and we were not under way too long when Ernst passed down the word for no talking. He had stopped his engine and was listening for a German patrol boat as they had stopped their engines too.

Birthe Petersen, their five year old daughter was talking and I remember putting my finger to my lips and saying shhhhh! . After maybe 5 minutes Ernst started the engine again and went all the way to Simrishamn, Sweden unhindered.

Arriving in Simrishamn, the SWAN had hardly come to rest, when the police were all over us. I hardly had time to say good-bye to Ernst, Helga and Ebbe.

I gave my "Hack Watch" to Ebbe Hasselholt, as the police pulled me off the boat. We were transferred to Malmö immediately.

The police here took immigration pictures and questioned us etc.

After that a Swedish intelligence officer took me to the train for a ride to Stockholm.

I was alone in the car with the officer. He wanted to know everything we saw on Bornholm. I told him everything I saw. I assume that the rest of the crew were on the same train because we all were at the embassy at the same time. All the crew was put up at a hotel.

A few days later in Stockholm, Ernst Petersen came to me and asked me to intervene for him with the Embassy to get him a work permit to fish. Told him I would and they did and Ernst got his permit. Only thing I remember of Stockholm was the motion picture "For Whom The Bells Toll".

The crew left Stockholm on the 8th or 9th June. We were due to go out on the 7th but D-day cancelled us . We left Sweden at night on a B-24 and arrived at a secret air base in Scotland in the early morning.

The air base was covered with a thin layer of water so that it looked like a lake from the air.

After security clearance I got to London and was roomed with Shelton.

I was moved to Bovington (replacement crews) for two weeks and lecture on Escape & Evasion.

On the night of the 4th of July ,1944 I arrived in New York.

As soon as I got off the plane and checked in, I called my parents. Got no answer so deduced that they had gone visiting friends in Connecticut over the holiday.

They knew that I had gotten back into friendly hands but they didn't know I was home. I figured they would be gone for a couple of more days so I put up at the Waldorf Astoria (on the army) for two days.

When I went down for breakfast, about four waiters hovered around my table, they could see that I was 8th A.F. and when I ordered a big mess of creamed Finan Haddie, they almost stumbled over each other to get the order in first, I had to laugh. They came back and apologized, they did not have it. Even the cook came out and apologized. When they learned that I was just back from the E.T.O., they couldn't do enough for me. I never got a bill for breakfast.

After two days I took the train out of Grand Central for home (Mt Vernon). I walked all the way from the station to 257 Gramatan Ave, I hadn't called the folks, thought I would surprise them, That I did.

When mother opened the door, she almost fainted, Mom, Dad and I had a great reunion.

I had a two week leave and reported to Atlantic City For R & R. From there I toured the country with permanent changes of station until I ended up in Drew Field, Tampa, Florida on the instructors training board.

This outfit would put out the training to the group instructors and then we had to check the crews to see that they had gotten the poop.

My job, being the newest member of the 5 man board, was to check the night flying. This scared the hell out of me. Some of these crews had over 400 hrs in the B-17 and couldn't fly it worth a damn. Some would land so hard, the plane would go so high you wondered if it would ever get back down.

Decided I was going to live through this war if possible and I would take a crew up for night landings. We were up until it just turned light and I would tell the pilot to take it in. As he was rolling back to take off, I had him stop, while I got out and told him he was checked out.

I had been on the board for about 6 months when I came into the shack we called our office and found a major at my desk.

I forgot to mention that all my crew was assigned to the interior of the United States that meant NOBODY could ship us out as we could be legally shot having escaped enemy territory, we were considered spies.

Now back to the major. I mentioned to the major that he was at my desk. He replied "Not anymore. I processed you for B-29s" . I asked the major when he had gotten back from overseas? He said he had not been overseas. With that I grabbed his kaki shirt and pulled him across the desk and said "I'll P—on your grave before I go over ahead of you".

The captain of the board saw what happened and had me sent to the psycho ward in the hospital with flying fatigue. He did this as a protection for me because the major filed charges.

The next morning the base commander came to see me in the loony bin. I told him my story and by afternoon the major was on his way to B-29s and I was back at my desk.

The war was coming to an end and after almost 5 years I had it up to my eyeballs.

I moved to Ft Dix N.J. for discharge in November 1945. Just 5 years. That was enough.

The Ringle Post War Story

Narrated by Seymour Ringle

Seymour Ringle February 1944.

After my leave at home I received orders to report to R&R at Atlantic City where airmen who had survived a 25 mission tour in the ETO (which was a 100% turnover of personnel) stayed for one month and then returned for another tour of duty.

I was then ordered to Instructors Indoctrination Unit in Galveston, Texas directly from Atlantic City. You see, evades, especially those who got to a neutral country, were not to be shipped out of the continental limits of the United States excluding Alaska.

From Galveston I went to Alexandria Air Force base, the same base where our crew had our phase training and learned to fly in a B-17 as an integral unit, where I served as a flight line and ground school instructor.

In March 1946 I went to Randolph Air Force base (where I had previously taken pre-flight pilot training) to demobilize. I needed to get 4 hours of flying in order to receive that quarters flight pay.

At the flight line I was told that an AT-6 training plane was about to take off on a training mission and there was room in the rear seat for me.

I took my position in the rear seat in this dual controlled plane and we took off. The captain in the front seat had a girlfriend in town and he started buzzing her house. We were tipped over in a steep bank when I observed another plane coming right at us from our right and slightly above us so that we were out of his range of vision and my pilot was absorbed in staring at the ground. I kicked us over with the dual controls into a tight left spin and avoided the collision. There were more training fatalities in the Air Force than there were in combat and, even though I had witnessed many of them while training as a pilot, navigator and bombardier, I was anxious not to be included in their number on my last flight. When he finally sighted the aircraft and stopped screaming at me, I pointed to the ground and walked away after we landed without saying a word and got the rest of my four hours in a C-47.

After separation, two of my friends and I went down to Vienna, Virginia to make our fortune raising tomatoes. This phase of my life is a tale onto itself. But the bottom line was that the blight hits the tomato crop every 20 years:—you guessed it!
After the tomato debacle I took the New York City police exam and finished 96th on the list of 20.000 applicants.

While serving my 20 years I did some moonlighting:—selling smoking pipes, manufactured by my father-in-law, on the road from Buffalo to Boston, through Connecticut, New Jersey and Pennsylvania; was a partner in R&S Investing Co. selling stocks and insurance; owned an ice cream truck with my radio car partner getting other cops to operate it on their off time; sold cigars and had peanut machines.

The Air Force contacted me in 1954 and asked me to join a reserve navigators squadron at Floyd Bennett field which was 5 minutes from my house in Brooklyn and filled my greedy head with the amount of money I could make by flying one weekend a month and two weeks of active duty a year plus 36 additional flying training periods a year for proficiency plus a pension after 20 good years which included my previous 3 years of active duty. I was also told that the law required the Police Department to allow me 52 working days a year with full pay for military duty.

I finally ended up as Major with a pension.

I retired from the police department in 1968 and went to work for various insurance companies as a claims adjuster. I sold my house in Brooklyn in 1988 for 20 times the amount I had bought it for and moved to Wellington, Florida where we live what we considered the good retired life.

My father was Max Ringel (I spelled mine the same way until I went into the service, where they discovered the spelling was Ringle on my birth certificate and since then, I am the only Ringel family with a misspelled name) who had emigrated from Poland and my mother, Jeanette Axelrod came from Austria.

My father died when I was 9 years of age and my mother when I was 17.

I was married to Florence Spiegel (Fay) January 8th, 1952 and we have a son Eric Jay who works at telephone marketing and is a dog show judge.

Our oldest son Marc died in 1990.

I am the middle son of three red headed boys. Both of my brothers are deceased.

The Whiteman Post War Story

Narrated by John S. Whiteman

John S. Whiteman. Photo taken in Malmö, Sweden June 2, 1944.

I went to work in Outdoor Advertising the day after I got out of the army.

Shortly after I also started up a charter airline, Westchester Air. We had two planes, a c45 & a twin engine training plane called the bamboo bomber.

Within a short time I found out that the public was not ready to pay the price of private charter so I sold the planes & the company. Didn't lose anything or make anything.

Then rented a Lockheed Hudson and tried flying lobsters from Boston to NYC. Lost my ass as half the lobsters died. Made three trips.

Got out of that and just banged around the country hither & yon in my own Gull Wing Stinson, a real underpowered dog with a 250 hsp. Wright engine. Couldn't afford to put in a new Pratt & Whitney 300. Because of that I had a few bad moments with it. It all got just too damn expensive so I quit in 1962.

I got married in late 49. Dorothy lived until November 53. She died of lung cancer. I was pretty broken up, and I got tired of the New York

agency people, asking how I was so I quit my job and packed everything I owned in the station wagon and headed West.

I planned on settling on the west coast. On the way, I stopped off in
Bismarck, N.D. and noticed a group of men milling around. One of
them came up to me and shoved a paper (legal) in my face and said will
you go $75 for this. Looked it over quickly and saw that it was a land
lease so I bought it.

I went off to study it and understood 95% . It was an oil lease. I went
over to a total stranger and said what do you think of this. His reply
was I'll give you $150 for it. He made a sale and I thought "man you
can't make money faster than this" and started buying.

Three weeks later I woke up to the fact that I owned $50,000 worth of
leases on paper and they were not worth anything until an oil company
bought them. I started selling as fast as I could but I was hooked on the
oil game. It took me three years to drill 7 dry holes. We would drill in
the summer and I would go to Florida in the winter. It was fun while it
lasted but I was going broke and lost a small fortune so I hotfooted it
back to New York City and started selling national advertising again.

In 1961 I remarried to Adele James. She is still with me, I retired in
1973.

On October 15th 1998 I flew back to Bornholm to honour the graves
of my helpers, Helga & Ernst Petersen.

I had been wanting to go back while they were living but many things
interrupted my doing so. One day I just rolled out of bed and made
reservations, got my passport, packed and waited for plane date.

A friend of mine, Eileen Marx, living in the same condo complex as I,
heard that I was going to Bornholm Denmark. She being Danish,
called Major Holger Pii and he was my mentor.

You would think I was a VIP !

I was entertained royally by Birthe Falt-Hansen (daughter of Ernst & Helga Petersen) & her husband Jorgen Ole Falt-Hansen.

I also met with the former farmhand Hans Christian West and last but not least one of my helpers, Ebbe Hasselholt. Ebbe and I were together every day during my trip to Bornholm.

John Whiteman and Ebbe Hasselholt at the point of no return.
The small harbor of Teglkas, Bornholm from where they sailed to
Sweden back in June 1944.

I flew away from Bornholm on cloud 9. It was a beautiful experience that I shall never forget.

Contact after Fifty Years

Narrated by Elizabeth Munch Petersen, daughter of Ernst & Helga Petersen.

The reason that I found interest in writing to the addresses on the old bills, were that my father sometimes told stories about how he and some other men had sailed American airmen and fugitives to Sweden.

My father told the stories so it felt like you were there, and I just loved to listen to him. I must have been around 10 years old, when I first heard him tell about it.

My father was born in Neksø. He loved the place and absolutely adored his mother. He didn't talk much about his father. He came from Sweden and worked as a cooper on the brewery in Neksø. On the other hand the mother was everything he wished for in a role model.

His youth consisted of a lot of hunting, fishing and by the time he was 10 he had his own little boat and fished for eel, which was shipped to Copenhagen. He made good living and he loved his life, especially Skansen and the Balka Bay.

He was an excellent student and got a scholarship for the college in Rønne. That didn't happen often in those days. It was terrible for him, not being able to use it, because of the distance—20 miles. In the summer he could ride his bike but he couldn't during the winter.

But one day, when he had turned 16, his mother died. At that time his father had to look for a new job, and the worst possible thing happened. His father decided to move to Hasle. The last place anybody wanted to live, except if they were from Hasle. It was horrible for him to say goodbye to his beloved home in Skolegade, the forest, the beach and to adventure and freedom. One cold December day they drove to the opposite side of the island, and took over the brewery in Hasle.

My father had plans to immigrate to America and one day when he was close to carrying his plan out, he was out walking with a friend, who was supposed to come along, and they walked across the town square. Here they met two beautiful girls from Hasle. One of them was carrying a box from the bakery, and my father who just loved cakes, asked her who the cakes were for. She said that he could have them, and then his trip to America was cancelled. It was my mother carrying the box of cakes.

My mother was very young when she moved in with my father and took care of all the housework and the two men. Later my parents got married and they moved to a house in Vestergade, and here the 3 children were born—Niels, Birthe and Jette. It was these three who were on the ship to Sweden that night in June 1944, where all of them had to run.

Due to a fire, they lost everything they owned and had to start from scratch. They moved to the house next door and it was in this house that they hid the American airmen in the attic.

When the war started, my father had to start fishing again, so he bought a boat. They made a fine living, and as I found out later from many of the people living in Hasle, they often helped where it was needed. My father was highly respected for his willingness to help and his boldness, but also because he knew how and when to keep his mouth shut—and you had to do that often during the war.

He was in a group of fishermen called "The Salmon", whose job was to help fugitives. It was Jews, Americans and whoever needed to disappear. I don't know how many people he had helped, because he didn't tell us everything, but the last trip he did tell about. That was the trip, which also brought my parents to Sweden.

Anyway, I saw the bills and because they were really there, the story got an eternal spark, which tells us about a time where people helped each other with their own lives at stake. I often looked at the picture, with the bills framed. Right next to it another picture hang, which was the

Letters of Honour from Winston Churchill and Dwight D. Eisenhower, which my father received after the war.

When my parents arrived at a camp for fugitives in Sweden, they were supposed to be separated to male and female camps, but that my mother wouldn't agree to. She was a very strong woman, but the scary trip and being alone with 3 children without the man she loved, was too much. My father managed to arrange a small apartment for them in town.

There were problems in getting a licence to fish, so my father went to Stockholm and met with the pilot, John Whiteman, and asked him to help him get one. He did and my father came back and could do his fishing.

He had asked the bank in Hasle to handle everything regarding the house, as long as they were fugitives in Sweden.

In Sweden my father met a sailor from Bornholm, Olaf Hansen. He was very good at fixing the sails, and my father employed him. He became a regular guest in the small apartment as well as Niels and Birthe in his small apartment further down Hamngatan in Simrishamn. My father told us that during a terrible storm, the only reason they came to shore was the great work that Olaf had done with the sails.

When the war ended, my mother went back to Bornholm with the children, while my father stayed another year, because he made more money in Sweden than on Bornholm.
Unfortunately the bank had sold the house, without telling my father, so my mother had to move into a small apartment to start with. I have read some of the letters that my parents wrote each other back then. It must have been a hard time for them, but they had made their own choices, and I have never once heard them complain—quite the opposite actually. But they both loved adventure.

Well, back to the present.

After my mother's death, I found some slides among my things. It was pictures of the bills, on which the American airmen had written their names and addresses. I sat there with them in my hands and thought of all the things that my father had told, but also of all the things that he hadn't told, things that never had come out in the open, and I think that the need to understand my parents and everything that had happened just grew inside me. What happened to the airmen, that I so often had heard about? It was as if something was missing.

I first wrote to John Whiteman in April 1994, and then everybody else, and never thought of whether they would be answered or not. 50 years passed and they could have moved several times since then. But still, it was very exciting.
I was very surprised when I heard from Liddle. It was like turning back time and suddenly become part of that time and the important thing in my parents lives. It just felt so good.

I sent pictures of the bills to Liddle, which he once had signed and a correspondence between him, his daughter Barbara and myself started.

In 1994 I was in California and talked to Barbara on the phone, and they would love it, if I paid them a visit. I didn't go for different reasons, but we kept in touch through letters after I came back to Bornholm.

One day my sister Birthe told me that she had been visiting a friend and there she met a woman who knew John Whiteman. We both thought that it was peculiar. I mean America is so big. I wrote a letter to John Whiteman and this time he answered my letter and we started writing each other regularly. He was the first one of the pilots I ever wrote, but he had never received my letter.

The first reunion came, arranged by Nelson. A short time after John announced his visit to Bornholm.

I contacted Ebbe Hasselholt Jørgensen in Randers, that my father had talked about, and we talked a bit about that time. I think, that I needed to, after both my parents had died.

Ebbe, who cared a lot about my father, was a policeman in Hasle during the war. He was also on the boat that night, because like my father he was also wanted by the Gestapo. He told me that in order to have fuel for the boat, he and my father had emptied the Germans barrels and filled them with water.

When John announced the date of his arrival I called Ebbe Hasselholt again, and asked him if he would like to join us. When he hesitated, I offered him my plane ticket from Copenhagen to Rønne, which was the last one on the same flight as John. He called me and accepted and said that his daughter Grete would be back from Switzerland to join him.

Later on both Grete and I got a ticket for the same flight, which lead to a wonderful meeting in Copenhagen airport, where Ebbe, Grete and I met and then welcomed John Whiteman, who came from America via Amsterdam.

The first thing he said to Ebbe was: "I wouldn't fit your coat today it would be too small". It became an unforgetable moment for all of us.

When the departure time got near, John Whiteman was suddenly called over the speakers. He was then escorted to the plane and into the cockpit, where he sat the whole time, and then they flew that route over Sose, which he had done when he made the emergency landing in 1944.

At the airport in Rønne, we were welcomed in a very special way, and John Whiteman was really surprised. He told me later, that he thought that he was just supposed to lay down the wreath and then go back home.

It turned out to be something very special for all of us. It was a big moment when John laid down the wreath on my parents grave. It was so beautiful watching him salute them. I told him that my father had been very strong. He looked at me and then said: "Yes, but your mother Helga, was a very, very strong woman too". he paused and then said: "They both had guts".

We had some wonderful days together. One evening Birthe had invited us all for dinner and I called Nelson Liddle and he and John Whiteman talked for a while.

When John and Ebbe left the island again, I think that they spent a few very important hours with each other.

John Whiteman, Nelson Liddle and I have kept in touch and we are cooresponding regularly.

The Liddle Post War Story and the Reunions
Narrated by Nelson Liddle

Nelson Liddle Harlington Gunnery School December 1943

I entered the air force in March 1943 and was sent for basic training in St. Petersburg, Florida for 16 weeks.

I then attended aircraft mechanics school in Gulfport Mississippi for 5 months and then to aerial gunnery school in Harlingen, Texas.

The next three months I spent at Alexandria, Louisiana. Then we picked up our brand new B-17 in Nebraska and then we were off to the E.T.O.

During our 3 months of training I met with another airman, Bernard Fridberg. Bernard Fridberg's story: "From Nazi Germany to the U.S. and the 8th Air Force"

After the escape from Bornholm to Sweden, we were flown back to England and then back to the United States.
After taking leave and a short stay in Miami Beach, Florida for R&R—rest and relaxation, we were assigned to air force bases close to our homes.

I was assigned to Langley Air Force Base in Hampton Virginia. I worked as a mechanic and flew as flight engineer on B-17 bombers, training radar operators on their way to combat overseas. This was my job until November 1945, at which time I was discharged from the Air Force. The war had ended and the armed forces were demobilizing.

I was married in November 1944 with Billie Jean Huffman and my daughter, Barbara, was born November 29th, 1945.

After serving an apprenticeship for watchmaking, I decided to re-enlist in the Air Force in 1947. I served 4 more years and was stationed in Frankfurt, Germany during the Berlin Airlift in 1948 and 1949. I worked as a mechanic servicing cargo planes flying supplies to Berlin. After the airlift, I returned to the USA until the Korean War began and

I was sent to Okinawa to work with the ground crews servicing B-29 Bombers that were bombing Korea.

I returned to the USA in September 1951 and was discharged as my enlistment was up. My second and last child, Heath Nelson Liddle, Jr. was born in September, 1948 while I was in Frankfurt, Germany.

After my discharge in 1951, we lived most of our lives in or near Blacksburg, Virginia. I worked as a machinist and tool maker for various companies in the Blacksburg vicinity. I retired in 1985.

In May 1994, exactly 50 years after our landing on Bornholm, I received a letter from Ernst Petersen's daughter, Elizabeth Munch Petersen.

I remember clearly how exited I was, when I read her letter and soon we, Elizabeth and I, were corresponding regularly.

Some day Barbara asked me why I did not try to find my crew members. I replied that I had no idea where they might be.

I did remember though that Lt. Whiteman was from Mt. Vernon, New York.

Barbara picked up the phone, dialed information and found that there were two John Whiteman's in that area. She got their numbers and the first call was to the right one!

After more than 50 years we were talking to each other. We both were very excited and soon after he came to see me in Newport, Virginia.

With the aid of the internet, my brother furnished me with names of people throughout the United States, who had the same names as my crew members and lots of post cards asking: "Are you THE JOHN DOE who was part of the WW II crew which crash landed on Bornholm, etc.

We began finding the surviving members of our crew. As the replies started coming back some were returned saying "No, I'm not THE JOHN DOE but I wish you luck finding him" and other similar messages like, He's my cousin or was my Father and he's passed away, on and on!

Someone suggested a reunion. I asked if they would like to come to Virginia and they all accepted our invitation except Horace Shelton who was not a regular member of our crew.

Our first reunion was on May 24, 1998 and all 6 of our surviving original crew members attended. We have had 2 reunions since, one in Washington, D. C. in 1999 and one in Savannah, Georgia in 2000.

The last 2 have been attended by 4 members each year.

If I had not received the letter from Elizabeth Munch Petersen in May 1994, I doubt that we, the crew, would have had our reunions. I doubt that we would ever have met again.

The Ebbe Hasselholt Story

Narrated by Ebbe Hasselholt

One of the first days in June 1943 I was called out at short notice for service on the island of Bornholm. I was stationed in Hasle as a coastguard, and my duties were to guard the harbour and patrol a district from Hasle Klinkefabrik northwards to Johns Kapel. I performed these duties unaccompanied so I could do almost everything unnoticed. When I had been in Hasle about one month I started having friendly chats with a fisherman who was known locally as "Bryggeren" ("The Brewer") (Ernst Petersen, skipper of "RØ 11 Svanen" (The Swan). After a few of these conversations we realised that we shared common ground. I was always on duty from 9 p.m. till 5 a.m. next morning, and I started helping Ernst when he took "passengers" on board the "Svanen". When Ernst gave the prearranged signal I was to wave to them to come out from where they were hiding—often the garden behind "Herolds Hotel", where I was staying myself. A staircase led through the garden directly to the harbour. A couple of times the passengers were hidden in Teglkås on the hill or in one of the huts where the fishermen stored their nets.

Ernst Petersen was both wise and cautious—none of his crew was told anything, and I don't even think that his wife Helga knew anything about my involvement. The owner of "Herolds Hotel", Ole Bidstrup, realised that I was up to something, as he once saw me with some passengers in the harbour, but he didn't say anything, and later he proved to be on our side.

The "Svanen" made quite a few trips from July to October 1943. After that period I lost touch for a while as I was transferred back to Copenhagen.

During my stationing on Bornholm I almost always helped out on the departure of the ferry, "Carl", from Hasle, which was the last harbour before the trip to Copenhagen. Several times passengers had to be brought on board without control because they had to leave the ferry in Falsterbrokanalen—often because they hadn't got off ship on the way out from Copenhagen. Sometimes these people, who didn't make it on the way down to Bornholm, were brought out of Denmark on fishing boats, among others the "Dana" from Nexø or the "Svanen" from Hasle. I remember that four people were landed in Hasle in the middle of August, and that a member of the crew told me that they had been too afraid to jump into the water in Falsterbrokanalen. Ernst had to transport them out of Denmark on board the "Svanen".

The above member of the crew on the "'Carl" knew me from the time when I was in charge of the police supervision on board and secretly involved in delivering mail and passengers in the channel. I remember that particular time because I was to be in charge of the supervision on board the "Carl" on its next trip to Copenhagen.

The following day the "Carl" had to sail from Allinge because of a storm from the west. Shortly after the departure I was contacted by a passenger who after some introductory remarks told me that he had to escape and that he wanted to get off in the Falsterbrokanal. He would like to know if it was really necessary to jump into the water from the ferry. I told him it was because of the Swedish neutrality, and that he just had to jump when the pilot boat pulled away. If we brought mail with us, we gave it to the crew on the pilot boat.

The man did make the jump into the channel. If he was the cause, I don't know, but when we arrived in Copenhagen the Germans had closed off the pier, and nobody was permitted to go ashore. German inspectors came on board, and they very quickly found an "almost cinnamon-coloured" jacket, which the man had taken off when he jumped over board. A woman—I shall never forget her and her square spectacles—pointed at me and said: " Ask that young police officer. He had a long conversation with the man wearing the jacket on the trip from Allinge to the channel. " The Germans brought me in for interrogation. I stubbornly denied being acquainted with the man and insisted that I didn't know he was going to jump over board. The German in charge of the interrogation gave up trying to make me talk and let me go. If this had happened 14 days later, i. e. after the 29th August, I might not have been so lucky.

I continued my service on Bornholm, and, among other things, I saw three barrels of oil being unloaded from the "Carl" and rolled to and hidden in a storehouse by a couple of workers. Ernst was informed, and the "Svanen" got 600 l of oil, which was replaced by water. The "Svanen" made a couple of more trips to Sweden, and I myself sailed to Copenhagen on the "Carl" a couple of times after this incident.

In February 1944 I was returned to Bornholm as a coastguard attached to the police station in Hasle. I resumed my work, but without regular night duty.

I continued my work as an inspector on the "Carl" for a while, and during this period I also served once on the "Østersøen" from Rønne. Things had become easier, and for the most part the passengers could climb directly on to the Swedish pilot boat in Falsterbro. Ernst Petersen had become very cautious and didn't want to take any more passengers to Sweden, but there were other contacts, and the ferries still offered hope of escape.

In the middle of April a collegue, Lund, from Vang told me that two American airmen had been seen south of Vang. He asked me for help. I told the owner of "Herolds Hotel", Ole Bidstrup, about the matter, and in the evening we went out to look for them. Bidstrup, who had worked as a steward on ships to America, spoke English fluently. As we walked around, we whistled English tunes, and suddenly somebody responded from the bushes near the beach. Bidstrup called out, and I hid behind a tree ready to shoot if it turned out to be Germans also looking for the airmen. Through the bushes came two American airmen who were then brought to Holm, a fisherman in Teglkås, and hidden in his attic, where they stayed for a couple of days. Then they were transferred via the beach to a powder depot just north of Hasle. I had a serious talk with Ernst Petersen, and he finally agreed to sail the two airmen to Sweden if I could get them to this boat the "Svanen". We decided to take them out early Monday morning. Bidstrup preferred not to go to the powder depot to fetch the airmen and bring them through Hasle town, and as my English wasn't very good, I had to ask somebody for help. One of my collegues, Erik Hansen, had been in the Danish air force, was a radio operator and was therefore fluent in English, so I chose to talk to him and asked him to go out with me Sunday night. I briefed him and warned him of the dangers, and of course I told him to keep quiet about it. He was willing, and I brought him up to the powder depot. He got emotionally carried away when he met the two airmen. He embraced them, and they all spoke at the same time. We arrived at "Herolds Hotel" after midnight, where we had coffee in the owner's private quarters. Then Erik left.

Early Monday morning I heard the prearranged signal and brought the airmen through the garden behind the hotel so that they only had a road to cross to get to the place where the "Svanen" was moored. It left without problems, and the airmen were delivered safely in Sweden. Their names were: Glenn Standish and Lauren Davis.

Gradually things became more difficult in Hasle harbour. A German patrol boat was now stationed there, and the Gestapo was present on the island.

I didn't really trust the new police sergeant who often came on inspection. He seemed very nervous and over-zealous, so we didn't take any more passengers out from Hasle harbour. However, it was still possible to use the "Carl", and Neksø offered good possibilities as a departing point for boats to Sweden.

At the end of May, just before Whit sun, I was again ordered to perform my duties as inspector on board the "Carl". I brought mail to Sweden on the trip from Bornholm, and on the way back from Copenhagen to Bornholm we brought both mail and passengers. On that trip I was contacted by a man in the gents. He said: "They are keeping an eye on you. You have to get out of the country."

When I returned to Bornholm, Ernst told me that they had hidden four airmen with Holm in Teglkås, and that these men had to be moved as soon as possible to another hiding place, preferably the following night. We tried to find a new hiding place, but in vain. Finally Ernst suggested his own attic. At daybreak Ernst and myself biked through Hasle town , each with an airman in uniform on the the cross bar of our bicycles, to Ernst's house next to "Herolds Hotel". We left the two with Ernst's wife, Helga, and then went back for the two others who were transported in the same way. (It is incredible that everything went to well). The airmen stayed in the attic for four days.

Both Ernst and I were warned again that we had to get away, but we hadn't had any possibility of sailing the four airmen out. In the meantime I was able to get hold of information about the German patrols and we agreed to sail out from Teglkås after dusk. Ernst's wife and their three children together with the fiancé of the leading seaman, Frede Olsen, were to go out to Holm in the afternoon. Ernst and his crew were to sail out from Hasle in the evening and later put into Teglkås where Erik Hansen, the four airmen and I/myself were expected to arrive between eleven and twelve at night—a "drop" in the German security patrol. After a very dramatic trip we all got on board the "Svanen" and reached Simrishamn early next morning, where we were all questioned by the local Swedish police. We were then sent by train to Malmø where we were separated from the airmen: H.H. Shelton—John S. Whiteman—M.L. Carraway and H.N. Liddle (I still have 4 hundred franc notes on which they wrote their names).

The rest of us were taken to a reception area in Malmø where we were further questioned by Danish and Swedish officials. We were told to sleep on beds with sheets and blankets of paper, but I made sure that the two women and the children were put up at a hotel.

Ernst and I had a contact address in Stockholm. However, we couldn't get permission to leave the centre in Malmø so we both jumped out of a window and found our way to the railway station where we took the train to Stockholm. We found the address. It turned out to be the British intelligence service. We gave them the information we had, but left out names and routes in Denmark. In any case they were mostly interested in the German occupation.

Ernst said that he would seek permission to sail under Swedish colours and the person who we contacted asked him to report back if he succeeded. We were given a meal and money for a return ticket as we had spent the money that I had managed to change in Simrishamn. In addition we were given some pocket money.

When we returned to Malmø we found ourselves in trouble because we had run away.

We were now separated. Erik and I were sent to a refugee camp in Nissafors, and Ernst and his family were sent to Løderup.

Idleness in the refugee camp made me relive the events in Denmark. My friends woke me up at night because I had nightmares and they said I was shouting. I asked for some kind of employment and was given a choice between forestry and agriculture. I chose agriculture and was sent to the state-run research farm "Ugerup" at Kristianstad where I stayed about a month. Then I went to Simrishamn to join Ernst and his family and Erik Hansen. Shortly afterwards I found employment on a Swedish trawler, "Øland", based in Hønø near Gøteborg. This was very unusual for the time and I think I was the only Dane who got such an opportunity. With the job came a permit that gave me free access to the otherwise closed Swedish ports.

The "Øland" trawled herrings in the Baltic and after a couple of trips I was asked to go to Stockholm and wait at the main entrance of the railway station where I would be picked up at a specified time. Here I met the person with whom I had the first contact. He told me that they had been keeping an eye on me and to prove this he gave me details of the places where I had been recently. He brought me to a building where, among others, the German embassy was located. We went into an office and I was asked if I was willing to report back as to the presence of German and also Finnish ships in the Baltic. When I agreed I was given a pair of binoculars and some tablets which—when dissolved in water—could be used to make your handwriting invisible, and other tablets which in the same way reversed this effect. I also received an address in Stockholm. I did manage to pass on some information. Three times our ship called at Christiansø. The first time the Danish police was still present and I registered the numbers of several German patrol boats. I passed on this information to a contact person who came to meet me in Simrishamn. (I could write a lot more about this episode and many other incidents).

I visited several Swedish Baltic harbours, among others Karlshamn and the heavily fortified "Sternø" where the "Øland" had to go to the shipyard.

In October when we returned to Hønø we had a lot of trouble with the Swedish port authorities who had been informed of the illegal presence of a Dane. The skipper, August Korneliusson, and I were ordered to Gøteborg. The telephone lines to Stockholm were red-hot, but in the end I got permission to go to Hønø.

At the end of October I was invited to join the Danish Brigade and at the beginning of November I learned that they had organized a police division in the Brigade. I was now urgently requested to join this division. I went to Ryd in Småland where the police division was based. A little later Johs. Hansen, a police inspector from Bornholm, joined the Brigade.

He had also been involved in helping American airmen to escape from Bornholm and he said to me that everything would have been easier if we had known about each other.

During the night between the 4th and the 5th of May I went with the Brigade via Helsingborg to Denmark. The 5th of May we had a highly memorable trip along Kystvejen (the coastal road) to Copenhagen. People lined the road cheering when they saw that we were Danish soldiers, the weather was splendid—fine and sunny—and many of us had tears in our eyes.

On arriving in Copenhagen we were sent to the brewery "Stjernen", which had served as a base for freedom fighters. After this we took part in a short exchange of fire with the enemy. I was in the first division that was ordered out to house-to-house fighting. The place where the gunfire came from was pointed out to us—some attic windows towards which we directed our fire. I fired three shots from my machine gun and a bullet grazed off the helmet of a friend, Simon, in front of me. The freedom fighters in the courtyard of "Stjernen" had emptied many magazines into the air. Our unit's training and drilling proved its worth, especially as regards consumption of ammunition.

We were then transferred for a few days to a school in Hellerup and subsequently to the State Police School from where we were sent out to perform various duties.

We held a large exercise (a show) on Amager Fælled to which the national Commissioner of Police and other dignitaries were invited. We used live ammunition and live hand grenades and they were very impressed with our precision. The Commissioner held a speech in which he said among other things:"You shall never be forgotten". (It later turned out that he was wrong). We were given many different tasks, among other things setting up road blocks, assisting at the King's opening of "Rigsdagen" (the former name of the Danish Parliament), handing over the supervision of Amalienborg (the King's and Queen's residence) to the royal guards, performing raids on German barracks and various arrests, etc.

"You shall never be forgotten"—we later experienced the shallowness of those words. When our salary was paid on the 1st of June 1945, about 30 men in our police division didn't receive any money. We were dismissed because we had left the country illegally. A colleague and I went to the Commissioner's pay office where we met the police superintendent, Heilmann, (later chief constable in Aalborg). To begin with he wasn't very receptive. I refused to leave his office until I received satisfaction and I threatened to go straight to the press. Those of us who had been dismissed because of our illegal departure from the country were all reserve police officers.

The permanent police officers' salary had been put into a bank account from the moment of their departure to Sweden and after the 19th of September 1944. The same thing applied to the reserve police officers who had left the country or gone into hiding after the 19th of September 1944.

With good cause we felt discriminated against. I was then told that they were going to make out a list with the names of the officers who would be entitled to their salary, which would be paid out to us the next day. From that day onwards we were reintegrated into the police force .

For me personally the timing of my departure from the country affected my seniority, which to begin with was calculated from the 1st of June 1945, but later—due to my protest—from the day I joined the Brigade in Sweden. As everything in those days was based on seniority, the consequences of this were significant, for instance in connection with promotions, attribution of a service telephone and many other things. As an illustration of this I was ordered out to guard refugees before my "younger" colleagues.

In 1947 or 1948, with the help of the Danish Police Association, my seniority was recalculated to take effect from the 5th of November 1942 (but I never saw any salary for the lost years).

That was a long story. I suppose I ought to have written it down many years ago when the facts were still fresh in my memory, but I just couldn't as I pushed many things that gave me nightmares and sleepless nights to the back of my mind. Many things I cannot remember and I have never spoken to anyone nor been member of any of the war veterans' associations.

I now had the necessary incentive to tell my story.

Randers, the 25th of October 1991 (signed) Ebbe Hasselholt Jør-gensen and Translated by his daughter, Grete Hasselholt.

Erik Dyreborg: Ebbe Hasselholt died June 25, 1999.

The Ernst Petersen Story—"The Brewer"

Narrated by Erik Dyreborg

Ernst Petersen thought that as few people as possible should know about the trips to Sweden, and therefore it was just a few remarks that came from him about the events during the Second World War, which he was involved in. After the war he was once again busy with new challenges and not much room for thinking about the past.

Before the war he made his living as owner of a quarry and at the same time also did business as a haulage contractor.

When the war broke out the quarry was put on hold, because it was hard to get oil for the electricity production of the diesel machine at the quarry. Instead he bought the fishing-boat "The Swan". The boat was sold after the war, when the work at the quarry started up again.

The fishing during the war made it possible to make the detours to Sweden and Ernst Petersen went several times with Danes, who for different reasons could no longer stay in Denmark and also Jews who had to go to Sweden via Bornholm.

Some of the American airmen who crash landed on Bornholm also got help from Ernst Petersen. The help he gave the crew of the "Sose plane" was also the last trip to Sweden, because Ernst Petersen and his family also had to go.

Regarding the "Sose plane" Ernst Petersen said that he had been told that American airmen were seen at Gines Minde approx. 4 km north of Hasle. Ernst Petersen looked into it and got in touch with the 4 airmen later on the same day.

At that time there was already an investigation going on several places along the coast where German patrols were looking for the crew from the "Sose plane". Consequently people were nervous about hiding the airmen and also taking them to Sweden.

Ernst Petersen was assisted by Ebbe Hasselholt Jørgensen, who was a coastguard, to move the 4 airmen to the Petersen house in Vestergade 55 in Hasle. Ernst Petersen and Ebbe Hasselholt Jørgensen took the trip twice riding their bikes, both times with an American airman in his uniform sitting on the handlebars.

Helga Petersen, Ernst Petersen's wife put them in the bedroom in the attic.

After several days with no food, the spicy food now had its effect. Stomach trouble and diarrhea. The airmen also had infections from insect bites and the town doctor had to step in.

At that time the family had 3 children. A 6 month old girl, a 5 year old girl and a 7 year old boy. They were of course told not to go up into the attic and were lodged with their grandmother and grandfather, whose house was close to the Petersen house.

The oldest girl, however, was a little bit too nosy and took advantage of the situation and ran home and up the stairs to the attic. The door was locked so she looked in the keyhole and saw two men lying on her parents bed and one man who was looking out of the window.

All of a sudden she stared into an eye on the other side of the door and then she ran downstairs and told her mother that there were some men in their bedroom, but Mrs. Petersen just told the girl that these men were electricians. The girl then answered "But they are not doing anything".

It was John Whiteman who was on the other side of the door.

Ernst and Ebbe had both been warned that the Germans might do house searches in Hasle and they realized that they had to go to Sweden very soon.

Suddenly, one night the Petersen family got a visit.

When Ernst Petersen opened the door, there was a man standing on the stairs. He asked Ernst to step outside for a minute for an important conversation.

Ernst Petersen sensed that there were two more men outside, he quickly grabbed the one talking to him and pulled him inside the house and shut the door.

There is no doubt that everybody was very nervous at that time. The German headquarters and interrogation rooms were at Pension Søhøj in Hasle and the visitor was known to help the Germans with different things.

After Ernst Petersen had questioned the man he was thrown out of the door and caught by the two men outside. They probably thought that it was Ernst Petersen who was thrown out of the door.

Now the Petersen family knew that they had to leave for Sweden as soon as ever possible.

In order to stop unwelcomed visitors at the attic, Mrs. Petersen had varnished the stairs.

They realized that they had to leave the next day—1st June 1944.

Then next afternoon Mrs. Petersen was to take the 3 children to Teglkaas. The family should go and visit Holm. Here they should stay until Ernst Petersen would come and pick them up later in the night with the Swan.

Ebbe Hasselholt and Erik Hansen, both of them coastguards, were to take the four airmen from Hasle to Teglkaas. The trip was done on bikes and Ebbe was able to get a hold of police uniforms, but Whiteman was too big for the uniform and was given a cape. They were also carrying rubber sticks and it was agreed what to do if they were stopped by a German patrol on the way.

Ebbe and Erik should arrive with the airmen between 11 and 12 p.m., where the Germans took a break with the patrols along the coast.

Ernst Petersen and two members of the crew were on board the boat.

In Teglkaas, Helga Petersen was waiting with her 3 children and one of the boat's crew members fiancée, who also was going to Sweden. In total 14 people were going to Sweden that night.

The Swan was being prepared for fishing and shipped out from Hasle and called at Teglkaas around eleven o'clock p.m.
The children had been given sleeping pills and were carried on board, but the departure became quite dramatic.

Ebbe was delayed, trying to help the pilot John Whiteman, whose pants were stuck in the chain. While Ebbe was trying to help the pilot, Erik proceeded with the 3 other airmen to Teglkaas.

Time was short!

Ernst Petersen was on board the boat in Teglkaas with the engine running and was told that everybody, who had arrived, was on board and below deck.

Ebbe and one of the airmen were still missing. The waiting time was becoming almost unbearable.

Then suddenly in the dark, they heard boots tramping on the dock and they really got scared.

Ernst Petersen thought that it might be a German patrol and had his rifle ready to fire, but at the very last minute he heard that it was Ebbe who was shouting: "Wait for us, we're going with you".

Ebbe and the pilot came on board and then, with the lights turned off they started their trip to Sweden.

Those who were not strong at sea got sick, but maybe the storm was a help, so that it was less likely that they would be searched for by the Germans.

The Swan arrived at Simrishamn, Sweden early in the morning on the 2nd June 1944. When the 5 year old girl came on deck she discovered that they were not in Hasle as she expected but in a foreign place.

She watched her father talking to some men and told her mother that those were the men she saw in the bedroom at home.

Marine soldiers came from a ship close by with gruel in milk cans.

After that they were questioned by the Swedish police, and all taken by train to Malmö. Here they were questioned again and put up at a place in Malmö with a big dormitory and the beds had paper sheets and covers. The women and men were separated. Here Helga Petersen had to take care of her 3 children which was hard in a new country and alone.

Ebbe who had a certain amount of power via his connection to the police, arranged that Mrs. Petersen, her 3 children and the other woman were put up in a hotel in Malmö.

Ernst Petersen went on the same train to Stockholm as the 4 airmen and they got to the American Embassy and talked to a Mr. Allen. Whiteman was present at the meeting and the family got financial support.

After the meeting Ernst Petersen returned to Malmö. Ebbe and Ernst also made a trip to Stockholm together in order to be questioned by the British Intelligence.

At this occasion they ran into Whiteman again and Ernst Petersen asked him to have the American Embassy put pressure on the Swedish authorities, so that Ernst could get a permit to fish from Sweden.

When they returned to Malmö Ebbe and Erik were sent to a refugee camp in Nissafors. Ernst Petersen and his family were sent to Loederup Strandbad, which also was a refugee camp. Here the family was given a small room and a couple of boxes containing the few necessary things they had.

For the first time Mrs. Petersen had a break down and she started crying.

One day Ebbe paid a visit to the Petersen family at Loederup and they were out walking. The 5 year old girl suddenly discovered something interesting on the other side of the road and just walked across the road. A car was coming and only Ebbe's fast reaction saved the little girl.

With the help from the Americans Ernst Petersen was now allowed to fish from Sweden and thus able to support his family. The Petersen family moved to Simrishamn, first at a boarding house and later in a small and cold flat.

The winter of 1944-1945 was very cold and there was ice on the walls in the apartment. When they went to bed they put all their clothes on top of the cover to try to keep warm during the night.

The Swan was now fishing under the Swedish registration number SIN 223.

In Sweden they didn't miss anything during the war. With the fishing the Petersen family now had the money to buy furniture and clothes for the children. They had things that were impossible to buy in Denmark, such as chewing gum, bananas, oranges and real chocolate. The Christmas of 1945 was celebrated with the Thorsen family also from Hasle. They were in the same situation as the Petersen family.

Mrs. Petersen and the children stayed in Sweden from June 1944 to August 1945, when the Swan brought them back to Bornholm. They stayed a short while with Mrs. Petersen's parents in Rådhusgade 3. Here the children played and dressed up in the airmen's uniforms, which they had saved.

When the children returned, speaking Swedish they were teased, but once they were back in Denmark, Danish came back to them very quickly and the oldest boy started school again.

On Bornholm the Russians had taken over. Ernst Petersen therefore continued to fish from Sweden until it was sure that the Russians would leave the island.

Then the whole family moved back to Bornholm.

Ernst Petersen left Sweden on the 19th March 1946.

When the family left Bornholm in 1944, the bank was supposed to take care of the house and business. The house had been sold and the money used for the quarry, so when they returned they had nowhere to stay and very little money.

They first rented an apartment in Hasle and when the quarry—later "Hasle Granit" was running again they bought a house in Storegade in Hasle.

There were given opportunities for financial support in Denmark after the war, in order to help the families who had lost everything because of their special effort during the war. Ernst Petersen was in 1947 granted an interest free loan of DKR. 9.000,-(1,100 dollars today) and a gift of DKR. 1000,- (125 dollars today) so that he could buy a truck.

The quarry turned out to be a good and healthy business and the company also exported to Germany. Here the family made some good friends, the Rickmann family, who could tell about how the German population suffered during the war.

Now times were changing.

Back in 1939 Ernst Petersen bought a new ship "Gudrun". On a trip where Ernst Petersen was on board as a crew member, she hit a mine in The Baltic Sea and exploded. One crew member died at the accident, which was in May 1940.

The payment of compensation was in slow progress and it was hard to do without the money, with which they were supposed to buy a new ship. Instead they invested in the Swan.

In 1950 payment of the compensation took place, but only after a long and hard trial.

The Petersen family also lost a 2 month old son in February 1941. He was born with spinal disease.

It was common for the airmen who received help to send a "thank you note" to the people who helped them. This thank you note was often written on a dollar bill or on other bills and the Petersen family have several of these bills.

In 1994 one of the children, Elizabeth Munch Petersen, started searching for the airmen, knowing that they could have moved several times since 1945.

Helga and Ernst Petersen's engagement during the war should be seen as a part of their natural readiness to help people in general who were in distress.

At the same time they were both adventurers, a quality which can be necessary, when you are running your own business.

Also the employees in the company "Hasle Granit" enjoyed the assistance from Helga and Ernst Petersen, which among other things could amount to a little extra on the weekly pay-day.

For families with lots of kids, lack of money often was the problem. People at that time didn't have the Danish social security as we know it today.

The Petersen's also looked after their staff when Christmas was coming up.

Helga and Ernst Petersen both had great interest in the nature on Bornholm and they themselves, their five kids and the remaining family really enjoyed the frequent picnics.

Helga and Ernst were a good solid team. Helga was backing up her husband 100% all the way. She actually gave Ernst the strength to deal with his daily business, his membership of the Hasle Harbour Committee, board member of the Rock Industry of Bornholm, and also as a member of the Bornholm Trade Council.

Due to his former relations to the brewery business, Ernst Petersen was nicknamed "The Brewer"—in Danish "Bryggeren".

Ernst Petersen died in 1980, 72 years of age and Helga Petersen in 1992, 80 years of age.

Erik Dyreborg: 2nd LT John S. Whiteman and his crew was the second American crew that evaded and escaped as a crew.

My Most Memorable Missions

Narrated by John Chopelas 452nd Bomb Group.

The Crew.

Crew of "Forbidden Fruit" Combat phase training Rattlesnake Field Pyote, Texas, 1943.
Front row L to R: 2nd LT Ed Skurka Pilot, 2nd LT Henry Krosnowski Co-pilot, 2nd LT Dwight Newton Navigator and 2nd LT Herbert Martin Bombardier.
Back row L to R: Sgt. Norman Burton Ball Turret Gunner, S/Sgt. David Bittner Engineer, Sgt. John Tinker Waist & Tail Gunner, Sgt. Norman Hess Waist Gunner, Sgt. Charles Hickman Tail Gunner and S/Sgt. John Chopelas Radio Operator.

April 11 Rostock, Germany

My second mission.

My crew never flew a combat mission together. On April 9, Easter Sunday, our ball-turret gunner Norman Burton, and tail-gunner, Charles Hickman, volunteered to replace two sick gunners on two other crews. Burton flew in the lead ship, *"Iron Bird"* (which was going to be renamed , *"Leading Lady")* carrying our squadron commander, George Oxrider.

It was shot down and last seen on fire diving into the Baltic Sea. No survivors. Hickman's plane, *"Dinah Might II"*, was shot up and he bailed out over Denmark, spending the rest of the war as a POW. It was their first and only mission. So, after all that training together, we lost 2 men before flying a single combat mission as a crew. The rest of us were immediately scheduled for a mission on—my first one. It was a relatively easy one ("milk run") to Courcelles, Belgium and I really didn't have a true idea of what combat was like.

So, on the 11th, when the curtain was drawn back to reveal the large map of Europe, with red ribbons stretching deep into the eastern sector, there were groans, moans and curses from the veterans and I knew right away that this wasn't going to be a "milk run"'!

The target was Poznan, Poland. But when we approached Poznan, the bad weather conditions prevented our bombing the primary target so we turned back to hit Rostock, Germany.

As we neared this city, we were suddenly jumped by the Luftwaffe. We were attacked by three waves of enemy fighters and it was one scary, hectic encounter. From the rear, we were stalked by a Ju-88 twin-engineer fighter that we called, "The Rocketeer" because of the missiles they launched.

He stayed just out of range of our guns then began moving in. John Tinker, our tail-gunner, was firing quick, short bursts while I tried to get in my own shots. Suddenly, my gun jammed. You talk about one mad, excited gunner!

I remembered from gunnery training that I could manipulate a part of the .50 caliber machine gun so that a cartridge was inserted into the chamber of the barrel, after which the gun resumed firing but only a few rounds when it again stopped. This went on for several minutes and I was jumping up and down in anger and frustration (too excited to be scared at that moment; the fear came later.)

In the meantime, the Ju-88 crept closer and closer and I could actually see the flare under its wing as the rockets were fired.

I'll never understand why that German pilot came so close to us; I could see the crew of the "Rocketeer" just before it suddenly winged up and plunged to the left, on fire. Meanwhile, the FW-190s were barreling head-on, then quickly flipping over and down.

From the sides came the Me-109s. These whizzed by so fast that I never had a chance for a shot. I kept looking around for our fighter protection but they weren't in sight. (We learned later that the P-38s missed the rendezvous). But they were there <u>after</u> we bombed Rostock, keeping the Luftwaffe from our formations.

Tinker was credited with destroying the Ju-88 while our bombardier, Herbert Martin, shot down a FW-190. Tinker had taken over Hickman's tail-gun position. They were "buddies" who had requested to be assigned to the same crew. When Hickman was shot down, Tinker asked for and was given permission to move to the TG slot. Tinker was killed a month later.

This was a long mission—10.5 hours and my "baptism" of combat.

The following are excerpts from the letters of Charles Hickman, my crew's tail-gunner, who became a prisoner of war, bailing out on his first and only mission while flying with another crew, April 9, 1944:

"Back to my half-mission. We bombed a Focke Wolf factory in Poland (Poznan) that wonderful Easter Sunday. From my understanding, they tried on several occasions to accomplish this feat without success. We did hit the target but got a little battered with flak over the target and lost a couple of planes over the target.

On the way back we were attacked by Ju-88's lobbing rockets from a distance. They inflicted some damage on a few planes. When they ran out of rockets they closed in on us with machine gun fire. I shot one down but never claimed credit even though the pilot confirmed it after the war. Someone else shot one down and they left.

We were then attacked by about 35 FW's from one o'clock high. We were over the Baltic Sea at the time. I saw "Shorty" Burton's (Norman Burton, our ball-turret gunner flying also with another crew) plane go down just before we peeled off.

We had two engines on fire and the ship was vibrating badly. I tried to open the tail hatch but it was buckled from the concussion of a flak burst. I crawled up to the waist where other gunners were lined up ready to jump. I was the second one out. My chute opened and I could see land below. I landed in the middle of a German naval training station on an island off the Danish coast.

The flight engineer broke 12 bones in his foot and ankle when he hit a rock on landing. The ball-turret gunner (not ours) was beaten severely by civilians who captured him. They injured his back in some way and he was in misery for awhile.

The co-pilot, who was not a regular member of the crew, and the bombardier bailed out before the order was given. The ship was banking to the left and the bomb bay doors were open. They went out the nose hatch and hit the bomb bay doors. They never opened their chutes.

We were questioned that night (no food since breakfast before the flight) then put on a boat to the Denmark mainland. We were put on a train headed for Frankfurt, Germany. There was 8 of us and 5 guards.

Two of us carried the flight engineer from station to train or train to station whenever we had to walk somewhere. The following afternoon we stopped in a station and the guards took us to a little restaurant where we got our first meal of lousy soup and black bread. We finally arrived at Dulog Luft in Frankfurt for interrogation.

When we walked thru the station we were stoned by the civilians. We remained at Dulag Luft for almost a week then we were packed into cattle cars where we lived for the next 6 or 7 days as they transported us to our new home in Kremz, Austria. Stalag 17—this was a story that could fill a book but I won't go into all the details. For the most part we were cold, dirty and underfed. But you know my nature, I made a good time of the whole affair."

"I have always wondered how many planes actually returned from that raid. Rumors in the Stalag were that none returned to the base but two had made it back to the coast and ditched. I read recently in a B-17 book an account of the raid and it said we only lost 2 planes. I know this was wrong because I know I went down. I saw "Shorty"'s" plane go down and I knew guys from a third crew that were in the same barracks with me in the Stalag.

They got shot up a bit so they headed for Sweden. Their navigator told them they were at Stockholm but when they landed they were in Copenhagen, Denmark. Presto, the Germans had a B-17 intact. The plane I was on was "Dynamite II". "Dynamite I" ditched off the English coast on the second mission. I heard from the pilot of the plane a couple of times and then I lost contact."

"I did receive those reports that you sent and I did notice that the pilot stated that we were at an army base on that island but all of the enlisted personnel that I was in the prison camp with thought it was a naval training base and I still believe this to be a fact. I do not believe that Burton's body was ever recovered or do not know how it could have been recovered.

That Baltic Sea was a desolate and cold body of water and they told us that you could not survive more than 30 seconds. If the plane sunk right away, I do not know how they could ever find it.

I do remember being interrogated and filling out forms and these look familiar but I did not know very much to tell anyone. I did not know where we were or even how everyone was captured until later.

I did not pass along information that was more or less hearsay from the camp. I figured the other crew members would tell their own stories which had been related to me while I was in the camp."

"In regards to "Shorty" Burton. He was shot down in the same sweep of fighters that shot me down. His pilot peeled off to the right and went down in the water and Lt. Boy peeled off to the left towards that small island and did not give bail-out orders till we were over it and could stay out of the water.

I started drifting out towards the water but kept spilling air out of my chute so that I would hit the land. Lt Boy almost sacrificed himself fighting to get over the island and by the time he bailed out it was almost too low. He said he pulled his rip cord, the chute opened, he felt the pull upwards and then he hit the ground. None of the others including me even saw his chute open. We thought he was gone until the Germans brought him in. "

"When I was in Gulfport, going to mechanics school, I would go to the hotel pool every afternoon and swim. I fell asleep in the sun and reported that night to sick call with a 104-degree temperature and they put me in the hospital with sun poison. They asked me how I got it and I fortunately remember that it was a court-martial offense so I told them I got it taking calisthenics and the P.T. instructor made us strip to the waist. (I hadn't reported for calisthentics for weeks.) They bought the story and when I was released from the hospital, the doctor gave me an excuse from calisthentics for 14 days. I put a "1" in front of it and never did go back to do them."

"As to the question of special awards for those who tried to escape, the answer is that we were not really supposed to escape. It was our duty to stay and harass the enemy and make them use more and more guards *and keep them from going to the front. We did our share of that. There were two thousand soldiers to guard 10,000 men of all nationalities. You dig tunnels and let them find them. You start rumors of escape so that they will hear them. There were many things you can do to keep them on their toes and keep them thinking, but if you get the chance to get loose, you just had to take it. I received my P.O.W. medal in the mail.*

"*Just before bailing out, we hooked those seat packs on that contained a rubber raft, cigarettes, food and other survival equipment. I bailed out and right after my chute opened the rubber raft and all the survival stuff passed me on the way down. I thought, 'what the hell was that?'. I reached back and my pack was empty. I had put it on upside down and it emptied out when my chute opened. It sure would have done me a lot of good if I had taken that cold dip in the Baltic. Guess God was looking out for me knowing I was a little stupid.*"

"*I remember 'D-Day'. We received the news and thought we would be FREE in a couple of weeks but that turned into almost a year.*"

"*I had a tussle with a big tough paratrooper in the P.O.W. camp. He slapped across the face and I went blind with rage. When they finally pulled us apart, I was covered with blood (his). they to sew a 4-inch gap around his eye. He removed himself as group leader, moved to another group and they elected me (the kid) as group leader. That guy never talked to me again.*"

"*Regarding the mission I was shot down on. The story answered a lot of my questions. The writer seems to have observed much more than I did. I have always been told that only six planes were lost on that mission but he states that the six were lost from group only and more were lost from other groups. From his letter our group only had 8 aircraft to finally go on the raid. What I though were Ju-88's he says were Me-410's and he says that we were shot down by yellow-nosed 190's but they went over my head too fast that I was not sure but my top turret gunner said they were 190's and so did my waist gunner.*"

May 8, 1944 La Glaciere, France

This was my ninth mission.

At briefing, my crew was scheduled to fly as a "spare" which meant we would follow our group to the English Channel where, if a B-17 had to abort, we would take its place and continue on the mission but since this didn't occur, we returned to base at Deopham Green.

I remember how relieved I was to skip this one because it was to Berlin and how I was looking forward to a day of "leisure"—napping, writing letters and, probably, bicycle to the local pub. But as soon as we landed, we were alerted for an afternoon mission.

Needless to say, all of us were rather disappointed. At the short briefing, we were assured that this would be a "milk run" (an easy mission with little flak or enemy fighters). Our plane, piloted by Ed Skurka, took off at 1622 hours. We flew the No. 4 position. Our target was La Glacerie, France, a missile-launching site ("Crossbow").

These afternoon missions were unusual for the AAF and normally flown by the RAF. All went well until we almost reached the "IP" (Initial Point where the bombardier would take over the plane for a straight and unwavering flight to the target.)

The tail gunner, John Tinker, announced on the intercom that the flak was "six o'clock and level". Not a very good sign since it indicated that the flak was at the same level with our altitude.

I usually sat at my seat in the radio room, facing forward but, for some unknown reason, on this mission I decided to stand up, facing aft, peering through the open radio-room hatch on which my single .50 cal. machine gun was located. This may well have saved my life. Before we reached the IP, Tinker reported again: "Flak, six o'clock level and tracking", the last words he would speak.

This was really bad because the flak battery had us locked in not only on altitude but was tracking in towards us. Suddenly, the B-17 shuddered from an explosion in the tail section. I bent down to look through the waist section into the tail and saw smoke and debris.

Before I could think of what happened, there was a second burst in the bomb bay behind me. I was wearing a steel helmet heard a "ping" followed immediately by sharp pain in the lower part of my head. I was momentarily stunned, then noticed that we were losing oxygen and I began shouting on the intercom: "Watch your oxygen! Watch your oxygen". Seconds later our plane began a sharp dive, finally pulling up several thousand feet below.

Skurka had deliberately dived the B-17 to lower altitude so that we wouldn't need the oxygen. I don't know how he managed to pull up the Fortress.

We assessed the damage and discovered that the rudder controls had been severed, plus damage to the ailerons and loss of the hydraulic system which meant no brakes.

Ironically, on this mission we had a flight surgeon aboard as a passenger. (The "Loading List" shows him, Edmundson, replacing our navigator). Since the briefing officers thought this would be an easy mission, they allowed the doctor to fly with us, probably to observe a crew under combat conditions. He went back to the tail section and when he emerged, shaking his head, I knew that our tail-gunner was dead.

The surgeon had patched up the co-pilot who had been severely wounded in the shoulder and fitted a bandage around my head to stop the bleeding. My wound was described as "moderately severe".

The pilot decided to try and return to base, informing us that anyone who wanted to could bail out, either over France or over England (if we got there). No way was I going to jump. I absolutely never had the desire. I had complete faith that Skurka would get us back.

The rest of the crew felt the same way. The second flak burst had prematurely released the bombs. We carried 12 500-lb GP (General Purpose) bombs.

When we finally reached our base (much later after the other planes had already landed), everyone except the pilot and co-pilot took crash positions in the radio room where I had stored my gun out of the way.

Skurka made a perfect landing but without brakes and rudder control, the B-17 started skidding to the right until we came to an abrupt halt. I was the first out of the hatch (bandage and all!) and took off as the rest of the crew followed me.

We feared a fire or explosion because of all the fuel that was leaking. Skurka would have preferred to make a belly-landing but because of the risk of a fire or explosion, he chose a wheels-down crash-landing.

Crash landing May 8 1944. Evening mission to "Crossbow" target (missile-launching site), La Glaciere, France. Two direct flak bursts—tail and bomb bay. Tail gunner killed, co-pilot and radio operator wounded. Landed without brakes, collided with crash truck, killing driver.

I finally stopped running after many yards when it became apparent that there was no fire. I slowly turned around and walked back to the plane. The gun section in the tail had broken off and I saw Tinker's body lying half out of the plane. Then I heard someone sobbing.

I walked to the other side of the B-17 where I saw Skurka kneeling beside one of our waist gunners who was suffering an emotional breakdown. (He was permanently grounded as was the co-pilot).

Then I saw why we had come to a sudden stop. We had collided with a crash truck that was racing along side of us when we landed. The collision killed the truck driver.

I spent a week in the hospital and another very relaxing, pleasant week at a "flak house"—one of the mansions leased by the English to the AAF for rest and rehabilitation of combat crews.

I returned to combat completing my 24 remaining missions. Skurka was awarded his first Distinguished Flying Cross for this mission. He had been recommended for a Silver Star which he should have received.

This was a short, 4.3-hour mission but my roughest one. The desk in my radio room and the radio receiver were perforated with flak holes. If I had been sitting there, as I usually did, I believe that I would have been killed or been severely wounded. (So much for milk runs.)

June 6, 1944
D-Day

About the D-Day missions. Although they were historic, they were rather routine. I flew two missions that day and with the passing years, they seem to "mesh" together.

I know the first mission took off very early. According to reports that I've read, the first planes of our group became airborne at 0201 hours. The 452nd put up three "groups", "A", "B" and "C" with a total of 41 aircraft. We carried 216 500-lb G.P.s and 608 100-lb G.P. bombs. Our bombing altitude ranged from 17,000 to 19,500 feet. Our target was on and behind Omaha Beach (between Pointe de la Percee and Colleville) and the huge coastal defense guns at Caen, France, the easternmost sector of the Normandy invasion beach.

The first bombs were away at 0701 hours, just 24 minutes before the assault troops hit Omaha Beach. Flak was very light and no enemy fighters were sighted. All aircraft returned safely, with the last landing in the dark at 2345 hours.

I can't recall when my crew took off on either one of the D-Day missions, nor when we returned. I seem to remember that it was getting dark when we landed.

As for the flight, itself, I do remember the overcast that hid from view most of what was occuring below, but a few breaks in the cloud cover allowed me to glimpse the huge armada heading for the landings. Even if it was a "milk run" (for which I personally was grateful), I realized the historic significance of this mission and like most of the other crews, I was excited and pleased that I was a part of it.

June 21, 1944
Shuttle Mission To Poltava, Russia (Operation "Frantic")

My 23rd mission.

This was my longest one—11.8 hours.

The 15th AF out of Italy had flown the first shuttle mission to Russia and we heard rumors of the 8th flying there. I think everybody wanted in on this one. I know I did. Only a few groups would participate so we were lucky to be picked. We took along our O.D. uniform and were instructed to be on our best behavior for the Russians. I've always thought this was more like a public relations effort. We also took along a ground crew chief, one of several mechanics to service the aircraft at Poltava.

We bombed an oil industry target at Elsterwerda while the rest of the 8t[h] hit Berlin. We did encounter some ME-109s that poked up through the undercast, taking pot shots at us as we continued east flying over Poland until we reached the vast wheat fields of the Ukraine, landing at Poltava on metal landing strips, parking the B-17s wing-tip-to-wing-tip, a dumb arrangement that was to prove very costly later.

After we landed, several Russian Yak fighters took off to chase a German recon plane that had followed us into Russia, spying from high altitude. What a sight the photos of all those B-17s must have been to the German brass! We had a short evening briefing for a mission the next morning, to Rumania I believe.

After a quick dinner, exhausted as i was from the long, noisy flight, I plopped on a cot in my tented quarters. I fell into a very deep sleep until abruptly awakened by loud whistles and yells of: "Air raid! Air Raid!".

The day after the German attack. 47 B-17s destroyed.

I leaped out of the cot in my underwear and ran to a nearby slit trench into which I dove headfirst. Then I heard the roar of the engines and the bomb explosions.

The Germans caught everyone absolutely unaware and unprepared. They bombed us for two hours, destroying 47 B-17s plus other aircraft and the fuel storage.

I can still see the brilliant white flare that was parachuted by the German bombers, lighting up the area like it was high noon. Fortresses were exploding everywhere and many Russian soldiers were killed trying to put out the fires.

Two Americans were killed. We were extremely lucky because the Germans obviously were concentrating on wiping out the bombers. For two days we couldn't get to our planes because of the anti-personnel "butterfly" bombs dropped by the Luftwaffe , that were still armed.

The Russian soldiers cleared paths for us. Our plane, *"Forbidden Fruit II"*, was one of the few to escape major damage.

I still don't know why another crew flew it back to England. I'm assuming it had to be repaired while we were being returned to the U.K. via Air Transport Command.

As it was, we never flew a mission out of Poltava and were "stuck" there for a week until the Russians gave the AAF clearance to evacuate us. We got along fine with the Russian G.I.s and civilians but the officers were more reserved and suspicious.

From Poltava we flew to Rostov then to Armivir and on to Tehran, Cairo, Benghazi and Casablanca where we spent a very pleasant several days' layover before boarding a C-54 for the flight to England.

The losses at Poltava were the most suffered on the ground by the AAF. It is a little-known episode of the war.

We hung around Russia for a week. At times, the Russians seemed puzzled as to what to do with us. In the meantime, we G.I.'s got along very well with the Russian soldiers (their officers seemed somewhat more reserved.).

Fraternization with the Russian women soldiers was prohibited, a rule that was, of course, frequently ignored. Russia in 1944 presented the classic example of the "scorched-earth" results of war. I don't think a single building in Poltava had its original roof. Most of them were shells of standing walls.

Each evening we all gathered at one of the bombed out structures where some danced to the music of a phonograph. There was also an old beat-up piano on which an American GI played popular songs that were quickly recognized by the Russians. The GI also did a good impersonation of Charlie Chaplin which was loudly applauded by our hosts. And we were surprised to see several Russian male soldiers dancing with each other.

The food, although not plentiful, was rather tasty—their borscht and coarse bread a daily staple. And, of course, the ever-present vodka was always a good excuse for a toast. And those Russians could drink!

I remember striking up a conversation with a woman in Armivir on our last stop before leaving the U.S.S.R. Although we couldn't understand each other, we managed to communicate by "sign" language from which I gathered that her husband was in the infantry. She had children with her and I gave her an American fifty-cent coin as a souvenir. I've sometimes wondered if she bought food with it or passed it on to her children.

We made only a brief stop in Tehran for fuel, spent a night in Cairo and refueled again at Benghazi. Here there was a small British PX operated by a lone soldier. Within minutes we bought every edible object in the place, including a large bowl of pickled hard-boiled eggs. The British guy could only look in astonishment as the Yanks departed with all his wares.

We enjoyed a longer stay in Casablanca where the sights were truly strange and intriguing.

This mission was one of my most memorable ones.

July 14, 1944
Supply Drops To The Maquis

The supply drop to the Maquis on July 14, 1944, Bastille Day. It was a 9 1/2 hour flight to the Vercors area in Southern France.

When we were informed at briefing that we would be parachuting supplies from about 500-feet, I became very, very nervous. I just knew we would be "sitting ducks" for ground fire from such a low altitude. But, fortunately, we didn't run into any problems.

As we released the canisters over the drop zone, I checked the bomb bay to see if it was clear and, looking down, I saw the Frence Resistance Fighters running out of the woods to gather up the supplies and waving up at us. I waved back at them. This was a "good-feeling"-mission because we didn't drop bombs for a change and I felt good about giving assistance to the Maquis.

I learned after the war that these soldiers were captured and executed by the Germans. That gave me a real sad feeling.

John Chopelas after having completed his missions 1944.

A Mission To Politz

Narrated by Warren Branch 492nd Bomb Group and written by his daughter, Karen Branch Cline.

"On May 29, 1944, one thousand bombers of the 1st, 2nd and 3rd Bomber Divisions were dispatched for visual attacks on aircraft plants and oil installations. Of the eight hundred and eighty-eight bombers which managed to drop their loads on the targets, thirty-four were reported missing after the raid. Six B-24's and two B-17's landed in Sweden."

The Crew.

Above the plane L to R: 2nd LT Robert L. Keehn Navigator, 2nd LT Charles R. Easton Co-Pilot, 2nd LT Frederick D. Gaulke Pilot, S/SGT Andrew J. Fry Engineer, SGT George G. Worthington Waist Gunner, and SGT Leon J. Sawyer Tail Gunner
Below the plane L to R: SGT Warren G. Branch Jr. Nose Gunner, 2nd LT John D. Murdock Bombardier, S/SGT Wernie O. Honberger Radio Operator and SGT Francis X. Baker Ball Turret Gunner

One of the six Liberators that made it to Sweden was a B-24H (42-95011) from the 492nd Bomb Group. The plane was hit by flak while on a mission over Politz, Poland. With the fuel tanks leaking and their flight engineer hit in the ankles, they decided to try to make it to Sweden. Their map showed only the southern part of Sweden, with a small airfield in the eastern region. On approach, the crew saw that it was a very small airfield and it had only one landing strip, with a lot of wooden areas surrounding it. Their first thoughts were that the strip was too short. They didn't think there was a chance to stop the plane before they reached the end of the strip.

The nose gunner, Sgt. Warren G. Branch and the ball turret gunner, Sgt. Francis Baker, came up with an idea to slow the plane down. They wanted to use their chest pack chutes. The pilot, 2nd Lt. Gaulke, okayed their idea.

They grabbed their parachutes and tied them to the waist guns' mounting brackets on both sides of the plane. On touch down, they released the cutes. Sgt Baker's chute pulled his gun out of the waist opening, along with his low cut shoes that had been tied to the gun. The plane stopped just before the end of the runway. There was indeed only about 100 feet between the end of the runway and the fence at the end. A large group of town's people had gathered to see this large plane come in for a landing. A jeep, pulling a small water tank on a trailer, arrived to extinguish any fires. The crew was not sure how effective this would have been had the plane caught fire.

The crewmembers exited the plane and Baker ran down the runway to retrieve his shoes (he was wearing his flight boots) from the waist gun. This took the Swedish guards by surprise. They thought he was trying to escape, but shortly learned that he only wanted to get his shoes.

The Swedish military personnel made the pilot wait before taxing to the grass so they could get the injured man (S/Sgt. Andrew Fry) off the plane. The crew was afraid that the plane was going to catch on fire (due to the leaking gas) while they were waiting to get S/Sgt. Fry off the plane. S/Sgt. Fry's ankle tendons were injured by flak. He was taken to the hospital in Kristianstad, just a few minutes to the north.He was later moved to the hospital in Malmö. (He was sent to Rattvik for internment after his release from the hospital in July.)

About 30 minutes after their plane landed, the crewmembers were sitting along the fence eating the cheese and crackers that had been brought to them. They looked up and saw another Liberator circling. It too, came in for landing, but did not use any chutes to slow the plane. The only way to avoid hitting the fence, and the crowd of people, was to loop the plane at the end of the runway. This plane was #42-110065 from the 445th BG, 703rd SQ, piloted by 1Lt. Edwin Peterson.

Ed Black, Flight Engineer on the Peterson crew, remembers "It was a short runway. The sun caused rising air currents. The plane was still in the air at 87 mph. We finally got it down at the middle of the runway. The plane thought it was a glider! We went off the runway at 60. There was not much room at the end of the runway and there were many people around the fence, so the pilot ground looped it. The inside wheel made a 50 ft. circle and was in the dirt to the bottom of the rim. The outside wheel was in to the top of the rim."

The crew of 42-95011 would later learn that their oil tank had also been hit. Even if they had enough gas to make it further, the engines would have seized due to lack of oil.

They spent the night on straw mattresses, in a barracks style house at the airfield. There was also a Farmhouse near the field that was used as the airfield's headquarters. The next day, they were taken from Rinkaby to the train to go to Loka Brunn Warren and the other crewmembers were interned in Sweden until the 21st of October, 1944. They returned to the states, from England, on November 24th, 1944.

Warren Branch at the lake, Loka, Sweden, 1944.

The Single Pilot

Narrated by Nicholas B. Kehoe 492nd Bomb Group &
Ingemar Melin, Trelleborg, Sweden.

The day was June 20, 1944 and take-off was at 0430. The 14th Wing of the 2nd Division was to be the lead wing over the target. That put the 44th Group with three squadrons as lead Group. The 492nd, our group, was second in with three squadrons. I was pilot on B-24J 44-40112 and was leading the low squadron of twelve aircraft.

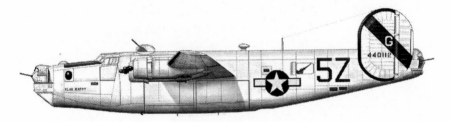

LT Kehoe's B-24 „FLAK HAPPY" Drawing by Ingemar Melin, Trelleborg, Sweden.

Assembly and Group, Wing and Division rendezvous were normal, but the "on course" air speed was slow—quote Major Losee, 492nd Group Command pilot (who also landed in Sweden), "we indicated 150-153 just about all the way". I had a little difficulty keeping my squadron in position, low and to the rear of our lead squadron, all the way to the Danish coast, due to this slow speed.

While crossing the Danish islands I placed my squadron directly under our lead Squadron, slightly in trail. I was gradually sliding out into position from trail when fighters struck. Reports on formation at time of enemy action seemed favourable; the tail gunner of Group lead ship and the navigator of another ship in high squadron said formation was in good position. Our altitude was approx. 21,000 ft.

The first indication I had of enemy action was the sight of hundreds of 20 mm shells exploding all around us. It was 0902-0915. The lead group was starting a turn to right, as scheduled, to hit I.P. I was getting ready to start into trail on our lead squadron.

A loud explosion was my indication that we had been hit. When I turned around the whole flight deck was in flames. For a moment, sky could be seen through the large shell holes above radio-operator's table.

Smoke became dense in pilot's and radio compartments as there was no escape for it. The co-pilot immediately left his seat to fight the fire, which proved to be too much for those on the flight deck (co-pilot, radio operator and engineer) due to heavy smoke and oxygen want (all rubber oxygen outlets were destroyed by the fire and walk-around bottles were not used). Sometime during these fleeing seconds I gave warning on bell and interphone system. Bombardier must have opened bomb-bays and salvoed bombs, as smoke was sucked out flight deck when draft was created.

It was only then that I was able to see that there was no one left on the flight deck and again gave bail-out alarm and inter-phone command. Don't know whether either was successful, but plane was sure empty later on.

Several flares caught fire and went off; the wiring that lined the wall behind radio table was burning as was upholstery and rug on both sides of deck. The flak suits and extra equipment on deck and behind pilot and co-pilot seats were burning. My vision was hampered due to smoke film on windows. I opened the side window, which seemed to draw much of the smoke back to cockpit.

As I remember, my turn after being hit was to the left and down about 270 mph. I gathered this excess speed while removing my flak suit, helmet, safety belt and looking for action on the radio deck. Don't know what prompted me to stay at the controls as long as I did, for great fear of explosion was experienced. Perhaps I was afraid to fumble through that smoke and flame. Thank heavens those bomb-bays opened to clear the smoke.

No. 3 engine was out (determined by back and forth movement of throttle without power response). With oil pressure around 10-20 on indicator, I feathered # 3 engine.

No. 1 engine registered about 30 where it remained. Later the throttle and rpm changes would not register—the system was out, I guess. I could not feather No. 1.

When the equipment behind my seat started smoldering, I reached for the fire extinguisher behind the pilot seat and armour-plating, but in doing so my ungloved right hand touched the hot metal armour plating and tore off pieces of skin from the back of my hand. I had turned my oxygen to emergency rich and had pulled down my goggles. I pulled the salvo handle so violently that the whole mechanism came out in my hand.

I left the pilot's compartment perhaps two minutes after the strike, when the plane was trimmed at 220 mph. I went to bomb-bays to jump. For some reason I hesitated to leave the aircraft and started back into the radio compartment. The front of the plane (carrying nose-navigator, bombardier and navigator) was deserted. I couldn't see into the rear of the aircraft because of the retracted Sperry ball-turret. I seemed to be the only one aboard.

I attempted to use fire extinguisher but co-pilot, radioman or engineer had used it all when the fire first broke out. I tossed out several pieces of burning equipment and attempted to stamp and beat out fire with little success. A yellow emergency case containing several cans of water was in the corner of flight deck. I split open can by can tossing water about on the flames. All my actions were jerky and without thought. I had to climb to the controls from bomb-bay and radio compartment several times to retrim plane.

The command pilot's seat, between pilot's and co-pilot's seat, was afire. I ripped it out. A piece of burning flak suit lodged between the bomb-bay bomb supports under gas tanks to add to the danger, but soon burned up and fell out. I used a large oxygen bottle on the flight deck as the oxygen hoses were burned up. Pure oxygen saved me from suffocation.

Back in the pilot's seat, I cleaned the front window with my arm. I was coming up on the Island of Bornholm (Denmark). I flew around it to the left as light flak was coming up.

I could see more land ahead through the haze. I put wheel handle to down position. Nothing happened, so I re-trimmed and went to the bomb-bay to manually wind down wheels. I could turn the mechanism only about 1 time. Guess I was weak. From the sound of the plane, it seemed to be slowing down. I dashed to controls to nose her down. A good share of the fire was out when I reached the coast of what proved to be Sweden. I wasn't sure that Sweden lay below because I hadn't been at controls much to watch the compass.

I definitely made up my mind to jump as I could find no airports or suitable fields and was losing altitude rapidly. The plane was still burning and the landing gear would not go down. I came in over land, turned 180 and headed plane to sea about 180 mph and went to bomb-bay and jumped. All went quiet.

The plane went straight and down for a few moments then gradually into a stall and spin. Spun into open field at Klagstorp two miles north of Aspo (= Äspö), Sweden.

I had bailed out at about 4,000 ft. And landed in sugar-beet field in the township of Vallby, village of Trelleborg, county of Scania, 20 June 1944, approximately 0940 (0840 LT), 20-30 minutes after attack.

Lt. Seitzinger, flying #4 in my squadron said that after we were hit smoke and flames were pouring from the bomb-bays and rear section. I presume that it was because of this that members jumped. I had been unable to see the condition of the rear of plane from the bomb-bays. Other airmen said that they saw chutes opening and that fighters were circling open parachutes at low altitude and that several boats were seen in the area.

We were hit by ME 210's or 410's—some say 150-180 attacked us in two three waves. I saw but three of them as they crossed my "nose" and left wing at about 100 ft.

I was met by several town people and home guard and was taken to a farmer's house to wash and eat (first fresh milk since I left the States—chicken too, and a brandy to steady my nerves)

Two Swedish officer's came and returned me to Trelleborg about noon. At my request, they took me to inspect the wreckage. I spent about an hour looking for traces of personnel (dog tags, etc.) that might have been in plane. None were found. The plane was a complete wreck having blown up on contact with the ground.

June 22, 1944, Rättvik, Sweden (1st Lt. Nicholas B. Kehoe)

LT Nick Kehoe (2nd from the left) just before leaving for Trelleborg.

The following articles appeared in the Trelleborg news papers, June 21, 1944:

"BURNING BOMBER CRASHED OVER SÖDERSLÄTT"

The crew had already left the aircraft over Germany. Only the pilot made for Sweden and was rescued. Over 20 American bombers to Sweden yesterday.

The southern part of the county of Skåne was during yesterday morning hours involved in the airwar. All the coast line from Ystad to Falsterbo. Never before had so many American bombers landed here in one day. About twenty bombers made for Sweden, most of them were going down at Bulltofta airfield.

In one case a bomber ended up in a complete break down. It was a burning aircraft, that just before nine o'clock on Tuesday morning crashed about 100 meters from the large granary in Klagstorp. It went down on the farmer Anders Persson's sugar beet field, and it was a mere chance that it didn't hit any of his cattle grazing close to the aircraft's impact spot.

When our special correspondent arrived to the crash site half an hour after the crash, the remains of the aircraft were still burning. It was an unparalleled devastation. At the impact spot of the aircraft there was now a 2 meter deep and 2 meter wide hole. Thousands of pieces was spread out on approximately one and a half acre large area. Everywhere ammunition from the guns could be found. Some shells had already exploded. A barring was immediately placed around the crash site by the military to avoid souvenir collectings.

It all started at eight o'clock in the morning when people near the south coast began to hear the typical sound of multi-engined aircraft. The Swedish anti aircraft-artillery had been in action from early in the morning. People had also heard the sound of heavy detonation from the other side of the Baltic Sea during the late night. The aircraft which crashed in Klagstorp had been observed by people from all over Söderslätt before its brake down. They understood that it was damaged and that it was intended to land. It made some wide banks near the coast before it went down and hit the ground.

According to several eyewitnesses the last banks were made over Äspö just before it ended up with a loud crash ended up at the Toarp field of farmer Anders Persson. At the same time a parachute was seen coming floating down over Vallby. The man landed with his parachute at the farm of Nils Larsson close to a small chapel.

The parachutist turned out to be the pilot of the aircraft, and he was a nice young guy who seemed to handle the situation calmly in spite of burns on one of his hands.

He was uncertain of the fate of his crew, who had left the bomber while they still were over Germany. There is a risk that some of them had landed in the sea. Concerning there is every reason to worry, as the Germans recently has made an announcement which stated that allied bomber crews should be treated as terrorists.

The pilot, a charming young man! He was saved thanks to his own courage and calmness.

It turned out that the pilot of the Liberator was a very charming young man. He is only 26 years old, with an university degree. He is married, and in his home in New York he has two small boys.

When approaching the target in Germany the bomber was hit and caught fire. At that moment all ten in the crew decided to parachute. It was above the German coast, but they were all wearing life wests, so the pilot could only entertain hopes of them being rescued by ships outside the coast.

Himself had made the very hard decision of trying to make for Sweden. He had barely got the fire under control while he was heading north after jettisoning the bomb load in the sea.

When he reached the coast he still didn't really know that he was on Swedish territory. He decided to make a force landing, but when he later found it impossible he made up his mind and bailed out. Just before that he had activated the autopilot with heading south.

For some reason it failed and the aircraft crashed on land instead of out in the sea.

The American pilot was received as a guest in Oscar Levin's home in Vallby. Oscar Levin showed the pilot great hospitality. The American was delighted when he understood that he was in Sweden. Since he had, as he said with a smile, "eaten an early breakfast in England" he ate heartily. He was later brought to Trelleborg by the military.

There was literally a queue in the air over Bulltofta

A total of 16 Liberators landed yesterday. Six men were killed in a crash.

For several hours yesterday morning in Malmö, there was an intensive activity in the air.

A large number of foreign aircraft invaded Malmö. It all started when the anti aircraft-artillery was heard firing just before 10 o'clock, and shortly after that a lot of heavy bombers came in over the city. They began circling around waiting for landing at Bulltofta airfield. According to unconfirmed reports not less than 16 Liberators landed there yesterday.

One of the Liberators hit against a hillock with its wing at the boarder of the field during the final approach. The plane caught fire and six men were killed. Four men of the crew was rescued.

The first aircraft arrived at 9.30, and then the others arrived in a steady stream. Periodically there was literally a queue of bombers in the air. The aircraft which crashed was the eleventh to land. Two of its engines were damaged, and shortly before touch down, the wing hit against the hillock and the plane rolled over and ended up as a wreck just about 300—400 meters from the air station building. It was completely destroyed.

Reports from the hospital said that they had received seven crew members from the force landed American bombers. One of the men was already dead at the arrival at the hospital. Two were seriously injured, but not gravely. Four were slightly injured.

Two Liberators were safely landed at Halmstad at around eleven o'clock. One at Helsingborg, and still another one crashed at Ljungby-hed. In that case the crew already had bailed out.

With such a great number of Liberators and Flying Fortresses force landed in Malmö, it's hard to find an empty spot at Bulltofta. It's not without concern that you think of what's going to happen during the next few days, if similar invasion waves as we've seen today will continue.

21 allied bombers to Sweden yesterday
A Liberator plane went down in a sugar beet field at Toarp, Klagstorp.

Tuesday the 20th of June entailed the largest invasion of allied bombers that ever has landed in Sweden. Already at half past ten in the morning not less than 21 four-engined Liberators or Flying Fortresses had force landed or crashed in Swedish territory. No less than 16 of these 21 aircraft were going down at Bulltofta. One of the last aircraft to arrive crashed near the border of the airfield and six men were killed.

One of the bombers crashed east of Trelleborg. It crashed just before nine o' clock in the morning in a sugarbeet field barely 150 meters north-east of Anders Persson's farm Toarp in the parish of Klagstorp. The only man onboard when the aircraft reached the Swedish territory, parachuted and landed just beside a small chapel in Vallby. The rest of the crew had already left the plane just outside the German north coast.

"The plane was not far from a collision with my barn" Anders Persson told the reporter from Trelleborgs Allehanda. " The big aircraft swept not more than about twenty centimetres over the roofs of my farmhouses, and actually touched the top of the barn, before it definitely ploughed down with its nose in the field about 150 meters north-east of the farm houses"

The time was 9.45 in the morning when the bomber first appeared. It was coming from the east, and seemed to be going west heading for Malmö, when it suddenly made a turn in the opposite direction. There was nothing indicating anything wrong with it.

All the propellers were running, and it went steady through the air. It flew on an altitude of approx. 3-400 meters when suddenly a parachute was unfolded.

The airman came slowly floating down towards Vallby with the eastern wind. When the plane was approaching the ground a wreath of smoke could be seen coming out from it. It was probably a fire onboard that had forced the pilot to abandon the ship. For a moment it looked like the plane was going to crash into the houses on the farm, but fortunately it passed just above. Several other houses were also in danger. Anders Persson and some other eyewitnesses consider it a miracle that no disaster occured.

At the impact a very loud explosion was heard, and in a few seconds there was a big sea of fire. It was only wreckage and small pieces left of the big bomber, and there was about one acre burning. Ammunition from the machine guns was exploding continuously. The plane created a crater with a depth of two meters.

Two persons were working on the sugar beet field when the plane crashed. One of these was Mrs. Zaar. In the last moment she saved her self from being buried underneath the burning wreckage. She was working exactly at the impact point.
Soldiers from the home guard arrived within ten minutes. Later on also men from the army stationed nearby, and besides, a lot of onlookers. During the whole afternoon huge crowds came to see the crash site.

But there was not much to see, the plane was completely destroyed. Only ashes and burnt wreckage remained.

The sugar beets nearby had been burnt. Mr. Persson, the farmer, estimates the total area of destroyed beets to a least two acres.

Since only one man was seen leaving the aircraft, the rest of the crew at first was believed to have been killed in the crash, but nothing was found among the remains of the plane to indicate that so was the case.

An unusual presentation

The parachutist landed just a few meters from the small chapel in Vallby. He was welcomed by the farmer, Oscar Levin who was in front of the airman even before he had time to get on his feet. Mr. Levin tells the reporter about his encounter with Lieutenant Kehoe:

"This man obviously didn't know where he was. But he got informed himself through a probably very unique kind of presentation.

"The American looked suspiciously at Mr. Levin for a few seconds, then hesitatingly gave Mr. Levin his hand and introduced himself: "New York!"

And when Mr. Levin immediately replied: "Sweden!" he became heartily hugged by the young airman. His happiness of being in Sweden knew no bounds.

After that Mr. Levin invited him to his home which was next door to the chapel. There he was given something to eat.

The American, Kehoe, told a little about himself: He is lieutenant and 26 years old, his home is in New York. In the civilian life he studies mathematics and chemistry at a the University in the State of New York.

After a while military staff as well as the district police superintendent Steen from Östra Torp arrived. After having his wounds attended (he had burns on his hands and in his face) Kehoe was taken by a military vehicle to Trelleborg, but before leaving Vallby he took the time to tell the story about what actually happened during the bomb raid over Germany.

A rumour that some more parachutists had been seen in this neighbourhood was wrong according to the district police superintendent Steen. He also said that it should have been a terrible disaster if the aircraft instead had crashed in the middle of the dense populated Klagstorp.

The Local People of Vallby meet with the LT Kehoe.

This is Tore Levin's story (son of Oscar Levin), narrated by Ingemar Melin.

My father and two other men from the village were working with cleaning up around the farm houses. Suddenly somebody was pointing in the sky at the east and shouted:

Look up! There is a parachute over there! What are you talking about, replied Oscar, I can't see any parachute!

But after a short while, everybody were seeing a man in a parachute slowly going down not far from the place where they were working.

Oscar started immediately to walk very fast towards the place which seemed to be the spot where the parachutist was going to land. So when he touched the ground, Oscar already was there. After the introduction (as you can read about in one of the articles) Oscar brought Kehoe with him and they started the short walk between the chapel and Oscars home.

At the same time an other farmer—a neighbour to Oscar, his name was Hugo Blomkvist—arrived was now standing beside the road looking at the two men who were approaching him when he suddenly shouted to Oscar:

Hey! Don't you see, he's carrying a knife! And that was true, Kehoe had actually a knife in his waistband.

And as Kehoe seemed to understand what Hugo was saying, he immediately took the knife up from his waistband and gave it to Oscar.

Tore also remember when they came to the house. There was a young man from the village who had studied English in school (Which was rather uncommon in Sweden at that time). He sat beside Kehoe during the whole meal, and they both were talking. When they finished, Kehoe went out in the kitchen where he found Mrs. Levin. He even thanked her with a "TACK SÅ MYCKET", meaning "Thank you very much" in Swedish.
(During their conversation Kehoe had asked the young man how to say thank you in Swedish).

And there was also a thing that sounded a little bit strange to me. Tore told me, that after a while a lot of curious people were coming to the house to see if the rumour was true, that there was an American pilot in Levin's house.

Two doors were opened up in each end of the house so people could pass through the room where Kehoe was sitting. Tore believes that this was going on for one hour's time.

I think it's important to have in mind that this was really an unusual and completely unexpected event in this little village at that time. There was no television, most of the older people had never even been to a cinema, and they lived their lives far from what happened in the world outside this village.

Survivors:

Besides LT Nick Kehoe, two other crew members survived the mission on June 20, 1944.

Nose Gunner 2nd LT Milton Grossman, was picked up in the sea near Sassnitz at 9:30 am. Left Waist Gunner S/SGT Lanta W. Redmond Jr. was picked up in the sea also near Sassnitz at 10:00 am.

Killed in action or Missing in action:

The remaining 8 of the crew are presume killed in action or drowned. The following is from the MACR:

Co-pilot 2nd LT Charles H. Bassin was found August 2, 1944 in the Bay of Tromper north west of Sassnitz. Buried at Altenkirchen.

Navigator 1st LT James P. Carroll—no information.

Radio Operator T/SGT William J. Seufert—no information.

Ball Turret Gunner S/SGT Herman E. Beasley. Parts of his body found August 3, 1944 and buried at sea near Göhren / Rügen, Germany.

Bombardier 2nd LT Armond L. Hankin. Found in the Baltic Sea and buried August 6, 1944.

Engineer T/SGT Charles W. Allen. Found in the Baltic Sea and buried July 24, 1944.

Right Waist Gunner S/SGT George S. Cavanaugh. Found in the Baltic Sea and buried July 19, 1944.

Tail Gunner S/SGT Elbert E. Ester. Found in the Baltic Sea and buried August 6, 1944.

On June 20, 1944, T/SGT Charles J. Ippolito was killed in action only 21 years of age. Charles was on the Politz-mission that day with LT Kehoe's 856th Squadron. His brother Frank served with the 15th Air Force in Italy and when he received the sad news about Charles, he wrote this:

Tribute To The Missing

To her they sent a telegram and then a national banner,
to remind the son she lost and the cause he did enamour...

"Missing" read the telegram deep pain without a sound,
lost he was to his country but to God he had been found...

A lifetime of ardent memories the dreams and future hope,
all ended so aruptly in a little tragic note...

There is no mound upon his grave no marker there to tell,
the world his cause, his age, his name
nor where or when he fell...

The clouds were red with bloodstains and the vapor trails were white,
the background blue of heaven gave credence to the fight...
it is a thought God put it there our colors of the sky,
When I salute my nations flag I always look up high...

If you one day are honoring the flag of your country
tilt back your head, look skyward and see if you can see...
red clouds and long white vapor trails etched on everlasting blue,

A tribute to those missing who gave their lives for you.

Frank J. Ippolito, 1944.

Afterword

When we started this book, Nels and I told the airmen who contributed their stories that the only thing we could offer them was that they would each receive a copy of the draft in book form.

After all the stories were gathered and the book had been designed and set up, the printing began.

I decided to print only 30 books and it took me more than 100 hours just to do the printing alone. Then all copies were sent to a local book binder who bent and cut the card board cover and put each book together with 4 screws and bolts. After that I mounted the front cover and the back cover.

Due to some misprints etc. I had to destroy 2-3 copies, but 23 copies were packaged very carefully, pre-labeled and finally packed in two cartons, more than 50 pounds in weight, and shipped over to Nels in Virginia. Upon receipt, Nels immediately mailed one copy to each of the airmen and others involved in the book.

Within 14 days, all the receivers of the book had responded (I asked them in a letter enclosed with the book, to let me know that they had received the book).

The response was overwhelming! I received e-mails and letters like:

> *"The book arrived in today's mail, and in excellent condition.*
> *A quick glance through the book indicates it is a superb publication.*
> *Congratulations Erik! More later, after I spend more time reading all*
> *of the narratives."*

"Just a quick note before I get to dinner. Dad just called to say he has finished reading the book you sent. HE LOVES IT! He said it is the best he has read regarding escape / evasion / internees. Back to dinner."

"I thank you. My wife thanks you. My children thank you. You did a superb job of compiling the data for the book."

"GREAT BOOK! Couldn't put it down…. Nelson sent me the copy…. MANY THANKS!!"

"The book arrived yesterday. Congrats for a really meaningful job. So many experiences and each one different from the next. This is probably close to "the last roundup" for those of us that have first-hand experiences to tell. In a few more years, we'll be a rarity. Thank you also for publishing my story. I appreciate it. Good luck, best wishes…"

And many more….

Receiving these kind of messages are the best rewards I could ever receive.

Even if this book project, from the beginning, was a coincidence, as are many things in life, I especially noted the sentence: *"Congrats for a really meaningful job."* This is exactly what it is, *"Meaningful"*, especially to me.

The airmen's stories are now all gathered in a book and have thus become immortalized and known to others than just their families and maybe a few other history buffs. This book will remind the readers of what these and thousands of other airmen did for us and our future generations.

As mentioned, it was a coincidence that I would be the one to gather the stories for this book. But again, you can't do everything alone and without the good help from all the participants in the book it wouldn't have been possible.

Being a history buff myself, I find it fascinating to read the stories of the airmen and it is especially exciting to be able to meet with some of them in person afterwards. It gives their stories a very special perspective.

What also fascinates me is that the airmen in this book, together with thousands of other young men, just joined up, ready to go overseas and fight the Nazis. I dare not even think about what would have happened if the Americans would have chosen "just" to fight the Japanese and left it up to the British and Russians to fight the Germans !? I do admire all those young men who joined up, came to Europe, and did what they did. They had guts!

When I talk with some of today's young men, I've come to the conclusion that they don't even know the meaning of the word "guts"! Guess the young people were quite different back in the 1940s.

Without the help of the brave young American Airmen, the world, or at least Europe, might look very different today, or the best case scenario would be that the war in Europe would have ended several years later with some sort of peace agreement between the East and West.

Fortunately the Americans did go to Europe. The German NAZI terror regime was crushed and all the European countries got a new start in a free Europe. Today the European countries are becoming more and more united in many ways, and this, I believe is an important factor to avoid future wars in Europe. But still, you never know......

The son of an American airman, who bailed out over France and spent one year in a German POW-camp, said:

> *"I firmly believe my generation owes its complete existence to all the young airmen who went into harms way—because it was the right thing to do."*

I agree with him !

This book contains stories from 24 airmen, which is only a fraction of the airmen in the 8th Air Force during WWII. Many people have written books about the 8th Air Force, the Bomb Groups, Fighter Groups, the airmen etc. but still there are (my guess) thousands of airmen out there, who will remain unknown forever. Their stories will go untold if they are not picked up and gathered into a book like this one—a lot of important stories about young airmen will be lost !

I would love to do a "The Lucky Ones II" and III or similar books, but at the same time I'll encourage other history buffs to do the same thing. It could even be done in cooperation with the various Bomb Groups Associations, there are 50—60 of them, other WW II Air Force related Associations, museums etc. However, the most important thing is that the experiences of these Airmen be documented for future generations.

Airmen of WW II, I salute you and encourage you to write about your experiences during the war and maybe even include your pre war—and post war stories of your life! Your families will be forever grateful to you for preserving your history for them.

Movies about bombers and fighters are very rare these days. The movie about the "Memphis Belle" is 12 years old and another movie, "Twelve O'clock High" is from 1949.

We have seen a lot of good movies about D-Day and WW II, films like "Saving Private Ryan" and the TV series "Band of Brothers" but we need a new movie about the Bombers, Fighters and Airmen of the Mighty Eighth and I wish that a Director like Steven Spielberg would create such a movie in the way he did with the paratroopers in "Band of Brothers". An "Airmen Band of Brothers" sort of movie or TV series and maybe even include some of the airmen and their stories from The Lucky Ones !

0-595-24990-6